D0321110

Ancient Epic Poetry

ALSO BY CHARLES ROWAN BEYE

Euripides' "Alcestis," translated with introduction and commentary

La Tragedia Greca: Guida storica e critica

Letteratura e publico nella grecia antica

Epic and Romance in the "Argonautica" of Apollonius

Ancient Greek Literature and Society

Ancient Epic Poetry

Homer, Apollonius, Virgil

CHARLES ROWAN BEYE

Cornell University Press

Ithaca and London

Copyright © 1993 by Cornell University

An earlier version of this work was published
by Anchor Books, Doubleday & Company, Inc., in 1966
under the title The "Iliad," the "Odyssey," and the Epic
Tradition, copyright © 1966 by Charles Rowan Beye.

All rights reserved. Except for brief quotations in a review, this book,
or parts thereof, must not be reproduced in any form without
permission in writing from the publisher. For information, address
Cornell University Press, 124 Roberts Place, Ithaca, New York 14850.

First published 1993 by Cornell University Press.

International Standard Book Number 0-8014-2673-1 (cloth)
International Standard Book Number 0-8014-9964-X (paper)
Library of Congress Catalog Card Number 92-28920

Printed in the United States of America

Librarians: Library of Congress cataloging information appears on the
last page of the book.

⊗ The paper in this book meets the minimum requirements of the
American National Standard for Information Sciences—Permanence of
Paper for Printed Library Materials, ANSI Z39.48-1984.

for
    Mary Willis Pendleton

Contents

Preface

In 1965 I wrote a book titled *The "Iliad," the "Odyssey," and the Epic Tradition*. Published in 1966, the book remained in print for many years in a variety of formats. When Cornell University Press offered me the opportunity to revise the text for a new edition, I knew I wished to make major changes. Homer studies and I are both very different now. New facts, new theories, new interpretations have made the Homeric poems seem to me quite otherwise than they did nearly three decades ago. My own critical stance has also changed considerably. My book on Apollonius, *Epic and Romance in the "Argonautica" of Apollonius*, has given me an entirely new perspective on the tradition of epic as it grew and changed from the Homeric poems to Virgil's *Aeneid*. Recent work on Virgil's understanding and use of Apollonius's poem has inspired a number of new insights into the *Aeneid*.

Instead of revising, I seem to have written an entirely new book. I have more or less changed every sentence. The most obvious difference, of course, is that I have added an entire chapter on Apollonius of Rhodes who, as I said, seems to me crucial for understanding Virgil's reading of the Homeric poems, as well as fundamental in the evolution of the European epic tradition.

Readers will note that there are three chapters on the origin, transmission, and context of the Homeric poems, then a chapter each on the *Iliad*, the *Odyssey*, the *Argonautica*, and the *Aeneid*. What may seem to be a disproportionate attention to the two archaic Greek poems will, I hope, not be found so upon reading. Since Apollonius and Virgil have made narratives that play off the *Iliad* and the *Odyssey* in line after line, and since for literary historians and theorists the very notion of epic poetry ultimately derives from the Homeric texts, there seemed to be ample reason for giving much space to the explication of things Homeric. It is also the case that the *Iliad* and the *Odyssey* seem to be in some way (not clearly understood and certainly arguable) specimens of narratives created in oral performance; the circumstances of their creation and perpetuation, so different from the thoroughly literate and literary poems of the Alexandrian Apollonius and the Roman Virgil, need to be explained, both as they are known and as they are theorized. Oral theory, of course, engenders a way of criticizing the two Homeric texts radically different from that employed in reading the *Argonautica* and the *Aeneid*.

Because I focused on heroic epic poetry, I have not included the *Metamorphoses* of Ovid, who, one might say, plays the part of a very witty Roman Apollonius to Virgil's Homer.

As before, I have tried to reconstruct the circumstances of the creation and reception of the *Iliad* and the *Odyssey* and to let my interpretation of the poems be instructed by what I imagine these to have been. In doing so I am perfectly aware that it is finally only my twentieth-century imagination at work. Because the authorship of these texts is so much in doubt, and because the historical moment in which they took shape is so unclear, there are far fewer controls on our imaginings than in the case of better-documented authors and periods. Homeric studies are perfect for those who insist that the author of any text is ultimately the reader of the moment, but those who are bent on contextualization, as it is now called, will suffer disappointment. In an absurdly circular way, certain facts about oral performance will lead toward an interpretation of the texts which, in turn, will be used to lend credence to the notion of the texts' having been orally generated. Critics can read into the poems what the more historically minded will argue could not possibly have been meant by the original author or understood by the original audience. But who would deny an intelligent interpretation? Who can maintain that an "original author" or an "original audience" can be conjured up with any authority? The *Iliad* and the *Odyssey*, like the Bible, have taken on lives of their own, become part of the mythology of Western Europe, and thus their meaning will inevitably be read back into them from the subsequent literary experience, not to mention the aesthetic and cultural history of the last two and half millennia.

Since I have no choice but to take complete responsibility for the interpretation offered here, I should perhaps have begun with some kind of confessional to help my reader assess its parameters: that is, my gender, my religion, my ethnic background, sexual orientation, social class—all those things that contemporary criticism insists upon knowing in order to establish the true authorship of what has been written. Instead, I shall hope that what I write is so clear and well argued that my reader will choose to agree with me, or that it is so provocatively off the mark as to impel my reader to his or her own reasoned interpretations.

Although almost nothing remains of the older book, the scheme of presentation is not very different. In the first chapter, "Oral Poetry," I examine such questions as reader reception, auditor reception, written text, and oral performance to find a mode of criticism. In the second, "The Poet's World," I try to conjure up what the Homeric poet or poets took for granted as the background to their stories and what their audiences might have understood easily in chance references that are hard for a contemporary audience to get. In the third chapter, "Poetic Technique," I review some of the techniques of narrative that are remarkable in the Homeric poetic tradition. The next four chapters are, as I said, individual essays on the *Iliad*, the *Odyssey*, the *Argonautica*, and the *Aeneid*. Taken together they furnish a kind of history of the emergence and recognition of a genre of poetry, its transformation from a popular poetry—presumably dependent on a public for support or whatever group controlled the public—to an elitist poetry that calls for a reader versed in the intricacies of a poetic and cultural tradition shared by poet and reader to the exclusion of the ignorant, uneducated, and nonacculturated. It is an irony that the best instance of this second category of poetry, the *Aeneid*, thereafter becomes an icon for the whole of Western Christianized Europe, surviving in this capacity down into the Romantic period, when once again the Homeric poems acquired a broad public and a popularity that they have not had to cede to any other ancient literary work since. In the minds of those, however, who love history, tradition, the sense of a past recalled, the city, church, and state, one world, and one destiny, the *Aeneid* will always remain the richest, deepest, most panoramic view of Western civilization. It is, as they love to say nowadays, totally polysemous. The book closes with some notes on further reading in which I direct my readers to various reference works that may illuminate and amuse at the same time.

The spelling of proper names and place names in this book has been Latinized. The Roman, hence Latin, appropriation of Greek culture is discussed a bit in Chapter 7. Greek names have passed down through the Latinized Western European tradition, and so they are known to most people in Latinized form: hence, Achilles, not Akhilleus, Ajax, not Aias. (Various translators and scholars, however, transliterate the names directly from the Greek.)

The designation of epochs which has been conventional in the West for centuries is in the process of undergoing change. B.C., which means "before Christ," and A.D., which means "in the year of Our Lord," have for the sake of convenience come to be used over the globe, despite the fact that they refer to religious ideas irrelevant or repugnant to so many. In their place, however, it is becoming customary to write B.C.E., "before the Common Era," and C.E. "the Common Era"; readers will see that these embarrassingly simpleminded terms have been introduced here.

All translations are mine. The reader should definitely get copies of these poems for reference. Richmond Lattimore's English translations of the *Iliad* and the *Odyssey* have the virtue of being close to the original Greek and translated line for line, even if, as some find, the translations are somewhat slowgoing. E. V. Rieu's prose translation of the *Argonautica* more than suffices. Virgil's exquisite Latin is notoriously impossible to translate successfully. Most translators, except C. Day Lewis, inflate beyond a line-for-line rendition (although the original Latin verse numbers are indicated on the pages of their translations). A mixture of Lewis, Robert Fitzgerald, and Allen Mandelbaum, with a heavy dose of Dryden, may be the best prescription.

As in the past I have been helped by splendidly generous criticism. I thank here Casey Cameron, Mary Campbell, Mary DeForest, Richard Deppe, Gregory Nagy, Natasha Prenn, Ann Rosener, Richard Sáez, James Tatum, and Craig Townsend. Frequently, despite their gentle imprecations, I have stubbornly persisted in the perversities of my style and my thinking.

I also thank the powers that be which make Widener Library at

Harvard University the efficient and pleasant place it is in which to work. In what many would argue is a constantly more degraded experience of living, Widener Library offers sanctuary.

CHARLES ROWAN BEYE

Cambridge, Massachusetts

· 1 ·

Oral Poetry

Pierian Muses, who give glory through song, come here, sing in me Zeus, hymning your father, by whom mortals are either unmentioned or mentioned, spoken of, made famous, or not by the will of Zeus.
                                    —Hesiod *Works and Days* 1–4

On the two of us Zeus set a vile destiny; so that hereafter we shall be made into things of song for the men of the future.
—Helen, speaking of herself and Paris, *Iliad* 6.357f.

Once he [the Trojan ally, Iphidamas] was married he left the marriage chamber, looking for glory from the Achaeans, coming with the twelve curved ships which followed along after him.
                                    —*Iliad* 11.227f.

It is ironic that the books of the Hebrew Bible and the Homeric epics, which are the most prominent and influential works of literature in the Western world, have such obscure authorship. It is easy enough to attribute the creation of the former to God, but readers of the latter have had to conjure up a human poet, wanting to imagine an author or authors for such sublime and authoritative narratives. Greek historical thinking always insisted upon ascribing every act, no matter how general or sweeping, to a single person; in Greek tradition the *Iliad* and the *Odyssey* were composed by a certain Homer, a blind singer from the island of Chios, whom they calculated to have lived at the latest in the ninth century B.C.E. The author of the so-called

Homeric Hymn to Apollo at one point identifies himself as this traditional figure, saying:

> Remember me later on when any man...comes here and asks you "Who do you think is the sweetest singer that comes here? Who is he who gives you the most delight?" Then be sure to reply all in one voice: "He is a blind man and lives in rocky Chios; now and forevermore his songs will be the best." [166–73]

Whether these lines are the source for the tradition or there is real substance to it cannot be known. Centuries of scholars have worried over the problem of the authorship of the *Iliad* and the *Odyssey*. Even in antiquity it was a subject of scholarly inquiry. A clever essay by the ancient Greek satirist Lucian recounts a journey into Hades, where he consults with the ghost of Homer on some disputed facts. Lucian certainly had the right idea. The only person who could satisfy our curiosity is Homer, and he is dead.

Twentieth-century research into the texts has raised a host of questions that bear directly on the way in which we read the two poems. Are they products of a time in which writing was unknown? Are they relics of a vanished second-millennium culture that survived in the tradition of court poets who recited from memory? Are they really true only to a later age in which they seem to have been composed? Are they written versions of oral performances in which a poet recollected, improvised, worked from memory with bits and pieces from a great repertory called the oral tradition? Is the oral tradition more the creator of these two poems than any one single poet? What is the relation of the oral performances to the written texts we possess? If every recital of an oral epic poem produced a demonstrably new poem, then are these two written texts evidence for two performances in which bards reinvented, as it were, these two narratives? What about reciting from memory? Could the poet or poets write? Did one poet create both poems or were there two? Were there lots of other poems that did not survive but were just as good, or from the same workshop? What kind of associations can we imagine the bards were making between the poems? What was the audience for these supposedly oral performances? Could they remember enough after hearing a poem to make associations the way literary people (or academics, at any rate) do? How often did they hear poems? how often these two poems (in any of their successive permutations)?

The reader by now may be moved to ask the really big question: does any of this matter? The facts surrounding the origin and transmission of the *Iliad* and the *Odyssey* are exceedingly meager; there is much speculation, much argument, much theory. Sound and fury signifying nothing? Well, no. Readers must, of course, rely upon their intelligence, taste, discernment, wit, and experience when they come to a text, but some may wish to know what facts we have and how they have been interpreted, so as to avoid as much as possible a facile assimilation of verbal constructs from a time and culture demonstrably and essentially alien to the contemporary world.

Research into the texts of the two poems during the latter half of our century has been decisive for most scholars in establishing that the poems themselves were created in a preliterate society, one that existed before the invention of writing. Although our only real evidence of the poems is the two texts of them—written texts and products, therefore, of a literate society—scholars postulate that the creation and formation of the poems took place in this earlier preliterate period. Innumerable mysteries abound, naturally, in accounting for their origin, transmission, and final reduction to written form. It is important at the beginning to establish the peculiarly oral nature of these poems, if for no other reason than to remind their readers that the aesthetics of oral narrative are not at all the same as those of Virgil's *Aeneid*, Milton's *Paradise Lost*, or, for that matter, Tolstoy's *War and Peace* or Proust's *A la recherche du temps perdu*. Written extended poetic or prose narratives such as these have been used at various times as the norm from which Homer criticism is quite mistakenly launched. Readers must understand as well that the poetic manner of the Homeric poems, which has sometimes been called "primitive" or "naive," is in fact the refined contrivance of a very sophisticated narrative tradition. Not for nothing did the ancient Greeks call Homer "the divine poet."

The theory of the oral composition of the *Iliad* and the *Odyssey* arose to account for two facts: (1) that over the several centuries in which it is assumed the poems took their shape there was no system of writing, and (2) that these poems describe or allude to a world that ended before writing was invented. Let us consider these in reverse order. Though the ancient Greeks got most of what they took to be serious information about their own prehistory from the Homeric poems, moderns rely on the findings of archaeology. Principally from archaeology we learn that Greek-speaking peoples settled in the area we now call Greece presumably toward the close of the third millennium B.C.E. In the second, those who had founded major settlements in the Peloponnesus created a culture that the archaeological remains indicate was a great empire. Historians call these people Mycenaeans after their principal city, Mycenae; they are thought to be the so-called Achaeans, the people described in the Homeric poems as fighting at Troy. Through the centuries credulity has alternated with skepticism about this great contest between the Greek and Trojan empires. We shall probably never know whether such a war was ever fought or whether Helen was indeed the cause, but the archaeological investigations begun by Heinrich Schliemann at Troy and Mycenae in the later part of the nineteenth century and continued there and at other Mycenaean sites to this day make abundantly clear that the world of Homer's Achaeans (our Mycenaeans) did in fact exist. Furthermore, there are artifacts and customs described in the poems which can confidently be assigned to that civilization and not to later times. Without writing, knowledge of these would have had to be carried in humankind's memory in some other fashion.

These poems, then, are part of a saga tradition that seems to derive from historical fact. It survived the collapse and breakup of this Achaean or Mycenaean world in the eleventh century B.C.e. and somehow had the means to maintain itself into a time when a Homer spoke, even to the moment when what he spoke was written down. From their experience of the Semitic writing system, the Greeks worked out an alphabet during the late eighth century. Long before that the Mycenaeans had adapted a Minoan system of writing known today as Linear B (its glamorous name bestowed by the archaeologists who first uncovered specimens of it). Linear B has been deciphered as a system of notation for the Greek language, a syllabary of about ninety symbols used, as we can tell from its surviving examples, for writing documents associated with administration. Nothing of poetry survives in it; no evidence of Linear B survives from a later time. The theory, therefore, is that the Linear B script was too cumbersome for any but a professional class of clerks and scribes to know and use and that it did not survive the decline in administration that followed the collapse of the Mycenaean empire.

Furthermore, statistical studies of the diction created by the poet or poets of these poems seem to argue for language usage utterly dissimilar to that of literate poets, usage designed to maximize the opportunities for creating line after line of metered verse spontaneously in what is assumed to have been performances like those described in the *Odyssey*. The poems are so long that rote memory cannot have been the vehicle for transmission. Some combination of memory and its creative application in performance would have been needed; or one might define it as performance, meditated but not rehearsed, of recollected material. It is in any case neither improvisation nor recitation from memory.

Examination of Homeric diction and style reveals that such an oral recital was made possible by the imaginative combination of inherited formulas: that is, repeated phrases. In ordinary human speech, individual words that are symbols of things are combined to create a larger concept. In epic Greek, however, more often than not the minimal element seems to be the formulaic phrase, the combination of a noun and an adjective. Any reader of the Homeric poems will immediately remember recurring components of the narrative such as "the wine-dark sea," "the hollow ships," "swift-footed Achilles." They are far more pervasive than most translations suggest. Still more important, each formulaic phrase is defined by its metrical value, which means it will fit some places in the line but not others.

Poetry differs from prose or ordinary speech by the fixed rhythms that identify it. The language of the *Iliad* and the *Odyssey* is cast in a metrical form known as dactylic hexameter. This is a system found also in Sanskrit poetry, and one may argue that the Greeks inherited epic poetry in dactylic hexametric rhythm from their Indo-European ancestors, from whom the speakers of Sanskrit also descend. The dactylic hexametric line consists of six units, or feet, as they are called by metricians; the first five of these are either one so-called long syllable followed by two short syllables ($-\smile\smile$), or simply two long syllables ($--$); the sixth foot is disyllabic, the first syllable invariably long, the second long or short ($-\,\overset{\smile}{-}$). Because it is distinct in its metrical shape, this disyllabic element marks a line end, even if the sentence continues into the next line.

The system of formulas in the Homeric poems shows the same breadth and economy that characterize the vocabulary of a language system: that is, all the words needed to express everything, and no two words that mean exactly the same thing. Although for different metrical positions within a line there will be different phrases expressing the same thing, phrases of identical metrical quantity which say the same thing are very few. The poet's language is made up of metrical phrases rather than individual words; each phrase is of course a larger unit of verse than each individual word, so these phrases drastically reduce the effort of the singer-composer, who does not have to juggle so many loose elements in each dactylic line. Individual words as well have metrical value and thus can hold only those places in the line where they fit metrically. The singer is aided by another convention: for every word there are preferred positions in the line even when other places are possible. This suggests that the poets combined a certain metrical feel of a word with a sense of the rhythmic shape of the line. As the unconscious and the conscious mind went through the nanoseconds of assembling the language that made the narrative of the story, the poet was helped by intuiting where to situate a key phrase or word in the line. Some studies suggest that the poet created phrases by analogy; that is to say, phrases phonetically or grammatically analogous to recognized formulas have been identified. It would be as though an English poet made the phrases "on the bone-dry land" and "in the snow-white room" on the analogy of the traditional "on the wine-dark sea." All three phrases, each with preposition, compound adjective, and noun object, are made up of monosyllablic words, all of them with the same accentual value.

The absence of phrases that are at once metrically and semantically similar seems to show that a process of selection and economizing was at work over a long period of time, that generations of poets—or bards, as they are often called—developed the best possible combinations: first to indicate their precise meaning, second to ensure flexibility in creating a line. The statistical analyses that showed this economic use of formulaic phrases fitting every metrical situation immediately shed a kind of theoretical light on the problem of the transmission by memory of so long a poem as either the *Iliad* or the *Odyssey* over so long a period of time: the solution was that no one had to memorize the poem. The poet or poets built with phrases, half-lines, and sometimes repeated whole lines rather than words. The earliest scholars who worked out the oral theory as it applies to the Homeric texts insisted that the adjectival part of the phrase—the epithet, as it is usually called—was essentially a neutral element that gave the line metrical value rather than important sense. In their view the phrase "he spoke winged words," which occurs relatively frequently, meant absolutely nothing more than "he spoke."

The notion that Homer, whoever he, she, or they might have been, was possibly no more than a collection of poets working on these poems over centuries, making their story out of half-remembered routines and stereotypes, coming up with phraseology to meet the mechanical need of versification, was more than many devoted readers of the poems could stomach. There has always been resistance to the extreme position advanced by the earliest adherents of the theory. The one aesthetic principle arising from this extreme mechanistic view of the process of Homeric versemaking is that over time the listener would develop a sense of what we might call "the rightness of things" or "the inevitability of things." The tendency of the ancient Greeks to look past reality to the ideal might be thought to derive from this principle, as well as the overdeveloped sense of irony that helped them arrive at a tragic view of life, in which what must be engulfs figures still naively indulging in what they fondly imagine to be free will. Perhaps nothing more vividly describes the irony of the human condition than individuals exercising what they imagine to be their personal sovereignty in language patterns so relentlessly fixed and thus inevitable.

While the phraseology of the poems seems often the most mechanical aspect of the poem's manner, this formulaic language too has its peculiarly realistic effect. Greek epic poetry, as stated earlier, is made up of phrases that seem to be the product of centuries of practice. The manner in which this phraseology is achieved is most clearly seen in the qualifying epithets. These pose a real problem for the translator. If they are faithfully translated whenever they appear, the poem will seem heavy and wooden for readers who are in the habit of reading every word and reading for sense. If they are omitted, the reader without Greek is often unaware of how important they are to the fabric of the poem, for they very substantially buttress an intricate system of metrical language. Greek, like Latin, is an inflected language (remnants of inflection appear in English, such as in the pronoun forms "he," "his," "him," or the second- and third-person verb forms of Shakespeare's "thou goest," "she goeth"), and naturally, not every form of noun or verb in an inflected language will be metrically the same. Analogies from English do not altogether work, but if we consider the time elapsed in the voicing of each syllable, it would be fair to say that the genitive form "man's" takes longer to utter than the nominative form "man." More obviously, "drove" is metrically quite different from "have driven." Consider a language in which a noun could conceivably appear in fourteen different forms and a verb in well over one hundred, where some forms are metrically similar but the majority are not. The problem of matching grammar to the metrics is magnified to the limit.

This feature of inflection is an important aspect of the system of noun-adjective formulas which the early researchers discovered in the poems. A series of ornamental epithets combined with names turned up in regular patterns of usage significantly tied to the differing metrical demands of each noun and verb ending: that is to say, every name has a specific epithet to be employed for each grammatical case that is metrically different. The semantics determine the syntax, which in turn determines the form of the noun, which finally determines the particular epithet used. In the *Iliad*, Odysseus is generally "shining" in the nominative, "godlike" in the genitive, "greathearted" in the dative, and "like unto Zeus in counsel" in the accusative case. A great many epithets are common to metrically identical names, but some are reserved for one character, such as "swift-footed," which with one exception is applied in both epics only to Achilles. These epithets are thought to be either more capable of characterizing or consistently attached to names of characters more completely individualized in the Homeric poet's mind.

It is hard to know in what sense the audience received these epithets. One would think that they recurred so quickly and were, so to speak, so shopworn as to go unheard in the positive sense. Because the audience anticipated an epithet in conjunction with a noun, its attention might be slacker in the split second of utterance. Certainly their ubiquity and inevitability render these epithets less potent in significance. The narrator, the audience will assume, sincerely believes that Achilles is the best of the Achaeans, yet from time to time the phrase is attached to another—to Diomedes, for instance. Like a Hollywood press agent who builds up whichever starlet happens to be in his company at the moment, the Homeric narrator magnifies Diomedes at that moment with the phrase. Many argue, however, that in oral poetry what the narrator says is true only for that moment, and the audience would not qualify the utterance by its recollection of other moments. This use of "best of the Achaeans" seems proof of the argument.

One must, nonetheless, be cautious. Sometimes it seems that the deployment of an epithet is true to the story as a subconscious revelation. Consider the very close of the first book of the *Iliad:* "Then up to bed went Zeus and down beside him lay Hera of the golden throne." Now Hera can also be described as "Hera of the soft white arms" in a slightly different metrical situation, and one might think that the narrator would work to create a line to accommodate the latter epithet. Since he does not, the reader will forgive Homer the awkwardness of the adjectival phrase qualifying Hera on the theory that this is simply another of the mechanical applications of epithets. Yet the scene preceding the line is one of great anger between the divine couple, a fight so ugly that the rest of the gods move in to restore tranquility. Perhaps the narrator unconsciously plays to that scene by depositing a bulky piece of furniture in the royal bed between the warring couple.

One might argue that these epithets go to establish the realism of the poem. They tend to attribute to persons and objects eternal, immutable qualities that the exigencies of the moment cannot alter. When this is so, what matter if ships rotting on the beach are called "swift," or the sea in a summer's calm is called "hoary with white caps"? Because the epithets are so particular in their focus, they do not idealize or generalize the object or person to which they are attached; they bring to attention only a facet, and from the constantly changing facets that the bard displays in the epithets there is created the illusion of change and of the unique, of the underlying reality of things which accident and surface temporarily distort or hide. The sense of shifting and variegated reality in these narratives owes much to this kaleidoscopic effect.

The depiction of the common events of the heroic environment are among the more obvious examples of how the epic poets gave formulaic expression to narrative. The arrival of dawn, for instance, when indicated as an isolated fact, is rendered by "Dawn rose from bed, from the side of illustrious Tithonus, so that she might bring light to immortals and mortals." But when it serves a temporal conjunction, the formula is "when early-born rosy-fingered Dawn appeared." The necessary addition of the Greek equivalent of the word "when" obviously establishes an entirely different metrical dynamic.

These ubiquitous expressions of the Homeric poems will not bear repeating for an audience of readers who savor each word, knowing that they can look back if memory grows dim or interest is piqued. A reading audience wants variety in successive expositions of the same idea. The audience of the oral poet, however, makes no such demands; the spoken word has at best a very brief past or future, and the voiced statement scarcely outlives the moment of utterance.

In addition, the hearing of a normal person misses about half of what is said, the mind filling in the lacunae unconsciously from a knowledge of the language and the presumed intent of the speaker. Clichés are therefore essential to any sustained session of listening, along with, we must grant, heightened attention on the part of the audience. In accounting for the continued enjoyment that Greek epic gives to generations of humankind whose temper and manner are more or less alien to the epic style, the formulaic element is an important consideration. In a poetic manner which is in so many ways artificial and unreal, the elaborated formulaic lines, depicting in clichés such common events as eating, sleeping, rising, or leave-taking, come to be apt representations of the real action, which, being both frequent and common to all human experience, is in itself a true cliché.

Roughly one-third of the Homeric epics consists of repeated lines, many of them of the sort that have just been discussed. Many more are routine one-line descriptions of maneuvers in hand-to-hand fighting. Some repeated passages consist of a speech delivered to one person, who in turn relays it to another. Neither a summary of the speech nor a simple reference to it would be consonant with oral technique, which must accommodate to the fact that everything that has been said no longer exists. Paraphrase, one might say, implies a past, while exact repetition insists upon the present. This seems true to the oral psychology. The sort of paraphrase that Homer tries is really not paraphrase at all. When in the first book of the *Iliad* Achilles recounts to his mother, Thetis, the events that led to his quarrel with Agamemnon, the poet uses line for line some of his earlier description of the event, omitting simply the intervening speeches of the priest Chryses and of Agamemnon. The absence of paraphrase, reference, or summary suggests that narrative once spoken not only no longer exists but on the conscious level never existed. The exact repetition over several hundred lines suggests that if this reflects real conditions of performance, then the poet's contrivance, much of it no doubt repeated from occasion to occasion of telling this particular story, remained in the brain as a palpable verbal construct for a real period of time before being dissolved once again into words and phrases no longer making an intelligible whole.

The repetition of certain passages of seemingly greater significance will impress readers, who look for motive, for intended irony, and the like. Is this search legitimate? Being trained to discover levels of meaning by slow, careful, and repeated inspection of the text, do we not read in a more sophisticated way than oral poets could possibly imagine their audiences to hear? For an auditor, how many lines of spoken verse can separate similar passages before the memory of the first one is thoroughly blurred? Does the epic poet attempt to direct the attention either back or forward, and, if not, would an auditor have the instinct to remember more than the plot? These are hard questions to answer, although in some sense it does not matter, since nothing prevents contemporary readers from making meaning as they choose, all the while ignoring questions of literary history. True knowledge of the past often has a decidedly deadening effect upon the contemporary aesthetic enjoyment of antiquity. Consider ancient Greek sculpture or temple architecture, for example: contemporary taste demands that they be damaged and fragmented and bereft of their painted surfaces.

Let us consider, however, another case of repetition in which it seems much more likely that connections are being made subconsciously. Would an audience of listeners in oral performance note these repetitions, make these connections? Some critics insist upon extraordinary powers of memory in an audience habituated to listening, unable to read, and ready for the infrequent stimulus of chanted verse. Eight extended similes are repeated in the two poems, six in the *Iliad* and two in the *Odyssey* (although, since one in the *Odyssey* occurs in a repeated speech, it can be discounted). Precise or nearly precise repetition in a work where the style displays repetition through *variation* seems striking. These repeated similes cannot be compared to an exactly repeated phrase like "rosy-fingered Dawn sprang from the bed of Tithonus to bring light to mortals"; nor, again can they be compared to the formalized repetitions of typical scenes of arming, leave-taking, banqueting, and so on. There are hundreds of similes in the poems, and only these few are exactly repeated. That seems significant.

Two similes seem so obviously functional in the structure of the narrative that one searches the others for a similar use. One is the simile comparing Agamemnon's tears to "dark spring water which trickles down black from the sheer rock steep even for goats" (*Il.* 9. 14–15), which is repeated to describe the weeping of Patroclus (16.3–4). Agamemnon cries as he ponders in despair what to do for the failing Achaean cause shortly before his council of advisers encourages him to send an embassy to ask Achilles to return to battle. Patroclus cries as he returns from learning of the desperate straits into which the Achaeans have fallen and asks Achilles to return to the fight. In both instances imminent destruction for the Achaean cause has produced an emotion that impels someone to petition Achilles; he refuses in the first instance and partially accepts in the second, sending his surrogate out to certain death, thus prefiguring his own shortly thereafter.

In the ninth book Achilles is asked three times to return to battle, and three times he refuses. As we can observe in folktales from many cultures, there is a certain fatal turn of events connected with the triad—in the *Iliad* itself, for instance, when Patroclus charges the Trojan walls three times. At the close of the ninth book the poet is poised for the folkloric turn from three to four. But the poet of the *Iliad*, telling a vast and complicated story, seems to mean to hold the tale together by laying out the narration on a grid of story structures, and this is one. The audience awaits this particular denouement, the move from three to four in Achilles' response to supplication. At the same time, the poet prepares the audience for Patroclus as the eventual fourth supplicator with the tale of a hero just like Achilles, the obdurate Meleager, who three times denies entreaties—first of the leading Aetolian political figures, second of his father and family, third of his friends—and then in the fatal fourth turn yields to the supplication of his wife, Cleopatra. Comparison with this story pattern in other cultures reveals that the *Iliad* poet has advanced the friends to third position and left the wife for last. This maneuver implies that the poet is intent upon making some connection with Meleager's wife and Achilles' companion; one may also note that their names are almost anagrams of each other, Patro-clus and Cleo-patra, both meaning "glory of the father." In the story Meleager finally relents when his wife entreats him, but it is too late for him to gain any benefit from it. Achilles, too, stands to gain nothing from relenting so late. Patroclus, his alter ego, will go to his death after having entreated his companion.

From the ninth to the sixteenth book the narrator brings into the story a variety of scenes having to do with the Achaean retreat and the Trojan advance upon their ships. At the beginning of the sixteenth book he returns to the narrative of the fatal refusals which he had inaugurated with Agamemnon's tears at the beginning of the ninth. The progression from Agamemnon to Patroclus is in this sense as immediate as that from the Aetolian elders to Meleager's wife. The intervening action, or the illogicality of Achilles' continuing bitterness at Agamemnon—for the studious reader will note that Agamemnon in Book Nine has offered gifts as amends, which Achilles in Book Sixteen seems to have forgotten—is only the surface of the underlying logic of the move from the third to the fourth request. The repeated simile describing the crying of Agamemnon and then the crying of Patroclus is the tip of that underlying structure, a mnemonic device for bard and audience alike by which the narrative is held in place. Some may consider this an all too casual dismissal of what seems to be a real contradiction in Achilles' refusal to remember Agamemnon's attempts at amends. Let them consider how often *structures* inform the Homeric narrative, much more dynamically than any psychological nexus seems to do. The great example is Penelope's decision to hold the contest of the bow (discussed early in Chapter 3).

The other simile whose repetition seems so clearly functional occurs when Athena's physical transformation of Odysseus is compared to a master craftsman's overlay of gold on silver, first at Scheria (*Od.* 6.232–34), then back at the palace at Ithaca (23.159–61). When Odysseus has washed the brine from his body, he steps out clothed in the borrowed garments, and Athena, who plays Fairy Godmother in this charming scene to Odysseus's Cinderella and Nausicaa's Prince, transforms him into a considerably handsomer fellow. Later in the poem, after Odysseus has killed the suitors, he goes to wash off the blood and the grime. He then emerges ready for the long-awaited meeting with his wife, and Athena once more transforms him. It has been suggested that the poet means to recall us consciously to the scene of Odysseus and Nausicaa's first meeting. Apart from the real unlikelihood that an oral poet can or would think to return his auditor to something now long gone in the saying, the notion seems crude. Should we and Odysseus confront his long-sought spouse with the memory of a desirable and desiring girl in his and our minds? That kind of reverie would be an unlikely reading of this repeated simile in the context of this momentous occasion, unlikely at least for all but the very cynical. More likely the repeated simile is part of an ensemble of events which has to do with the wooing of a princess. The *Odyssey* poet is clearly intrigued with repetitions. One thinks of the arrival scenes, or the disguised Odysseus's false autobiographies, or the Circe/Calypso/Penelope replication. The repetition directs the reader of the scene of Penelope and Odysseus in reunion to a subconscious recall of the erotic undertones which had been so much on the surface in the beach encounter between the hesitant, naked hero and the eager, nubile princess. As Odysseus confronts Penelope, the unlikely underdog has won the princess and he is being transformed. He washes off the filth as he washed off the brine. Penelope awaits him; now it is she who is hesitant, he who is eager. The wooing commences.

The *Iliad*'s most celebrated simile is also repeated. In the first instance (6.506–11), Paris, who is leaving Helen to return to battle, is compared to a horse galloping forth into pasture, freed from his stable. This is a remarkably precise statement of Paris's mood and attitude as he emerges from an amorous encounter with Helen. The scenes involving Paris in the third and sixth books have established him as a sexual artist and athlete who owes his special nobility to a splendid body and the natural use he brilliantly makes of it. As Paris dashes forth to join Hector on his way to the battlefield, all the qualities of masculine sexuality well used are evoked by the simile. He has obviously come from Helen's bed ("from the stable, sated at the trough"); he experiences the freedom and vigor that are the aftermath of sexual intercourse ("snaps his halter, rushes out on the plain, stamping hoof"); he will wash away the sweat of lovemaking in the sweat of the battle ("accustomed to wash in the fair-flowing river"); he is proud and happy in the knowledge that he is good in bed ("proud, head held high, . . . he knows he's splendid"). The simile is remarkable because every element exactly fits the moment, whereas Homeric similes generally are fitted to a theme and only then to a context. So close is the fit here that one might remember it over thousands of lines. Particularly if it were a well-known piece from the poet's repertory, if it were always a way of describing Paris, then it might become a powerful element of irony when it is later applied to Hector, because Hector is not the Paris of this narrative, a man who leads a charmed life.

The simile reappears in the fifteenth book (15.263–68) when Hector is animated by Apollo to reenter the battle. Struck down by Ajax, Hector lies on the ground spitting blood; when he finally recovers enough to sit up, he is directly encouraged by the god. Here the simile is specifically apt only as it compares Hector freed of his disabilities to a horse freed from the stable, and Hector rejoining his fellow soldiers to a horse going with the other horses in the meadow. As we have seen, the repetition of a simile can have some significance. Ignoring the possible ironies that are likely to occur to the reader, let us consider this repetition as part of a larger pattern with which the poet is dealing. Here we can talk in terms of a repetition of narrative structure: the return to battle; we have in both cases the entry of the hero into battle. Are there, however, more precise correspondences to suggest that the second passage is in some way a restatement of the first, as seems to be the case with the other two similes? In its first appearance the simile marks Paris's reentry into battle, which precedes the duel between Ajax and Hector. The poet is giving a vast background review of the Trojan War before moving to the immediate story in the eighth book. At the point when the simile occurs, the poet has only one last detail to introduce and that is the cause of the animosity between the Trojans and the Achaeans: Paris's refusal to give up Helen. The refusal is described after the duel; it is a refusal calculated to follow such a duel. One might have expected it following a duel between husband and paramour—but Ajax and Hector are fighting for Helen as a possession, not as a sexual partner. (Here Helen is a variant of Briseis, the woman Agamemnon takes from Achilles not for lust but to show his power.) Paris's refusal does not follow altogether logically and naturally from the duel, since Helen is his sexual partner. The poet needs to emphasize Paris so that he will not be upstaged by the duel; he furthermore needs to qualify Paris as the man who possesses Helen sexually. Hence the long and evocative simile, so particularly fit to the circumstance, which accompanies Paris's entry into battle.

In the fifteenth book a similar turning point makes the reappearance of this particular simile altogether satisfying. Hector, once encouraged by Apollo, returns to the battle and, surpassing even himself on previous occasions, brings the fight close in to the Achaean encampment so that at last he lays hands upon one of the ships. This is the crisis moment that even Achilles had envisioned. Hector's furious dash is the very provocation that leads Patroclus to beseech Achilles, which in turn leads to Patroclus's death and thereafter to the resolution of this narrative. So it is that the selfsame simile is used to describe the entry into battle of the two major Trojan figures and to mark the entry as fundamental to the story of Achilles and of the Trojan War. The first time the simile appears, Paris opens up the plot by refusing to return Helen; in its second use Hector acts to bring the story to its conclusion by bringing furious fighting down to the ships.

The same deep structure lies beneath a repeated simile that describes first Ajax being forced back in battle, then Menelaus leaving battle, as a hungry lion at a cattle pen who is kept out and finally forced away by the farmers and their dogs. The simile first occurs in a scene (11.548ff.) in which one after another of the Achaean chieftains has been wounded in battle and drops out until finally Ajax is left alone. At this point Nestor, the old king of Pylos, is told to withdraw with the wounded medicine man, Machaon. Then in the renewed fighting Ajax is forced to retreat, and the simile occurs. Moments later the poet reminds us that Nestor has set off with Machaon. It is this that Achilles notices, as the narrator tells us, and the reason he sends Patroclus out to learn what is happening. In the battle over Patroclus's body in the seventeenth book Ajax is again prominent in battle, and he sends Menelaus out to tell Achilles that Patroclus is dead. The simile (17.657ff.) is not altogether apt, since there is no reluctant lion in Menelaus's willing departure. Think, however, of the structural position of the repeated similes. In both scenes Ajax is prominent. A fellow Achaean is asked to withdraw for some reason other than fighting. The withdrawal in both instances is bound up with Achilles' gaining information. In the eleventh book when Achilles notices Nestor withdrawing, he sends Patroclus to get information and report back to him. It is this request that causes the chain of events which leads to Patroclus's death. Here in the seventeenth book Menelaus is sent from the battle so that Achilles can indeed get the final report of something begun so long ago in the action of the eleventh book. One might say that this is a rather grand example of what is called ring composition in epic poetry, where the end of the narrative is implicit in its beginning and the beginning returns at the end. The simile in its second appearance does not fit so well—in fact, it blunts the sense of the passage—but is obedient to other narrative values. These are the architectonic strategies by which the poet determines the shape of his story.

The reader is not exactly sure how to interpret exact repetitions when they occur in passages that are formally very similar. Compare Agamemnon's speech to Menelaus, after the latter has been wounded in the deceitful breaking of the truce in the fourth book of the *Iliad*, with Hector's farewell to Andromache in the sixth book.

AGAMEMNON TO MENELAUS:

Dear brother, now it seems that it was your death that I   4.155
    was forging in the truce,
setting you out in front of the Achaeans to fight the Trojans
    alone,

since the Trojans have attacked you and trampled on the
    oaths we trusted.
But the oath and the blood of lambs are not at all in vain,
nor the libations of unmixed wine and the right hands we
    clasped in good faith.
For even if the Olympian has not immediately brought the   160
    consequences,
soon he shall, and they will pay greatly for this,
with their own lives, their wives, and their children.
For this I know full well in my mind and in my heart:
There will come a day sometime when holy Ilium shall perish,
and Priam and the people of Priam of the ashen spear.   165
Zeus, son of Cronus, in his high throne, dwelling in the
    sky,
he himself shall shake his threatening aegis at all of them,
angry at this deceit. And these things will not go undone.
But for me there will be a dreadful ache because of you,
    Menelaus,
if you should die and accomplish the term of your life,   170
and I were to return blamed and despised to thirsty Argos.
For the Achaians will immediately begin to think of their
    homeland,
and we would leave to Priam and the Trojans their
    triumph,
Helen of Argos, while the earth will rot your bones
as you lie in the land of Troy, your goal unreached.   175
And some one of the exulting Trojans will say,
jumping upon the tomb of glorious Menelaus:
"Would that Agamemnon might vent his anger in this
    fashion always,
he, who led an armada of Achaeans here,
and now has gone home, back to his dear fatherland   180
with empty ships, leaving the noble Menelaus."
Thus sometime will someone speak. But when that
happens let the wide earth open for me.

HECTOR TO ANDROMACHE:

I, too, my wife, am thinking of these things. But dreadfully   6.441
shamed would I be before the Trojans and their long-
    gowned women
if like a coward I were to slink away from battle.
Nor does my spirit allow it, since first I learned to be
    courageous
always, and to fight in the forefront of the Trojans,   445
gathering great glory for my father and for me as well.

For this I know full well in my mind and in my heart:
There will come a day sometime when holy Ilium shall perish,
and Priam and the people of Priam of the ashen spear.
But it is not so much the grief that will come to the Trojans   450
   that moves me
nor that of Hecuba herself, nor of Lord Priam,
nor that of my brothers, who many and noble
have fallen in the dust at the hands of enemy men,
as your grief, when some one of the bronze-clad Achaeans
leads you off in tears, taking away your days of freedom.   455
Then perhaps in Argos you will work the loom for another
   woman,
and perhaps carry water from the spring Messeis or
   Hypereia,
much forced, and heavy necessity will lie upon you.
And then sometime someone seeing you crying may say,
"There goes the wife of Hector who used to be the finest   460
   warrior
among the horse-taming Trojans, when they fought over
   Ilium."
Thus someday will someone speak. For you it will be yet a
   new grief,
bereft of such a man who could have warded off your
   slavery.
But may the earth, heaped up, cover me dead
at least before I hear the sound of your cries and your being
   led away.

The two speeches have many similarities. Both are speeches of compassion delivered by the stronger of two related persons. Roughly the same length, they begin by acknowledging one point of view (4.155–57; 6.441) but preferring another (4.158–62; 6.441–46) for the same reason (the identical lines, italicized here). After a few more lines, the concern of both speeches turns to the person being addressed (4.169ff.; 6.454ff.); a situation in which each is humbled (Menelaus dead; Andromache enslaved) is envisioned, imaginary remarks delivered at each in their humbled state (4.178–81; 6.460–61). In both cases the imaginary remarks reflect back upon the speaker (Agamemnon; Hector). Both speeches end with a prayer for death if the alternative is to witness the misfortune being conceived.

The logic that calls for the introduction of the parallel lines is quite obvious in the case of Agamemnon's speech. Troy's wrongdoing in having broken the treaty is only another outward manifestation of the moral inevitability that will destroy the city. Hector's use of the lines is somewhat awkward, but the logic must be that since doom is inevitable, vigorous fighting is the only possible course of action. Strategic retreat (which is what Andromache is advocating) has less glory in it and under the circumstances would accomplish nothing. The speeches therefore are integral unities; there is no need to consider the possibility of an interpolation in Hector's speech.

The speeches are separated by roughly one thousand lines; that distance—or we might consider it length of time in performance—seems to cancel out the possibility that the similarity is something to which the Homeric poet is playing. And yet not only are the speeches much like each other; they seem unlike any other stock speeches of the poem. The *Iliad* devotes so much attention to the inexorable processes of the cosmos that one is inclined to see the two speeches as conscious representation of two aspects of Troy's doom. The exactly repeated lines would be a definite mnemonic signal. On the other hand, one may imagine that the first speech inspired the second; that is, the shape and logic of the first may have become a kind of template for another. The speech to Andromache, once under way, began to assume the shape of the earlier speech possibly because the poet, instinctively realizing that this was Hector's farewell to his wife and that she would next appear in the poem as a widow, thought of the lines that I have italicized. It is doubtful that an auditor would have noticed.

How would an auditor take in Athena's directions to Telemachus in the first book of the *Odyssey* (1.271–97)? To a reader her words seem so muddled, so inconsistent. But can we assume an entirely different response from those hearing the poem in performance? The instructions in effect offer a direction for the plot in the next several thousand lines. As a program they may be followed, or for purposes of suspense and surprise they may be overturned, but they are so contradictory that no action could possibly result. Athena tells Telemachus to summon the suitors to a public meeting, to tell each to go to his home, to send his mother home to her parents who will arrange a new marriage for her; then she tells him to sail to the mainland to seek news of his father and, if he hears that Odysseus is dead, to return to pay funeral honors to his father and give his mother a new husband; and finally after all this is done he is to consider the means to kill off the suitors who throng in the palace. Poor Telemachus! How is he to proceed? This peculiar advice must be accounted for.

The nineteenth-century solution was to imagine a later composer who joined the first book to the second and in so doing took from the speeches of the suitors in the second some of the contrary advice Athena offers in the first. But this is to misunderstand the mentality of any so-called "later composer," which is to say, the mentality of a copy editor devoted to bringing order out of confusion, clarity out of obscurity.

It seems odd that these earlier critics of the poems defined as the work of the later editor what they saw as inconsistencies, outright contradictions, and glaring error, when editors have an objectivity that creators rarely possess. Undoubtedly, these nineteenth-century critics were much influenced by Bible criticism of the time. But the Torah narrative is fundamentally different from the Homeric poems because it is *sacred text*. Those who compiled the verses we possess were compelled in preserving what was sacred to sacrifice narrative values to religious ones; that is, they had to accept every inconsistency. The Bible scholar therefore has the obvious task of separating out variant narrative by using the inconsistencies as clues. It is an approach thoroughly unsuited to the problems of the transmission of the Homeric poems. Whatever the role of the sixth-century Athenian tyrant Pisistratus in the making of public performances of the *Iliad* and the *Odyssey*, he and those around him were not a rabbinical council.

Athena's contrary advice is the poet's doing, and he had his reasons; it seems unreasonable to update the inconsistency argument and make it congruent with the oral theory by imagining that the poet during performance was thinking ahead so hard that he inadvertently introduced some of the suitors' advice from the second book into Athena's speech. Rather, one might expend a little critical goodwill and consider that in a legend well known, every conceivable opportunity for suspense or surprise must be explored; that in so long a poem some sort of outline of the plot needs to be offered to the auditor, an outline which at the same time allows the poet some freedom to maneuver. The poet of the *Odyssey* has managed exactly that in Athena's speech. The goddess's arrival in Ithaca upsets the status quo and sets the action going; the poet, however, wishes to introduce a sense of crisis on the human level. All the remarks in the first two books alluding to Penelope's impending remarriage do this; time is running out for Telemachus and for Odysseus, and the son must act. Thus the assembly and the plans for his trip are overhung with a real sense of urgency.

At the same time the voyage of inquiry is made suspenseful, because on its outcome somehow the fate of Telemachus and Penelope will be decided. Finally there remains in the background the tantalizing fact that the suitors may be killed. Upon *reading over* Athena's speech anyone can say that its contradictions nullify any emotional impact it might have. The poet, however, has no intention of its being read over; he would not even consider repeating it. Each successive step in Athena's directions may contradict, but there is no way the auditor can stop the performance to go back and check. This speech is an excellent proof for some kind of narrative style that derives from expectations and makes demands quite different from those of a written text: that is to say, verse creation in performance.

Nonetheless, the oral theory for the origin of the *Iliad* and the *Odyssey* is finally no more than theory. A considerable amount of empirical evidence taken from contemporary living oral traditions has been assembled to give it substance. Most persons imagine on the basis of it that during the Mycenaean period there flourished court poets or bards whose principal occupation was to sing about the exploits of the famous and powerful men of the locale. Demodocus, the singing poet at the court of Alcinous (*Od.* 8.471ff.), is what we imagine them to be like. Blind, he is led forth with great respect, his lyre placed in his hands, and he composes a song—on one occasion a tale of the events of Troy, on another, a rather saucy account of Ares and Aphrodite caught in adultery by her husband Hephaestus. The bard was no minor retainer; he held a high position. Agamemnon, the *Odyssey* tells us, left his court bard as guardian over his wife, Clytemnestra, a task to which the poet proved unequal. Of course, one might argue that since in the *Odyssey* story, as we have it, there is considerable emphasis on the importance of singers, singing, storymaking, it would be consistent to elevate the poet to the role of confidant and intimate of the king.

The *Iliad* and the *Odyssey* are specimens of what is called heroic poetry. Presumably these narratives arose from the need to celebrate the deeds of famous local men, now dead and sanctified, the objects of a local hero cult. Heroes of the neighborhood were no doubt the local strong men, possibly similar to the Mafia dons of our own history and legend, who gave protection in return for the various services weaker or milder folk were prepared to render. The extraordinary emphasis on physical violence in the *Iliad*, the obvious correlation between immortal glory and mayhem, seem to suggest what kind of men were being celebrated. Modern readers should not, however, lose sight of the fact that in a world of limited political controls and no police systems or state militias, the welcome peace is kept by those who kill and control. A remarkable fact of the two Homeric poems is that they project considerably loftier concerns than the satisfaction of neighborhood domination.

There survive two other dactylic hexametric poems which are thought to be from the oral period. These are *Works* and *Days* and *Theogony* (Origin of the gods) by a certain Hesiod, who is much more willing to identify himself than is the narrator of the *Iliad* and the *Odyssey*. Although it is not clear how contemporaneous the Hesiodic poems are, they are valuable as specimens of some of the other poetry that was perhaps going from mouth to ear during that time. Hesiod describes himself at one point as going overseas from mainland Boeotia to an island to sing in a competition, which suggests a far broader arena for poetic activity than what the reader imagines from reading about Demodocus. Hesiod's poems are not unlike various pieces of Eastern oral poetry that have survived in texts, such as the Babylonian *Enuma Elis* or portions of the *Mahabharata*. *Theogony* is a poetic account of the origin of the gods and humankind, organized into a series of what the Hellenistic critics called catalogues: lists of proper names. Many of the deities included are no more than abstractions of natural phenomena. Consider, for example, the following genealogy:

> Night bore hateful Doom and black Disaster
> and Death, she bore as well Sleep, she bore the race of Dreams;
> then again she bore Blame and painful Misery, these
> without sexual intercourse did dark Night bear.
> [*Theogony* 211–14]

The reader will note that from time to time something very like this passage crops up in the Homeric narratives. In the eighteenth book of the *Iliad*, for example, when Thetis arrives to comfort her son, Achilles, she is accompanied by other Nereids, whom the narrator then proceeds to list. The celebrated Catalogue of Ships in the second book of the *Iliad* is a passage of several hundred lines in which the narrator lists the contingents of Achaeans and their allies who came to fight at Troy. The so-called Catalogue of Women is a list of famous women from myth whom Odysseus sees in the underworld (*Od.* 11.225–330). Something like the abstractions of natural phenomena which abound in Hesiod's poems occurs in Phoenix's speech to Achilles in the ninth book of the *Iliad* as he tries to define the psychology of having to say "I'm sorry": "Entreaties for Forgiveness are the daughters of Zeus and they come along scuffing and dragging their feet, their faces all scrunched up, unable to look one in the eye" (9.502–3).

Works and Days is a mélange of maxims, fables, agricultural lore, rural calendars—all bound together in dactylic hexameters to serve the greater end of a disquisition on the nature of justice. It is considerably more overtly philosophical than anything the reader will find in the Homeric narratives, yet the instinct to render experience in axiomatic or epigrammatic sayings is not unknown to the narrators of the *Iliad* or the *Odyssey*.

Heroic poetry, sung in praise of famous men, could conceivably have had immense social value, first, in a culture that had no access to written archival records and had to get its history from those who claimed to remember, and second, for those men whose justification for existence came from their hopes of posthumous fame. There are so many forms of social communication today that it requires a great effort of the imagination to envision a world of absolute silence, empty of telephones, television, cinema, the printed word, and all the other instruments that work to maintain a verbal construct of our shared reality. The quotations at the head of this chapter speak to the value of a poetry that rescues people and places and actions from anonymity, from the death of being forgotten. Even Iphidamas came to Troy so that he could get into history, so to speak, by dying in an Achaean heroic praise poem. Helen realizes that all the misery and madness she has had to endure since leaving Menelaus were simply the means by which she entered the true realm of story, not the death-in-life obscurity of sitting out her days in the backwaters of the Peloponnesus. People in preliterate societies cannot read about their celebrities in the check-out lines of supermarkets. Celebrities must be sung about to exist. We may also say that Helen realizes, as a character in a story (which is what she is), that she was invented by its author for all the misery she has caused or suffered so that she would be part of the narrative. That is yet another form of justifying the ways of god to man. It is also a way by which the poet reminds his audience of his signal importance to the community.

The *Iliad, Odyssey, Theogony,* and *Works and Days* share a common language based on formulas, although there is diction peculiar to each of the four poems. The language of the Mycenaean bards, we may assume, was a highly stylized, contrived, and formulaic language, hardly the same as the Greek that can be deciphered from the Linear B syllabary writing. Nonetheless, it was, we may also assume, pure Mycenaean, whereas the language of our *Iliad* and *Odyssey* is an extraordinary amalgam of several different dialects of Greek. Although it seems to be essentially a construct of Ionic Greek, there is a strong admixture of Aeolic and Attic, touches of Arcado-Cypriote and Doric, and others as well. It is an artificial language that came about through wide circulation in many environments in the enormous political and social upheaval that followed upon the collapse of the Mycenaean kingdom. Two contrary facts, isolation and commingling, are important. When the Mycenaean system of communications fell apart, the various areas of the mainland became isolated, and in this isolation speech patterns began to grow distinct and different in each area; eventually dialect variations came into being. At the same time an opposing process commenced. New peoples moving into the Peloponnesus from northwestern Greece displaced the older inhabitants. They migrated out of the area, eastward over the mainland and finally to Asia Minor. During the period of movement one dialect group mingled with another. These centuries of migration and relocation much affected, we assume, the language of the professional bards. They too must have moved away from the old Mycenaean court centers in the general human flux of the times. As they met with emergent new dialects, these bards made up formulas from them, some of which passed into the common stock. Thus Aeolic forms persist in the Homeric poems even when metrically equivalent Ionic forms are available. The Aeolicisms are embedded in archaic phrases as flies are caught in amber. Some words entered the epic language stock for the first time as they appeared in a dialect form of suitable metrical shape. This cross-pollination of dialect—a process of centuries—produced the hybrid language of the Homeric, not to mention the Hesiodic, poems. The English translator of these poems does not have the means to render this dialectal mosaic into English, so it is not possible to reveal this important aspect of the poetry. The epic language is something totally artificial and totally alien to common speech, the charm of which is seductive and addictive.

Over time we may assume that epic language became increasingly artificial, made up as it was of repeated formulas in a variety of dialects. Used only for epic purposes, a thing apart from natural speech, an artifice handed down from the past, given over to describing what is lastingly real and permanent in a distinctly unreal fashion, the Homeric language created a very special world and vision. Perhaps in fifth-century Athens and certainly in third-century Alexandria, this epic language must have had something of the sanctity and grandeur of aged obscurity that is akin to the qualities of the English of the King James translation of the Bible. For this reason, modern translators of Homer have sometimes used a kind of King James English, which manages to convey that peculiar blend of something utterly familiar yet very alien. King James English, however, tends to seem quaint in the twentieth century; more and more, it is becoming incomprehensible, whereas the language of epic remained alive for the Greeks—partly because the *Iliad* and the *Odyssey* were so fundamental a staple of their education, partly because the poetry of tragic drama and the lyricists was founded upon epic dialect and shaped by the epic style. Of course, by the third century, B.C.E. among the Alexandrians, some Homeric Greek vocabulary had become incomprehensible.

The advantage of using a variety of dialects for making poetry might be illustrated with a somewhat absurd example from the English language. If we were to measure the time that an English person, a New Englander, and a southerner take to enunciate the several syllables of the word "magnolia," we would very likely find that they could be schematized as măgnōlyă, măgnōlyēr, and māgnōlyă (I suppose that in reality no southerner outside of motion pictures says măȳgnōlyă). Dialect variations are not an obvious feature of written English because there is little attempt to spell phonetically; in any case, even if we had strong dialects in English, which we don't, mass communications are rapidly obliterating what differences there are. Nonetheless, the example shows the metrical possibilities of dialect variations of the same English word. The dialects of ancient Greece vastly increased the range of metrical possibilities. The verb "to be," for instance, appears in an enormous number of variants. Consider the possibilities for verse construction when the infinitive can be rendered *ĕmĕnăi, ēmmĕnăi, or ēinăĭ* (and when the poet sometimes neglects to observe the rules).

Epic poetry is thought to have been chanted, although the poet calls out to the Muse to sing. Chanted Greek, however, must have been distinctly musical because of the pitch accent. Ancient Greek poetic rhythms were not primarily accented with stress beats, as is generally true of English poetry. The distinction between long and short syllables was just what the terms imply: a long syllable takes twice as long to sound as a short syllable. The dactylic line, with its five feet of one long and two short syllables (sometimes with a substitution of two long syllables) and one final foot of one long syllable and one short syllable, is well suited to the earliest Greek, which contains a relatively high number of short syllables (as opposed to English, which, with its many more long syllables, is better suited to iambic verse). The pitch accent of ancient Greek, unlike the stress accent of English, marked one syllable of a word in which the pitch either rose, rose and fell, or remained constant. As any singer will tell you, changing the pitch of a word slightly but inevitably changes the quality of the vowels. This helps explain the marked musicality of Greek. Since vowels are held either long or short and are sounded with either normal pitch or raised pitch, the range of variation is great. The chanting poet then would be using time, beat, and pitch, just as modern musicians do.

The theory of oral composition of the Homeric epics was worked out in the 1920s and 1930s. Since then, studies of oral poetry around the world have proliferated, as have theoretical arguments about the nature of orality, which have been in turn applied to the Homeric poems. There is a certain bothersome circularity to this procedure. The fundamental fact that we can know nothing or very little about the circumstances of production of these two poems is also troublesome, as is the exceedingly slender field for sampling—there are only these two poems of exceedingly obscure origin to supply all the data for any statistical work. Classicists are not statisticians, of course, and used not to understand statistical mathematics. Although this state of affairs seems to be changing, the advent of computers is a positive blessing for students of these poems, since formerly the statistical evidence was collected in exceedingly haphazard fashion.

The principal problem in ascertaining the orality of the Homeric poems is defining a formula. Exactly repeated phrases seem obvious enough, but how many times must the phrase be repeated to count? What about analogous phrases? When the economy of the system is confirmed by noting that a phrase made up of a personal name and epithet, such as "swift-footed Achilles," is almost never duplicated in any one grammatical case in any given metrical position, what are we to say for the use of a word or phrase in the same metrical and grammatical situation which denotes the person without naming him? Achilles, for instance, can be called Peliades, "son of Peleus," which in any statistical survey ought to be noted as a variant of the name Achilles. Some contemporary critics have detected what they believe is considerably more freedom in the invention and use of the language than the earliest proponents of the oral theory would allow; they argue for the existence of a poet or poets of the *Iliad* and the *Odyssey* who came late in the tradition, perhaps could write, and thus play around with the possibilities of this style in a way the original oral poet could not. Despite what seems to be an impossibility in certifying anything, contemporary critics are often only too ready to call the question of orality settled and turn to other considerations: perfor-mance theory, for instance, or sociological interpretations, or the in-tertextual relation of the two poems.

A tradition stemming from antiquity that the sixth-century B.C.E. Athenian tyrant Pisistratus caused to have collected and written down the various songs of Troy which go to make up what we have as the *Iliad* and the *Odyssey* has exercised considerable influence on the way in which the poems are interpreted. In the nineteenth century, before the oral theory was argued for these two poems, scholars working from the tradition of a Pisistratean recension generally assumed that it was possible to go through the texts and, using a number of different criteria, identify earlier and later accretions. (This approach was sim-ilar to textual studies of the Bible by means of which, for example, nineteenth-century scholars identified the so-called J, E, and P writers of the Genesis story.) These analysts, as they are called, were largely discredited by their clumsy claims for diverse authorship of different parts of the two poems—and by the fact that they were mostly Ger-mans: as an aftermath of World War I the enormous hostility against Germans in the Anglo-American world spilled over into the scholarly community. World War II did not help things. The oral theory grew to become an article of faith sometime in the 1940s in American ac-ademic circles. One wonders how much this represents the triumph of reason and how much a reflection of international politics. In its radical form the oral theory has never had much vogue in Germany. Germans or those educated in German schools tend to practice what is now called neoanalysis. Neoanalysis accepts the notion of an oral basis for the origin and early development of the poems but sees the *Iliad* and the *Odyssey,* as we have them, as texts partially derived from other texts, all generated by writers.

The relation of literacy to orality has never been resolved. Strict oralists maintain that the poet or poets must have been preliterate in order to gain real mastery of the oral style, that once corrupted by writing, preliterate poets could not have sustained their narrative technique. An oral poem is fixed only by the performance that begets it; in every performance there is essentially a new poem. Strict oralists deal with the problem of having what is orally conceived finally exist only as written text by positing a moment in time when writing had only recently been invented and a literate person persuaded the oral poet to perform for dictation. (Transcription of oral performance has, of course, been done in the twentieth century by anthropologists in the field.) A refinement of this argument is that the writer to whom the poet dictated would require a very long time, during which the reciting poet would have the opportunity to improve upon his usual performance; this would help to account for the fact that never in any other culture have oral epic poems revealing the universally acknowledged genius of the *Iliad* and the *Odyssey* been discovered.

Relative to most oral epic poems that have been recorded, the Homeric poems are very long. What was the occasion of their performance, and who had the energy and invention for two poems so complex, so subtle, so controlled from first to last, so many thousands of lines later? One theory has it that narratives that started out as praise poems for local heroes became sufficiently popular to be chanted beyond the range of the immediate neighborhood. These narratives slowly began to lose their topicality, their regionality, as the two stories grew and became constantly more refined, more elaborate, more complex, spreading throughout a larger and larger region. As they lost their narrow local focus, they also took on more and more the universality of view that marks the Homeric poems as we know them. These poems were so popular that despite generations of subtle experimentation and improvement the telling was increasingly fixed, as it must be with preliterate people, who have a tenacity of memory far superior to that of readers. (Anyone who has ever read or told stories repeatedly to small children will know this: one cannot change even a word without causing an uproar.) Eventually the two poems, grown large and refined to a culture's satisfaction, now recited more and more verbatim and less and less improvised, were committed to writing for the Panathenaic Festival by command of Pisistratus. This view requires its adherents to accept the (to some slightly, to others highly) improbable notion that the evident mastery of the narrative throughout both the *Iliad* and the *Odyssey* is not that of any one or two persons but the result of generations of poetic improvisation.

Neoanalysts take for their starting point the fact that we have fragments of a number of epic poems, known as the Epic Cycle, which they believe left traces in the narrative of the Homeric poems. Although the poems of the Epic Cycle are said to have been composed after the time of the Homeric poems, the neoanalysts argue that they may have existed as fixed poems in some kind of oral state from which the Homeric poets took material. The neoanalysts are attempting to suggest the same kind of intertextuality that exists for written texts—a possibly dubious belief, since it is not clear how audiences or poets in the (as we imagine it) relatively fluid world of epic narrative improvisation and recollection would have any one narrative so firmly fixed in mind that it was there to be borrowed from or played to. Nonetheless, the neoanalysts take our knowledge of the Epic Cycle poem *Aithiopis* to read various meanings into the *Iliad*. For instance, in the *Aithiopis* the poet evidently described the moment when Paris killed Achilles by shooting him in the foot with an arrow. He also described a scene in which Antilochus, the son of Nestor, saves his father from battle but dies himself; the death of this dear friend motivates Achilles' return to battle. The neoanalysts argue that the *Iliad* poet has used this material for the scene from the eleventh book in which Paris shoots Diomedes in the foot with his arrow, and again when he describes Diomedes rescuing Nestor from battle in the fifth book. Achilles, in the twenty-third book, is portrayed as especially friendly with Antilochus, again something the neoanalysts claim comes from the *Aithiopis*. Their argument for the relation between the two poems helps assuage the doubts of those who cannot believe that poems of the length and complexity of the *Iliad* and *Odyssey* survived through time more or less in their present shape but in a fluid state, much as a human body is made up of myriad cells that constantly die and are renewed. Furthermore, it allows for a kind of foreshadowing, suggesting a poet and audience who would recognize the irony of these scenes in the *Iliad*, knowing their denouement in the *Aithiopis*.

Aristotle, Callimachus, and everyone else who mentions the Epic Cycle poems remark on their obvious inferiority to the Homeric poems. They seem to have been composed in order to create a chronology in epic narrative of all the events from the origin of the world to the death of Odysseus, which is what we might call the end of the heroic period. Aristotle congratulates Homer for focusing on a small time span in the grand scheme of the Trojan War while managing through allusion to remind his audience of all the events before, during, and after the ten-year war. The poets of the Epic Cycle had no talent for such sophisticated narration, it seems; their aim was the simpler, more straightforward one of furnishing a chronicle. Certainly the last, Eugammon of Cyrene, manages to tie the strands of saga into a marvelous bow. His *Telegonia* is the story of Odysseus's son by Circe, Telegonus, who goes in search of his father. When the two meet on the shores of Ithaca, unknown to each other, they fight— one to protect his land, if not to act out the masculine obsession with territoriality; the other to have his way, if not to respond to the inborn masculine need to kill one's father. Needless to say, son does kill father and proceeds to the palace to marry Penelope, while Telemachus, clearly *de trop* in this menage, sails out to Circe's isle and takes her as his bride. Where could the saga tradition go after this minuet had been danced?

Presumably the more talented poets in the oral saga tradition could hold vast numbers of stories, themes, formulas, stereotypic people, and actions in their heads. Demodocus in the *Odyssey*, for instance, can sing a variety of songs, and he is available for audience requests. Hesiod recounts that he goes to contests and sings heroic poems which are very unlike the two of his that have been preserved; of these the *Works and Days* is a veritable mélange of poems and stories which one imagines may often have been delivered in larger format from the capacious treasure-house of Hesiod's repertory. Correspondences identified by the neoanalysts and intertextualists are better described as the result of using stock material in more than one place. It is axiomatic that oral performance creates a product that has absolutely no shelf life: once enunciated, once heard, forever gone. For an audience to confront a performance with the precise memory of another or many other performances requires a kind of fixed text in writing, it would seem, as a tangible object for study. Or it requires a truly constant repetition of performance inconceivable in this ancient society. Even if the poet were literate, how would we describe his audience? To what degree does the invention of writing guarantee a reading public, even a small one, as we understand the term? Where were the materials that could be read? The writing implements? Sustained writing, sustained composition on the scale demanded by the size of either of the two Homeric poems implies material conditions and a special psychology which no effort of the imagination will assign to the eighth or seventh century B.C.E. Or the fifth for that matter. The notion of persons managing to read long texts written on the materials available at the time, let alone going back and forth in these cumbersome texts to locate allusions or significant repeated passages, is truly ludicrous.

Many will object that the auditors I hypothesize here are a group of people incapable of attending to nuance or subtlety or allusion in poetry, demeaned by a critic who will not grant that they are as intelligent as a hypothetical audience of readers. This misses the point entirely. Critics study the text of these poems over considerable time and are convinced of their reading, which is sustained by such study. They want the hypothetical "Homer's audience," which they conjure up in their imagination, to share in the delights of their subtle and supple imaginations. But they will not grant to such an audience the difference that comes from entirely different circumstances of apprehending the poem. Hearing a long narrative in performance, without the opportunity to hear it over a second time, is not the same as reading a book, an act that is always completely controlled by the reader. These critics imagine that their Homeric audience hears the two poems often enough to be able to store them up in memory. But one must assume that these poems changed their shape sufficiently in details so as to be new poems upon each hearing, and that the occasions for performance would hardly exceed more than one or two a year.

Scholars who argue that a scene such as that of Thetis coming to her *grieving* son and holding his head is actually taken from another narrative in which Thetis crying over her *dead* son cradles his head in her arms miss the point of oral narrative. Let us say for argument that the poet most often has been using this little detail in a scene after Achilles is dead. Some inner voice tells him at this moment in the *Iliad* to pull out all the stops, since now that Patroclus is dead, it is all over for Achilles as well. Constant retelling of this story in one form or another allows both the poet and the audience to participate in the scene with an instinctive feeling of the larger whole. After all, older members of the audience must have had a relatively firm knowledge of the principal stories, motifs, stereotypes, turns of phrase— all the tricks of oral performance. The poet remarks that Briseis and the other women who are keening over the body of Patroclus are crying for him as a pretext; more to the point they are crying for themselves. The poet is letting his audience cry over Patroclus while crying for Achilles as well. He is being hyperbolic, enlarging Thetis's grief as though it were Achilles who had died, and now he includes a few gestures that are equally extravagant. But the whole scene works: he himself is carried away; audience and poet participate in the extreme grief Achilles feels for Patroclus, Thetis for her son. Her gesture, which spans two occasions for grief, moves the audience to the larger view. But no one, not one person, is sitting there thinking that he or she well remembers this detail from a narrative performed last night, last week, last year, and how well it foreshadows Achilles' eventual fate. The oral poet tells his auditors exactly what to think, and in the fleeting moment of his delivery they have no chance to be reflective. They are obedient as ever: Thetis is grieving over her son's grief for Patroclus and nothing more.

Present-day critical interest in intertextuality has inevitably led to speculation about the relation between the *Iliad* and the *Odyssey*. Once they were assumed to have been composed by the same man, the Homer of Greek tradition. Today few favor that idea. As has long been observed, the narrator of the *Odyssey* never alludes to events that occur in the *Iliad*. Some would call this profound ignorance of the *Iliad*; others would argue that such a pointed refusal to acknowledge the other poem is tantamount to accepting its intrusion into every scene. More recently, various scholars have drawn attention to what they imagine to be subtle allusions to the *Iliad* in the *Odyssey*. One may compare the scene in the *Odyssey* (*Od.* 5.203ff.) when Calypso chides Odysseus (who is delighted to learn that he can now leave) with the rhetorical question about his wanting to go home and a scene in the *Iliad* (*Il.*2.173) when Athena chides Odysseus (who is part of the mob scene as the men rush to the ships) with a similar rhetorical question. The verbal parallels as well as the similarity in situation raise real questions for the reader about the relationship of the two poems—but only for a reader, a reader who has copies of the two poems for study. This historical truth seems to rule out the possibility of there being any consciously meaningful relation between the two poems.

In no way, however, should this inhibit the reader from making associations. The two poems are far too mysterious not to engage our liveliest imaginations completely. For instance, any reader of the *Odyssey* is free to enjoy the delicious irony that the language in which the disguised Odysseus replies to Eumaeus's suspicions about the possibility of his lying exactly repeats the haughty disdain for liars which Achilles directs at Odysseus in the *Iliad* (*Il.* 9.312–13; *Od.* 14. 156–57). More to the point, as Thomas Flesher points out, Odysseus in qualifying his contemptible liar as motivated by poverty reminds us that he himself lies for fun. Yet it would be very difficult to imagine that the circumstances of reading in the archaic age made such a witty bit of intertextuality possible, and more's the pity for that archaic audience!

But what is the *Iliad* to the *Odyssey* and vice versa? How is it that two such long poems of such genius exist when they do not seem to be the work of one single person? Why are they so complementary? The *Iliad* is imbued with what we may call the tragic sense of life, an understanding that human endeavor is measured only by the fact that humans must die. The *Odyssey*, by contrast, is the tale of one man's triumph over adversity and evil; as such it expresses much more the comic sense of life. The ancient critic Longinus called the former a poem of the poet's youth and the latter a work of his old age. There is yet another way to consider their symmetrical relation. They are much alike, each one beginning with an action that gets the plot underway and then disregarding the central figure for several thousand lines. The plot structure is very much the same: a man goes out and stays away and finally comes home. One must understand the going out as Telemachus's traveling in search of his father and Achilles' withdrawing to his tent, the staying away as Odysseus's vain attempts to get home while traveling about the Mediterranean and Achilles' petulant sojourn in his tent, and the coming home as Odysseus's return to Ithaca and Achilles' return to the battle. Some critics see the two heroes as participating in some kind of transcendent dialogue that sets the poems face to face. If we remember that these poems were most probably paid for by the authority figures of the society, we may want to consider how they immediately benefited such a group. Clearly there was something far greater than praise at stake. What was it in each poem, but more to the point, how did the two poems together satisfy whatever it was that the powerful men of the community wanted? What kind of society was it which over time selected these two narratives from among what we may presume were the myriad creative offerings of their poets? Why these two? What was rejected? The critic who would answer those questions definitively is a bold person indeed. Renewed reading of either poem will more often than not lead the reader to reconsider and change ideas that were previously thought to be fixed.

Throughout the *Iliad* and the *Odyssey* the narrators allude to other stories and other hero figures. One thinks of the Meleager story in the *Iliad*, Book Nine, or the reference to the Argonauts in the *Odyssey*, or the references to Hercules everywhere. We do not need the fragments of the Epic Cycle to remind us that the two Homeric poems are part of a grand mosaic of saga stories and myths that constitute a kind of history of the Greeks. There is yet another dimension stretching across time and cultures to the Sumerian-Akkadian-Hittite fragments of tablets telling the story of King Gilgamesh. The story of this man who is thought to have been king of Uruk between 2700 and 2500 B.C.E. is known today as the Epic of Gilgamesh. It is nowhere complete, but from various clay tablet fragments—some of them dating back to the third millennium not long after Gilgamesh's lifetime and the best and latest from 1600–1000 B.C.E.—scholars have put together what seems to be a reliable narrative. When the tablets were discovered roughly a century ago, they shocked the world because they contained a description of a great flood and a kind of Noah figure (Utnapishtim) that closely parallel the biblical account. It seems the Almighty was a more prolific author than previously imagined! Of interest to classicists, however, are the remarkable correspondences between the Gilgamesh story and the Homeric narratives. Most surprising, indeed uncanny, is that Gilgamesh in the agony of grief over the death of his friend, Enkidu, is compared to a lion who has lost her cub, exactly as Achilles is compared in his grief over the death of Patroclus!

The story of Gilgamesh as it is pieced together describes a man who, like Achilles, is the son of a human father and a divine mother; her name is Ninsun. He despairs of ever achieving the fame that will guarantee him some kind of immortality once he is dead. He is an arrogant king who oppresses his people. In their distress they call out to the gods, who decide to create a double to fight with Gilgamesh: Enkidu, a child of nature, who runs with the wild animals and eats grasses. To bring him into the city, a temple prostitute is sent out with a hunter to the watering hole where Enkidu and his animal comrades will come. When Enkidu encounters the prostitute, he has intercourse with her for six days and seven nights. Thereafter, he changes his ways; she teaches him about civilization, offering him wine and bread to eat instead of animal milk and grasses. He wants to fight with Gilgamesh now, and they proceed to the city. He meets Gilgamesh in the streets as the latter seems to be on his way to deflower new brides, and they wrestle. When finally Enkidu is pinned, he and Gilgamesh kiss and pledge eternal friendship. They set out on an adventure to kill the giant Humbaba. As they are about to enter the cedar forest, decisively breaking the gate to do so, Enkidu is afraid. When they encounter the giant, however, it is Enkidu who urges Gilgamesh on and even delivers the last blow himself.

In something of a narrative lurch, the goddess Ishtar now offers herself to Gilgamesh, who declines, citing the various other men who have enjoyed her favors and then come to grief. Spurned, Ishtar is furious and seeks revenge through her father, the god Anu, who sends the Bull of Heaven down to fight Gilgamesh and Enkidu. The heroes are victorious and celebrate.

The gods now decide that Enkidu must die in return for the death of Humbaba and the Bull of Heaven. Enkidu's death plunges Gilgamesh into deep despair. He begins the long journey to Utnapishtim. On the way he meets Siduri, a barmaid who, though warning him of the perils of his trip, suggests that he go across the waters of death to Utnapishtim. In another version she questions the value of the trip, saying it is better to make merry, drink, eat, make love. Gilgamesh continues to Utnapishtim, who tells him that there is no permanence, that death is inevitable. He describes the Flood. He challenges Gilgamesh to a test: stay awake for six days and seven nights. Gilgamesh fails the test and prepares to depart. Utnapishtim gives him a plant of eternal youth, but a serpent steals it from him. He and his boatman sail back to Uruk.

Readers will note several parallels with the *Iliad* and the *Odyssey*. Obviously, Enkidu is a double, a shadow figure like Patroclus, whose death reminds the hero of his own mortality. Gilgamesh's arrogance recalls Agamemnon saying that Achilles wants everything; his straining after fame that will give him some form of immortality echoes Achilles' anguish over life and death, which is the spine of the narrative. Gilgamesh's inability to stay awake is some kind of surrender to physical limitations, a theme with which the narrator of the *Iliad* plays when he uses eating in extreme grief as a statement of acceptance in the face of death. One could say that Enkidu's early years as a child of nature and his introduction to civilization through sexual intercourse parallel the loss of innocence of Adam and Eve and their departure from the garden. Both stories are about growing up, so one might then compare them with the early books of the *Odyssey*, which describe the young boy Telemachus, followed by the grown man Odysseus and his adventures, and then the man reinstated with wife, child, and home—just as Gilgamesh has adventures and wanders and finally comes home. Ishtar is refused as Calypso is refused. Gilgamesh lists males who meet disaster with Ishtar; Calypso begins a list of males whose contact with goddesses is disastrous. Circe sleeps with Odysseus and then, like Siduri, gives him directions for a perilous trip. On his journey to the underworld Odysseus meets a wise man, Tiresias, whose advice about the rest of his life and his death is somewhat like Utnapishtim's advice to Gilgamesh. In a parallel to the killing of Humbaba, Odysseus blinds the giant Cyclops and suffers a god's anger as a result. Nausicaa and her enchanted island of Scheria offer Odysseus the temptation of the full and sensual life, not unlike the advice to be happy which Siduri gives to Gilgamesh.

These are remarkable parallels. What is more important, however, is that the Gilgamesh narrative is sparse and suggestive, not unlike the several dreams it describes. The reader must make a spiritual investment in the story—for instance, by imagining motives for behavior or emotional reactions—which is not required by the Homeric poets, who bombard their hearers with so many details that they feel satisfied they have the entire story. The way in which the Gilgamesh tale is narrated produces a truly profound spiritual experience. By contrast, in the Greek oral poetic tradition a similar narrative structure is fleshed out thoroughly and thereby transformed into something considerably more profane, yet for that reason more accessible, more instantly popular in the greater sense of the word. The extraordinary abundance of detail gives the Homeric narratives a kind of solidity— the illusion of realism, we might call it—that the Gilgamesh story does not have.

The Gilgamesh story is part of the Mediterranean cultural inheritance. The more immediate myth and saga world of the early Greeks is something to which the Homeric poets allude throughout the poems. The *Iliad* poet is particularly skillful at reminding his audience of the principal antecedent events of the Trojan War story. With great discretion he makes them into a suitable opening to his narrative. It is this that Aristotle held to constitute the superiority of the Homeric narrator over other epic poets: the ability to center a story within a narrow compass while at the same time referring in one way or another to the major events of the larger history. The early books of the *Iliad* are an exact illustration: the time span of the few days in which Achilles retreats to his tent and then rejoins his comrades at war is filled by the poet with material that gives his audience the entire Trojan War.

The poem begins with a quarrel between Agamemnon and Achilles which results in Achilles' refusal to fight and his entreaty to his mother to get Zeus to turn the tide of battle against the Achaians. When Zeus agrees, the story line is set. The narrator sends Achilles out of the narrative until it is time to enact this story. In his absence the narrator uses flashback material recomposed for the present moment. A scene of anarchy in the army motivates a regrouping of the men into their military units. The army review is presented in the form of a versified list of the ship contingents that sailed for Troy from Aulis and a smaller catalogue of the Trojan forces and their allies (2.483–877). The third book begins with a march of the Achaeans into battle, at which point Paris challenges Menelaus to a duel over Helen. Helen herself appears on the walls and proceeds to describe the various Achaean leaders for the benefit of old King Priam. Again the poet seems to have recycled a piece of the story originally meant for the early days of the war. That in the course of the nine years preceding the time of this narrative Paris and Menelaus have never thought to have a duel and that Priam has never met the Achaean leaders in various parleys and truces—to one of which he is in fact about to go—are considerations quite irrelevant to the narrator's establishment of the scene. He does not apologize, he does not overmotivate; he simply insists that this is what is happening. The narrator can do this so well partly because he has given the responsibility for the poem to the Muse from the very beginning. He is just the mouth. Furthermore, in a narrative that we assume derives from the manner of oral performance, there is no time for the auditor to speculate on these matters.

In the fourth book Agamemnon holds a review of his troops which functions as yet another list of participants, a kind of third catalogue. This *Iliad* narrative, as we know, will be very long, and one could argue that the poet is establishing this as a very long poem through

the monumental introduction he is creating. In any case, as the Catalogue of Ships describes the political and military identity of the
participants, and Helen's review from the walls concentrates upon
the heroes' physical attributes, Agamemnon's review serves to show
the psychologies of various leaders. The fifth book presents Diomedes
in a solo battle performance, what the ancients called an *aristeia*—just
the kind of individual bid for glory which defines these heroes and
which Achilles has temporarily forsaken. Book Six takes us inside the
walls of Troy for an introduction to the women in Hector's life. Seven
presents yet another duel, this time one with a more realistic twosome
doing the fighting, the tough Ajax and the manly Hector, instead of
the definitely second-rate and fearful Menelaus and the pretty-boy
Paris, who is meant for better things. At its conclusion Paris rejects
the idea of returning Helen to the Achaeans, an action which again
must have happened in the very earliest days of the war and which
by rights should have been the consequence of the duel between Paris
and Menelaus but is here established as the event that causes the
battle to be resumed.

Finally, the war is on. Notice that the narrator has managed by this
time to bring together all the important antecedents to this late day
in the Trojan War, as well as to contrast the hero-destroyer with the
city and its protector. He has even managed in two scenes to bring
in the gods, whose ridiculous behavior generally increases the overall
importance and seriousness of the human order. All this, and the
story has scarcely been begun. Anyone who will give Books Two
through Seven some careful study cannot help but come away awed
not only by the tight control exercised over material that could easily
come apart but also by the narrator's insistence upon a story logic
that is not really there.

The tight control and the insistence suggest that a master narrator,
secure in all the techniques of oral performance, is fashioning this
story. Of course, we will also assume that the poet is performing
for an audience so familiar with the details of the foreground and
the background that the chronological priorities of the narrative can
be ignored. The bard may choose to depart briefly or at length into
the side avenues of the saga tradition. Often the digression has a
mechanical motivation, such as the brief description of Olympus,
to which Athena returns after reappearing to the sleeping Nausicaa
in the sixth book of the *Odyssey*. A temporal transition from the
night of Nausicaa's sleep to the dawn of her awakening is needed,

and the epic narrator has the habit of leaping over periods of time by introducing interludes. The detailed description of Olympus is just such an interlude, but, in fact, it is more: within the epic scene it is a reminder, hardly conscious, of the absolute infinity in which human existence plays out its drama. While the central narrative unfolds, we are forever being shown other scenes occupying other places in other times, so that the effect is a cosmic vision encompassing the totality of experience. In this respect, epic achieves a realism that other forms of literature which narrowly restrict the scene cannot produce.

The saga background permits the poet to make allusions that are often obscure to us but probably were not so for the poem's original audiences. They would know this material as a small-town resident knows the town gossip. Reading through a handbook of Greek mythology is not unlike listening to some old person in a small town recite a lifetime's supply of local gossip. Mythology, after all, is really nothing more than the projection onto phantom or ideal neighbors of all the behavior and attitudes the human psyche is capable of. In any case, Homer's audience, having had the opportunity in the course of a lifetime to hear every episode of this almost endless chain of story, could make clear sense of any chance reference. So in the ninth book of the *Iliad*, when Phoenix gives a relatively scant narration of Meleager's behavior at the time of the siege of Calydon, its very sketchiness suggests that the narrator has said enough to recall the story to the audience's mind.

Brief allusions to elements of the culture from which the epic poem springs became one of the hallmarks of literary epic. The emphasis changed from the simple description of oral performance to the use of such allusions for symbolic purposes. The *Aeneid* is almost a compendium of Greco-Roman civilization, as *Paradise Lost* is a composite of Greco-Roman and Judeo-Christian learning; so much of the meaning of these two poems comes through the allusions that only a knowledgeable person can read them successfully. In our own time, the general absolute decline of knowledge about our European past means that only a pedant could read or compose a poem like *The Waste Land*. Homer, however, uses allusion not for symbolism but to spread out the panorama of his vast story over still greater space and time, obliterating in his audience's mind the sense of boundary or focus that is the intrusion of art into reality. The story line is there, but the poet successfully obscures it.

The ancient Greek capacity for viewing things separately, the inclination to honor whatever is being recited, a certain kind of disingenuous passivity such as yielding up to the Muse the authority for the narrative at hand—all this is akin to the commonplace Homeric style known as "parataxis." The word is Greek, used by the ancients to denote a system in which each idea is contained in a separate simple sentence; these may be juxtaposed with a conjunction or with nothing at all. Parataxis allows for ideas to be added on as they occur to the speaker, a common enough phenomenon in simple talking and a boon to listeners, who are not then caught up in complicated sentence structures. "Hypotaxis" denotes a sentence structure in which certain ideas are subordinate to the central idea in clauses of time or of cause in relative clauses. The difference between the two can be seen in the following: "Achilles is angry with Agamemnon, and he is determined not to fight" is parataxis; "Since Achilles is angry with Agamemnon, he is determined not to fight" is hypotaxis. In the first example the two ideas lie side by side, equal in their value; in the second, Achilles' determination not to fight is given priority over his anger with Agamemnon. (One could have written it quite the other way, of course: "Achilles is angry with Agamemnon with the result that he is determined not to fight" reverses the priorities.)

The opening lines of the *Iliad* unfold in what we might call the appositional style, one image laid beside the next, amplifying and redefining what went before. Here they are, literally translated:

> Wrath sing, goddess, of Peleus's son, Achilles,
> destructive, which on the Achaeans many woes imposed;
> many powerful souls it sent to Hades before due
> of heroes, their bodies as prey it fashioned for dogs
> and all the birds; and the will of Zeus was fulfilled.

Here "destructive" qualifies "wrath," and the subsequent clause defines "destructive," whereas the following two lines imagistically define "woes," and the whole thing is summed up in a new definition ("the will of Zeus was fulfilled").

Consider the following randomly chosen remark of Priam's (22.46ff.), very literally translated, set out in the demonstrably separate grammatical elements (numbered for convenience) in the Greek:

(1) For even now two sons   (2) Lycaon and Polydorus
(3) I cannot see   (4) among the Trojans sheltered in the city
(5) whom Laothoe bore   (6) a queen among women.

Phrases one and three make the narrative skeleton, although well separated both by phrase two and by the formalism of their parallel positions at the beginning of a line. Phrase two is a redefinition or expansion of phrase one, just as phrase four is a redefinition or refinement of three. Phrase six stands in a similar relationship to phrase five, while the entire third line redefines the first line. This very common rhythm in Homer is like a rock tossed into a pond, clear and sharp, followed by softer ripples. Action is posed, persons are indicated, then ramifications or implications are noticed. It is as though one were to look at something suddenly and then let the object come into better focus, to see the object and then its surroundings.

Parataxis is yet another of the mannerisms that produce a kind of reality in the highly artificial epic style. Consider this simile. Menelaus has just been wounded in the thigh by an arrow.

> Straightaway the dark blood flowed from the wound. Just as when some woman stains a piece of ivory with purple, a Maeonian woman or Carian, in order to make a cheekpiece for horses, and it lies in a chamber, and many are the horsemen who long to carry it, but it lies there to be an adornment for some king, both an ornament for the horse and a thing of glory to its rider, just so, Menelaus, your thighs were stained with blood. [Il. 4.141ff.]

The immediate comparison is excellent, but the act of staining the ivory has a reality, a history, a vitality of its own, and we are made to move away from the shouting moment at Troy to the quiet of a woman's chamber anywhere in the Eastern world (two places are suggested), then to the living desire that the beautiful object engenders, and finally to its universal and ideal function, its inner virtue—an ornament for the horse and a thing of glory to its rider.

The example makes clear the Homeric disinclination to make hierarchies of human experience. Every experience is of equal value, one placed against the next, a progression of equivalence. We may say this is in essence the highest realism, for it is true that in the daily living of our lives no editor cuts or shapes anything; we must experience each thing and live through each moment, and when all is said and done, it remains true that the consummation of a great love affair can often occupy far less time and command far less concentration than the picking of one's teeth.

The Poet's World

Then upon this much nourishing earth still another
    generation, the fourth,
did Zeus make, more just and nobler,
a race of heroes, godlike, who are called
demigods, the previous to our own upon this
    boundless earth.

        —Hesiod *Works and Days* 157–60

Like any other artifact the Homeric poems belong somewhere in time and space. The earliest pieces of written text of the poems that survive, however, are dated to the third century B.C.E., hundreds of years after the poems seem to have taken shape. References to them, allusion to them in lyric poems and vase paintings go back to the archaic age. Beyond that, scholars employ educated guesswork to try to establish some kind of historical context for the poems. Because of the presumed length of time of their gestation or evolution, the poems seem to describe a world of their own making more than a context identifiable from other sources. It is not unlike the blurred countryside that appears to the passenger peering from the window of the high-speed railway train from Paris to Lyons.

Linguists hypothesize a common original language from which sprang most of the languages spoken in the area from the Atlantic Ocean to India. Called Indo-European, it is the mother of Celtic, Germanic, Italic, Greek, Slavic, Hittite, Sanskrit, Persian, and many others, from which evolved in further permutations English, Latin, French: that is to say, most of the contemporary languages spoken in this same area, except for the Semitic languages of the Near East. The process whereby languages proliferated has to do not only with the natural change in speaking from generation to generation but, more important, with the lack of communication between one language group and another. It is hypothesized that the original speakers of Indo-European migrated out of a common area of habitation as the population grew and in successive centuries lost contact with each other. During this time a common language became a series of mutually intelligible dialects that eventually became distinct languages. So it is thought that around 2200 B.C.E. Indo-European peoples came down through present-day Albania into northern Greece, speaking a dialect of Indo-European sufficiently differentiated from the mother tongue so as to be well on its way to becoming the distinct language that we call Greek. These people brought with them a common cultural ancestry. Among its features, it seems, was the dactylic hexameter poetic line. They must have brought as well, therefore, the practice of singing or chanting verse. Some scholars believe that the Homeric poems contain linguistic features that can be traced back to the earliest formation of a Greek language and its use in dactylic hexameter verse. Some identify features of the narration that are common to Sanskrit poetry. Some see features that may be found in all the poetic traditions of the peoples who descend from the Indo-Europeans.

Western Europeans have always thought of themselves as descendants of the Greeks through the subsequent Roman tradition. The *Iliad* and the *Odyssey* are so vivid a part of the shared experience of Western Europe that few can resist imagining that they constitute a detailed portrait of our earliest cultural ancestors. In the nineteenth century Heinrich Schliemann set out to make this portrait a tangible reality. Convinced of the reliable historical truth of the Homeric world, he set out to excavate at Mycenae in Greece and at Hissarlik, the mound of land near the Hellespont in present-day Turkey. The ruins of habitation he found at the latter site he called Troy; the numerous gold objects he found in the graves at the former convinced him that he was unearthing Agamemnon's palace; and the archaeologists who succeeded him identified what is known as Troy VIIa as the very level containing the ruins of the Troy that the Achaeans sacked. The romance of the excavations of Mycenaean centers is paralleled by the decipherment of Linear B, an event that occurred after World War II, when men who knew Greek had been trained as cryptologists. Code breaking was the skill they employed in the deciphering.

Although at first there was resistance to the belief that the Linear B system of notation was showing Greek, there is little today. The notion, however, that the war Homer describes ever took place as he described it at the site of Hissarlik—that there ever was the kind of Trojan kingdom he describes, or that Agamemnon and his Achaean colleagues ever set out on such an enterprise—is still a matter of considerable controversy. One side argues that the excavations prove enough to substantiate the Homeric Trojan War; some argue the more extreme view that Homer knew the topography of the plains of Troy. The other side insists that the meager, impoverished settlement of Troy VIIa could hardly be Priam's Troy, that the chronological imprecisions invalidate any secure identification of the remains of a war or an expedition or kingdoms, that Homer's descriptions are far too generic and never specific enough to be used as identification of anything. Certainly Homer tells us very little about topography when he describes Mediterranean sites in such noncommittal terms as "sandy," "steep," or "surrounded by sea."

Archaeologists learn a great deal about history from the most minute evidence. Bits of pottery can establish elaborate systems of reliable dates and trade routes; garbage dumps furnish important information about diets and crop patterns. Archaeologists have an irresistible urge, however, to glamorize their subject for a larger audience, if not to justify to themselves the hours of tedium sifting through minutiae. Thus, they will approve an artist's conception of elevations of buildings based on excavated wall bases that resemble twentieth-century palaces, as in the case of Pylos; or they will rebuild and paint for grandeur as at Knossos, or endow ruins with the glamor of past history as in the case of Hissarlik and Mycenae, two otherwise singularly uninteresting and uninspiring tourist attractions. Any tour guide with any sense will take his charges a scant few kilometers south of Mycenae to the ruins of ancient Tiryns, the extraordinary power and grandeur of whose architecture immediately suggests great Mycenaean kings and high doings. If only they could move the superb and impressive Lion Gate entrance from Mycenae to Tiryns, the site would perfect!

Homer's Trojan War is really a generic war, the kind that must have been fought over and over again throughout the second millennium. More to the point, it is the stock war for a poet of stereotypes; the Homeric poems do not describe a war lodged in time, implicated in a context of causes—economic, social, and political—which define the conflict. That observation provokes the question: to what degree in fact do the poems mirror the second millennium? On the theory that over centuries a succession of oral poets kept alive a tradition of dactylic hexametric verse narrative, one may legitimately imagine that there were embedded in the inherently conserving yet constantly renewing narrative certain practices, attitudes, and artifacts of this second millennium, called variously the Age of Mycenae, the Bronze Age, or the Heroic Age. In fact, there is very little indeed that can be secured beyond doubt for that period. There is the boars' tooth helmet that Meriones gives Odysseus (10.261–65), a perishable item that would no longer have been seen by poets in the later centuries, but which has turned up for the archaeologists' record as an indisputable Mycenaean find. The Homeric description is so exact that archaeologists can easily figure out from the remaining fragments of these helmets found in graves how to reconstruct them. Allusions to the richness of Egyptian Thebes must go back at least to the fourteenth century, B.C.E., which was the last time the Achaeans had direct knowledge of its glory. The woven metal corselet for the chest and the greaves, the shin protectors that have given to the world the ubiquitous "well-greaved Achaeans," are military gear unknown to later ages. And bronze, which gave its name to the age, used in cutting tools and weapons of war, is an archaism that the poets insist upon, even though they describe the use of iron in similes that generally reflect more closely a time assumed to be contemporaneous with the later stages of the evolution of these poems or their stories.

If, as seems to be the case, the poets were using traditional language and situations, their confusion from time to time in matters inherited but not understood is quite reasonable. Homer has chariots in his traditional, highly formulaic battle narratives but misunderstands their function: he has his warriors ride out to battle in the chariot, then dismount to engage their enemy. Archaeological excavation suggests that over time there occurred a change from the heavy thrusting spear used in Mycenaean hand-to-hand fighting to the two lighter throwing spears carried centuries later by fighters who stayed in tight groups, but Homer sometimes seems not to register this difference. In the duel between Paris and Menelaus, for instance, the two men cast lots to see who will use his throwing spear first, but then Paris is armed with one thrusting spear, which he proceeds to throw.

Details of fighting are perhaps essentially a kind of decor which can be set up as the poet needs them to establish other dynamics in a scene. For Homer's audience the formulas for weaponry may have indiscriminately inspired images of fighting which took their more specific shape from the experience of the auditor. No doubt the words came to mean something that they do not literally mean. There is the confusion in the *Iliad* on the matter of shields. For instance, Mycenaean shields are thought to have been large, covering the entire body, tower shields, suited to hand-to-hand combat. No man could go far on foot with such a shield; he needed his helpers to set him up, and then he was more or less immobile. Centuries later, however, when soldiers moved about on foot in a phalanx pattern, used throwing spears, and relied more on their swords, their protection consisted of a much smaller (easily portable) round shield, that, together with the shields of his neighbors, gave each man security. It was this shield that called for greaves and breastplates.

As a rule, epic poetic convention has converted to the newer shield, but occasionally the older tower shield appears. When Hector goes to Troy to tell his mother to supplicate Athena, he is described as marching the whole distance with a shield that "bumped as much against his ankles as his neck"—obviously a large body shield, particularly impractical and unnecessary here, since Hector is passing on foot through friendly territory. One could argue that the poet wants to give substance to Hector's going to Troy, wants to give the hero himself stature. The scene is at best ill motivated, and the principal Trojan hero is reduced to errand boy; yet for narrative purposes other than pursuing the story line, Hector must go to Troy. In the rest of the *Iliad* he is always described with a small shield; here the narrator is intent upon other narrative strategies.

This explanation is based on the notion that the poet was consciously aware of the distinction between the shields. Some would argue that it is probably more reasonable to assume that all formulas involving shields are in essence mechanical; it is the fact of the shield that gives the formulas meaning, not the type of shield mentioned. On the other hand, when the large shield appears consistently as part of Ajax's armor, one might label this an example of the mental process that modern psychologists call word association: the thought of Ajax triggers the appearance of such a shield. One can also speculate that Ajax, who is consistently described as exceedingly powerful physically and is often singled out as fighting alone in the midst of a group, is the man naturally suited to the older style of equipment. The Epic Cycle portrays him as the soldier who, by a vote of the army assembly, loses out to Odysseus for the arms of Achilles; Sophocles portrays him as a kind of anachronism. Perhaps the seeds for these two portrayals lie in his loyalty to the old tower shield. The army assembly looks to his love of outmoded weaponry and thinks that he does not at all suit Achilles' gear. Sophocles can understand the tower shield metaphorically as Ajax's incapacity to change with the times.

The poet of the *Iliad* takes for granted his audience's knowledge of heroic warfare, if for no other reason than that they have presumably heard versions of it so many times. If the details are blurred, one might argue that the poet himself is unclear about what he is saying, although it does seem better to assume that over time, clarity of detail has been sacrificed for an impressionistic description of hand-to-hand fighting. In the Mycenaean period, war was fought by individuals who could command the necessary equipment and retinue. The image of a few persons actually doing battle surrounded by groups of men forms the perfect context for the heroic ideal. As in a tapestry, on a field of massed men a glorious few are picked out for notice. The heroic chieftain is driven into the thick of battle in a chariot; his loyal friend/servant often manages the reins. Once at a battle station he steps down and hunts out a target for the spear he carries. His armor includes a metal helmet, crowned by a plume of horsehair that continually waves and nods, a fearsome thing adding considerably to the dimension of the man beneath. The helmet comes down to cover the vulnerable parts of the head; in front the full cheekpieces create slits for the eyes, contributing further to the grim war look. The chest is covered by a metal breastplate, beneath which the man wears a corselet of metal or tough leather to help protect the parts of the torso exposed by the necessary joints of the breastplate. On his legs are greaves of metal, protection against hostile blows; these became confused in the tradition with the much older shin pieces that gave protection against the inevitable chafing caused by the large Mycenaean tower shield.

Two modes of warfare are confused in this narrative, but so confidently does the narrator describe the battles that they seem integral and consistent to all but trained archaeologists. Scholars may devise a chronology and try to place the Homeric poems in it, but the narrator himself rarely acknowledges any distance between the time of the action of his poems and his audience's own time. Essentially, the events described occur in some temporal limbo. But when Diomedes picks up a heavy rock to throw at the enemy, Homer calls it "a big thing, which not even two men could carry, such as mortal men are nowadays" (*Il.* 5.303f.), an idea he repeats twice, once in connection with Aeneas, once with Hector. The observation carries the hint of that rather common ancient melancholy perspective in which better times and grander people are in the past. It comes again in an exchange between Zeus and Hera in which Homer even seems to be making real use of historical change in his narrative. Zeus rebukes Hera for her constant hot hatred of Troy and threatens to destroy a favorite city of hers someday, to which she replies: "As you well know, there are three cities by far my favorites: Argos, Sparta, and Mycenae with its wide streets. Destroy these, whenever they become hateful to you in your heart." (*Il.* 4.53). Imagine the chill running through the archaic-age audience who knew that Mycenae stood in their time as a magnificent hill of ruins.

The narrator once again steps back to acknowledge change when in the twelfth book of the *Iliad* he describes the future destruction of a protective wall around the Achaean ships, which were at this point being seriously threatened. As long as the war lasted, he says, the wall stayed, but then Poseidon and Apollo caused flooding rivers and high tides to wash it away, returning the beach to its appearance before the war began (*Il.* 12.12–18). The poet seems anxious to square events with a real landscape, even though it seems impossible that he knew any real landscape for these events. More to the point, perhaps he wishes to disassociate the wall from the tradition, so to speak. His remark that the wall had been built against the gods' will might be another way of saying that he, very innovative poet that he is, has decided to describe the siege of the wall in a poem taking place on the open plain in order to vary the formulas for fighting, and this is his way of acknowledging that it is not part of the tradition. The passage is remarkable for the fact that the poet only at this point in the two poems refers to his heroes as demigods, "a race of men half-divine." Like the notice of the destruction of the wall, this appellation has the ring of history: the wall does not exist in the singer's day, and the men of his time are not like the men of his narrative.

One must turn to Hesiod, whose *Works and Days* includes a description of the ages of man, using metals for metaphor, from the golden or best age and in descending order through silver, bronze, and then to his own time, iron. This seems like a traditional conceit into which Hesiod, aware as he is of the saga tradition, inserts just previous to this last the age of "the race of hero men whom they call demigods" (quoted at the head of this chapter). Scholars who object to the Homeric usage of this term, particularly the fact that it occurs only the one time, call the passage in the twelfth book spurious. But they miss the point, perhaps. Just as Hesiod does not use the term precisely but includes many whose parents were both mortals, so Homer uses it to mean that generation or race of men who were close to the gods. Yes, Achilles is the son of a goddess, but more to the point, he can speak with her; Athena comes to him, as well, just as she actively helps Odysseus and talks with him, just as Apollo talks to Diomedes. When Homer describes the destruction of the wall, rather than the event he is focused on its actual obliteration. That relates to what he goes on to mention: the corpses of those half-divine men whose bodies fill the riverbed. These dead men are emblems of an age that no longer exists, just as the wall has disappeared from history. Certainly the word "hero," which Homer uses now and again, carries the sense of those great men of the community, now dead, about whose tombs a cult has been established. Heroes, therefore, are part of past time.

Whatever minimal sense of the past one finds in the Homeric poems, there is no ethnographic curiosity at all. It is true that Odysseus moves among some very strange people on his travels, but all of them speak his Greek. In the *Iliad* there is no difference whatsoever between the Achaeans and the Trojans. Occasionally Homer will note that there are two names for some person or some place: Paris and Alexander, for instance, or Ilium and Troy. Modern linguists recognize that one is Greek, one non-Greek, but that is not a distinction Homer would make. The Trojans speak Greek; more important, they live among the very same gods as the Achaeans do.

In the fifth century the historian Herodotus remarks (2.53), "Homer and Hesiod created a geneaology of the gods for the Greeks. They gave the gods the epithets which qualify them, established what were their honors and what their special attributes were, and they gave them their form." Certainly Hesiod's *Theogony*, with its exhaustive lists of all the divine creatures born into this world, is an authoritative account of their gods, nymphs, sprites, and intellectualized abstractions that pass as divine. But the *Iliad* and the *Odyssey* play an even more important role in this process. We assume that the earliest narrative poetry celebrating local heroes or hero cults was so grounded in the immediate locale that the religious surround to the story would derive from the cults and myths of the neighborhood, whereas the Homeric stories as they were disseminated over an ever wider area, began to displace local deities in favor of those featured in the poems. There was not in ancient Greece either a priestly caste or a dogma promulgated by some religious institution. A variety of cults and beliefs vied for the allegiance of the populace. Cult involves propitiating a god to some end; it does not provide the means to savor the identity of the godhead. People rendered something to the gods in return for favors, whether that meant finding a lost necklace or renewing the crops of the family farm or the whole community. The concern was to get the titles of the god correct; the formulas for the transaction between human and god were what was important. With no fixed theology created and promulgated by a priestly caste or a church, poets and all storytellers were central to the creation and maintenance of ideas about the gods. The gods were a part of the myths that rendered for the ancient Greeks a simulacrum both of the world in which they lived and that other world in which their subconscious dwelt. Myth stories were fixed, and the poets could not alter their outcomes; along the way, however, they could sketch many a nuance. Probably the single greatest contribution of the poets of the *Iliad* and the *Odyssey* is first their focus upon what came to be called "the Olympian gods" (because they were thought to reside on Mount Olympus), and then the extreme anthropomorphization of these deities.

The god Hermes is a good example of the process of anthropomorphization. The name comes from the Greek word *herma*, meaning a pile of stones used as a boundary mark. It was the custom for those passing on the road to add a stone to the pile, a kind of religious act of demarcation. From this inert and inanimate object comes a god who is a trickster god and a messenger god in poetic narrative. The trickster Hermes is like the Norse god Loki; he is also an emblem of deviant behavior. Hermes is what one might call a kind of patron saint of Odysseus's grandfather, Autolycus, "the greatest liar and thief of his time" (*Od.* 19.395–98). The gods themselves look to his talent for stealing when they urge him (*Il.* 24.109) to steal the body of Hector away from Achilles, who won't return it to the Trojans. Just as he is the patron saint of cattle rustlers, who must violate boundaries, so he is the patron of cattlemen, who look to boundaries to protect their stock; Eumaeus, the swineherd, sets aside a portion of the evening meal for the god. (One will note that these gods often function in roles later assigned to Christian patron saints, which is not the least bit odd, since the early Christian church evolved its pantheon of saints to fill the need previously satisfied by the pagan polytheistic religious system.) As the messenger, Hermes crosses boundaries when he is sent by Zeus to Calypso to tell her to let Odysseus return home. He meets Odysseus at the boundary of Circe's property to give him a charm to protect him from her magic (*Od.* 10.275); he meets Priam on the boundary in no-man's-land, to use a modern military term, and accompanies the old king as Priam goes to seek his son's body from Achilles (*Il.* 24.334); and he leads the souls of the suitors down from the land of the living into Hades at the end of the *Odyssey* (24.1–14).

Anthropomorphized as they are, the gods enter the human drama of the *Iliad* and the *Odyssey* more sparingly than one might imagine. Their fastidiousness may well be an extension of Apollo's reasons for not wanting to fight in the battle at Troy. He is made to say to Poseidon, who has been encouraging him (*Il.* 22.462–66), that he will not fight with mortal men who are like leaves: they come alive, feed on food from the earth, then fade away and die. Divine aloofness seems yet another manifestation of the fundamental indifference of the universe. The *Odyssey* narrative is distinguished by the presence of Athena, whose constant appearance and motivating action in the poem mark her as a supporting character as significant to the story as Telemachus. A much smaller but significant role is played by Poseidon, whose unremitting hostility works as a principal obstacle in the progress of Odysseus's homeward journey. By contrast a variety of gods make their appearance in the *Iliad*, but as a group they remain aloof (Zeus particularly never enters the fray as partisan of one side or the other), portrayed more as indifferent spectators than anything else (how well Christopher Logue has caught this in his adaptation of the *Iliad* in the lines "And them above, their faces pressed against eternal glass, / The Gods . . .").

The principal god is Zeus, whose name has a clear etymology. He is the light of day, the shining one, as such the god of the sky, the god of weather, whose rain and storm can be beneficial to crops or destructive, just as sun makes things grow or too much burns the tender leaves. His thunderbolt is the power that no thing can withstand, the sign that he is at hand. In Hesiod's account of him Zeus wins the throne of power from his father, vanquishes the Giants and Titans, finally securing his own power to all eternity by swallowing the woman pregnant with the fetus that could grow up to overthrow him in another act of a son's destruction of his father. He is the god of victory, the all-invincible god. Yet Homer depicts him bowing to necessity when he sees his favorite son about to be killed, holding up the scale of fate when Hector and Achilles meet on the field of battle, letting fate take its course rather than succumbing to his own partiality. In these moments he is made to transcend his anthropomorphic emotional yearnings and be identified with the abstract and severe principle of *moira*, fate or destiny. Zeus is described as the father, the king, and the husband. In his court at Olympus all the gods defer to him; all people of the earth honor him first. His wife, Hera, despite her grumbling, acknowledges his power. When he nods in assent to a petition, it is described as already then accomplished.

Hera, his wife, is also his sister. This gives her a position of parity that no mortal woman enjoyed in her own marriage but does not stop Zeus from having physically abused her once or threatening to repeat the abuse (*Il.* 15.16–33). Her grievance against him stems principally from his aggressive sexuality, from which neither woman nor handsome boy seems to be safe. As a cult figure Zeus is an emblem of fertility; stories of sexual vigor are a natural manifestation of this power. They will, of course, conflict with the depiction of a god so highly anthropomorphized as to be locked in the bonds of marriage.

Numerous are the stories of his female conquests. The women are in fact often quite unsuspecting, since he does not hesitate to approach his victim in disguise—as a shower of gold, for instance, or as a swan. The young Trojan prince Ganymede is snatched up and carried off to Olympus to be his cupbearer, so that Zeus will have a handsome young boy to fondle to all eternity when the wine is being poured (from which we might imagine every ancient Greek male's fantasy of the perfect banquet waiter). The reader of the *Iliad* needs to remember these stories when considering Hera's cold, calculated, and quite hostile sexual seduction of her husband in the fourteenth book, or her shrill, contentious assault upon him at the end of Book One. Homer has so presented Hera, one imagines, to satisfy the conception of a wife which the men of the time might have entertained. They were no doubt striving for the effortless and extraordinary promiscuity of their principal male deity, in their erotic fantasies if not in fact. His constant exhibition of virility through oppressive acts of sexuality would certainly enrich the fantasy life of the ordinary puny male auditor, who might thereby entertain spurious notions of his own superiority by confusing easy oppression with genuine eroticism. In cult, however, Hera appears as a far more powerful, important, and sympathetic deity. She is worshiped far and wide as the Great Goddess, her connection with temple architecture is very early and ubiquitous, as we can see from the early wood temple at Olympia, later replaced in stone, and from the two splendid archaic temples dedicated to her in the same precinct in southern Italy at Paestum. She is the goddess of marriage, presiding at weddings. All these serious roles lie far behind and are much beclouded by the ill-tempered shrew of Homer's conception. Is this not yet another sign that Homer is playing to a distinctly male audience?

Poseidon is of the same generation as Zeus and Hera. Homer has him recount (*Il.* 15.186ff.) how he, Zeus, and Hades divided up their patrimony by casting lots, Zeus getting the heavens, Poseidon the sea, and Hades the underworld, while the three of them share the earth and high Olympus. (In early myth, Olympus tends to mean no more than the locale of the gods on high, until finally it becomes localized to the top of a mountain in Thessaly.) Poseidon is also connected with earthquakes (one of his special epithets is "the earthshaker") and with the horse. There is a superb portrait of him in the *Iliad* (13.17–38) as he harnesses his horses and drives his chariot to the place where the Achaeans are fighting. The glitter of the chariot as it progresses through the sea with dolphins playing about it contrasts with the notice of Poseidon's care for the horses once he has reached his destination; it puts the thoroughly anthropomorphized soul of a humble horse trainer into the surface portrait of divine majesty. In the *Odyssey*, a description of Poseidon making a storm at sea (5.291ff.) is a fine example of the religious sensibility that is intent upon domesticating the irrational and awesome forces of the universe by making them human. Poseidon is a Mycenaean god; Linear B tablets identify him as the principal god of Pylos, which is probably why, when Telemachus arrives at Pylos, Nestor is discovered sacrificing to Poseidon (*Od.* 3.4ff.).

Pallas Athena is a protector of cities, much like Notre Dame de Paris or Nuestra Señora de Guadalupe; she is the patron of Athens, as the one reference to her on a Linear B tablet has it. The meaning of her name Pallas is unknown; she takes the rest of her name from the city, which was an original Mycenaean site. In the *Iliad* she is also protector of the city of the Trojans; Hector's mother and the other women form a procession to supplicate her. She is a powerful force in battle; the *aegis* she carries, a goatskin, is terrifying to her enemies when she brandishes it aloft. When she is not a warrior goddess, she is a patron of the arts of civilization: weaving, for instance, and cultivation of the olive tree. In the *Iliad* she appears to Achilles (1.194ff.) as a kind of external projection of his struggle with self-control; in the *Odyssey* she appears to Odysseus (13.288f.) in her true form as goddess, "a tall woman skilled in handicraft," after he cunningly lies to her about his identity. Athena is thoroughly asexual, having been born not from a woman's womb but from the head of Zeus. He had swallowed her mother, and Hermes or Hephaestus split his head open with an axe; this act of extreme hostility (which would be fatal for mortals) was the catalyst for her arrival into the world.

Apollo and Artemis, sister and brother, children of Leto and Zeus, have less personality in the Homeric poems than some other deities. Apollo uses an arrow, brings sickness, plays the phorminx, a kind of lyre. Perhaps the narrator's choice to describe Apollo as the god who disdains to fight in a human battle represents a disinclination to put a less well anthropomorphized figure in the human arena. Certainly Apollo has fewer attributes than other deities. While Apollo reminds his fellow god Poseidon that human beings are inconsequential, seen from the divine perspective, from the human perspective, divine intervention in battle is definitely ennobling. A reader might think that Apollo, who beguiles Patroclus at his dying, is cruel or treacherous. The death is preordained, however, and Apollo's participation translates Patroclus's death into something greater, just as the bull who is brought to his death by the greater bullfighter makes for a more thrilling "moment of truth" on a hot, dry afternoon.

Artemis in cult is known as the *potnia theron*, mistress of the beasts. She presides over the world of nature; she is the protector of animals and their hunter as well. Her virginity, unlike Athena's, is emblematic of the constant promise of fecundity, the unploughed field, ripe with potential for harvest. Virginity is, indeed, so important an aspect of fertility that goddesses such as Hera, who are manifestly not virgin, have annual rites to reinstate that condition. It is perhaps surprising that Artemis, who seems so strong a figure in cult, is reduced in the *Iliad* narrative to a silly weakling in the humorous battle of the gods. That may be again the male narrator playing to the prejudice of his masculine audience. In the *Odyssey* Artemis assumes greater dignity and importance in a comparison with Nausicaa, the idea being repeated by Odysseus in his address to the young maiden. It is one of the great similes if only because of its literary progeny, beginning with its use by Apollonius in describing Medea (*Arg.* 3.876–84), then again by Virgil to describe Dido (*Aen.* 1.498–502). Here is the Homeric version:

> Nausicaa of the white arms led the dance,
> just as Artemis who delights in arrows over the mountains,
> either the Taÿgetus range or on steep Erymanthus,
> delighting in the wild boar or swift deer.
>
> [*Od.* 6.101–4]

Aphrodite is associated with the sexual act; her son is Eros, the Greek word for physical desire. As such she is a Greek version of the Near Eastern goddesses Ishtar and Astarte, emblems of fertility, reproduction, and sexuality. Hesiod tells how she was born from the foam floating in the ocean around the lopped-off genitals of the god Uranus. Hesiod's epithet for her is *philommedes*, "loving male genitals," which has been changed in the Homeric tradition to *philommeides*, "laughter loving." In the third book of the *Iliad* she snatches Paris up from battle, deposits him in his bedroom, and searches out Helen to go to him for lovemaking. This scene may be the poet's reminder to his auditors of the contest in which Aphrodite competed with Hera and Athena for title of most beautiful goddess, and won. The judge was the boy shepherd Paris. Bribed with offers of power by Hera, of brains by Athena, of the most beautiful woman in the world by Aphrodite, he did what any kid would do and voted with his hormones. Aphrodite, of course, gave him Helen.

Hephaestus, god of fire, god of the forge, makes for Achilles the resplendent shield so lovingly described in the eighteenth book of the *Iliad*. Crippled from birth, Hephaestus was thrown out of heaven by his disgusted mother, Hera, who bore him without male participation in the reproductive process. In the divine family on Olympus he is the commonplace runt and butt. And yet, although he is the object of laughter at a divine party in the *Iliad* and cuckolded by his wife in the *Odyssey*, Hephaestus is nonetheless given dignity and wit in the poet's description of him.

Ares, the god of war, has a name that is also a common noun and most likely means something like the adrenal rush that overcomes anyone about to do something especially daring, such as a charge into battle, or knocking someone down in a barroom argument. He is the negative side of warfare, one might say, as Athena is the positive. Zeus calls him the most hateful to him of all his offspring. The narrator has Ares play brawn to Athena's brains, and twice (*Il.*

5.890ff., 21.391ff.) the poet brings them together in conflict on the field of battle with sad results for Ares.

The Homeric gods differ from humans in being first of all immortal, then ageless, and finally superhumanly powerful. Otherwise, they seem capable of any mortal emotion or impulse. Truly the Greeks created gods in their own image. At a very early stage, however, objections began to be raised against the epic poets' depiction of a group of gods who are capable also of every crime and perversion that mortal mind can devise. Later ages failed to understand Homer's brutal objectivity. His conception of the gods accounts for a world in which every kind of emotion and action is possible. There is no ideal to which mankind should strive, just as there is no beneficent deity who has a loving concern for humans.

God is all things. So Homer can describe Hephaestus as a laughter-provoking cripple, patronized and tolerated, in the first book of the *Iliad*; as a frightening ball of fire in the twenty-first book's account of Achilles' battle with the river; and as the exalted craftsman, maker of all things beautiful and complex, who creates a shield for Achilles in the eighteenth book. Again in the *Odyssey*, Aphrodite is first described in the most amusing way when a metal trap designed by her husband, Hephaestus, catches and holds her in the middle of the act of sexual intercourse with the god Ares, while all the male gods come to gawk and laugh. After this humiliation, this touch of the common, when Hephaestus has let them loose, Homer restores her majesty with these words: "Laughter-loving Aphrodite went to Cyprus, to Paphos, where her precinct and fragrant altar are. There the Graces washed and anointed her with immortal oil, the kind that covers the gods who exist forever, and then dressed her in beautiful clothing and she was a wonder to behold" (*Od.* 8.362ff.).

The Alexandrian critics tended to remove lines from the Homeric epics which to their mind diminished the majesty of the gods. One such passage from the third book of the *Iliad* describes Aphrodite pulling up a stool for Helen so that she can sit and converse with Paris. The Alexandrians who did not like the picture of Aphrodite as a serving maid quite missed the point, for in fact the scene shows the goddess as all powerful and quite sinister. Helen, who is sick to the death of her role at Troy, has just remonstrated with Aphrodite, threatening rebellion, and the goddess has reminded her in the harshest terms whose protégée she is, then sent her on in to Paris. In Aphrodite's placing a stool for Helen the poet emphasizes the hovering insistence of this powerful goddess, who will not allow her erstwhile client to imagine for even a second that she has a will of her own.

Aphrodite's interference is an elaborated version of the more frequent kinds of reference to the divinities, such as "Zeus put a thought in my heart" or "the nymphs roused up the goats so my comrades could eat." In the great battle from the eleventh to the seventeenth book of the *Iliad* the poet specifically tells the reader that Ares does not enter the fighting yet remarks that Ares enters Hector and fills him with ardor (17.210–11). Obviously it is the essence of what Ares represents, the animal energy of aggression rather than the god himself, which the poet has in mind. Athena's importance to the plot of the *Odyssey* is offset by her disappearance at certain strategic moments. When Telemachus plans to continue to Sparta for more news of his father, Athena, who has been with him in the disguise of Mentor, turns into a bird and flies away (*Od.* 3.371ff.). Likewise in the travel narrative Odysseus makes no mention of Athena, for which the poet, in a conversation between Odysseus and Athena, feels compelled to apologize (13.318–19, 341ff.). In fact her departure from the narrative must be in both instances due to the delicacy and aesthetic subtlety of the poetic tradition which prevents authentic Olympian gods from colliding with lesser supernatural beings. Odysseus meets with nymphs, witches, and other fairytale creatures on his travels; Telemachus at Sparta will meet Helen, whom present-day students of religion call a faded goddess (a term for a local supernatural being with a cult whose authority and divinity have declined over time until she becomes simply a human being of unusual power and authority). The story tradition, we must assume, assumes the subconscious truth of Helen's godhead, which causes the poet to send Athena away.

The gods are an inheritance from the Mycenaean period. Stories about them no doubt began to be told very early, and as the epic narratives developed and the gods were made to take on roles in the action, they presumably assumed an ever more anthropomorphic character. Some saga stories must also be a Mycenaean inheritance, since they center on cities that were important then, such as Pylos, but not at all later on. The Linear B tablets tell us very little about Mycenaean civilization. The gold found at Mycenae and other sites betokens a very rich culture, and a hint of that bygone grandeur may be embedded in the description of Alcinous's palace in the *Odyssey*, an especially rich and decorated habitation that awes Odysseus. Mycenaean artworks tell us nothing very specific, however, although the technique of metal inlay described in the making of Achilles' shield seems to illustrate a Mycenaean technology.

The Minoans, whose culture was already in place on the island of Crete when the Mycenaeans began to develop their own, seem to have been a strong influence on the younger culture. With their highly developed sense of ornament the Minoans used images and scenes from the natural world in every kind of art they produced. These themes reappear on Mycenaean cups, breastplates, sword hilts, and gravestones. Their use of the natural world will remind the reader of Homer's depiction of images from nature in his similes. Since he does not otherwise describe nature, one can think of the similes as so many discrete works of art, decorated with scenes from nature, set into the text—inlaid, as it were, a kind of elaborate ornamentation. The bull especially seems to be a Minoan borrowing, since the bull is central to Minoan religion.

The lion, so frequent in the Homeric similes, is problematic, however. Lions seem not to have been part of Homer's actual world. It is argued that their frequent appearance in the similes is an inheritance from the long past of the epic poetic tradition. Yet the extended similes are not themselves necessarily part of the older inheritance. At least in the form in which they appear in the Homeric poems, the similes contain a number of words that linguists classify as late and, because they often mention artifacts and practices that are thought to belong to the latest period, seem to be a stylistic innovation in a long tradition. Still, the lion appears to have been a Mycenaean heraldic symbol. To this day two majestic lions stand rampant over the great entry gate at Mycenae. Perhaps the lion is a lingering reference to Mycenaean power, embedded in pictures of the ravening beast attacking the weaker livestock. Certainly the image of the attacking lion was attractive to the ancient Greeks. Numerous surviving pieces of archaic sculpture depict a lion upon the back of another large animal, it claws sunk deep into the flesh, its jaws open, pushing in, about to break the spinal column.

The style of art that followed the Mycenaean is called geometric. It too is thought to have left its traces in the narrative, although in a more profound way: it has been likened to aspects of the Homeric narrative style, and critics assume that they reflect a common aesthetic. Specifically, geometric art reveals an obsession with filling the entire field of the surface. Critics have felt that what they would call

Homer's obsessive need to tell his auditor everything, even about matters for which detail seems quite unnecessary, is the verbal equivalent of this phenomenon. The great objection to this equation is that a surface to be painted or drawn upon is finite, and one can honestly say that geometric decoration fills the entire surface. But what is "entire" in the Homeric narrative? Its field is by definition endless, and a plethora of detail is finally that only in the mind of the auditor or reader. Another feature of geometric art even more frequently linked to the Homeric narrative manner is its symmetry. The technique of ring composition (discussed in Chapter 3) is considered to reflect the relentless symmetry of geometric vase painting.

The artist's marauding lion also seems like a metaphor for the Mycenaean habit of attacking and plundering, if the reader can assume any reality to the frequent references to it in the two poems. Plunder may well have been a significant source of income, alongside the extensive trade to which remnants of Mycenaean pottery from the Atlantic to the Near East attest. Coinage had not yet been invented; the rudimentary economy was based on barter, and the poems—especially the *Odyssey*—are filled with references to gift exchange. Every visitor brings a gift and expects one in return, a custom widespread in humankind's history, as anthropologists report. That gift giving is a form of payment for services rendered is obvious in the traveler's gift to the household that receives him, but in return that household might reward the traveler with a gift for his not having come as a thief and murderer—the ancient version of our protection money. The Homeric convention of gift giving reinforces the fundamental reciprocity in human society.

Archaeological evidence implies that in the last centuries of the second millennium the social, economic, and political unity we call the Mycenaean Empire was dissolved. The cause is not clear, although the Greeks themselves maintained a tradition of a so-called Dorian invasion, which has been understood to refer to the purported movement of another dialect group of Greek-speaking people coming down out of northwestern Greece to enter the Peloponnesus, eventually dominating the rich centers of culture there. The original inhabitants fled, either up into the mountains of Arcadia, where a kind of Mycenaean Greek persisted in the local dialect, or across the sea to Cyprus, where another dialect presumably of Mycenaean Greek is to be found; it is so like the Arcadian that the two constitute a dialect in the linguists' handbooks known as Arcado-Cypriote. Still others went in the direction of Athens and then on across the Aegean to the coast of present-day Turkey near present-day Smyrna, the area known in antiquity as Ionia. The Mycenaean practice of inhumation was replaced by cremation (the practice we find in the Homeric poems)—reasonably enough, since peoples on the move who had a religious attachment to the remains of their ancestors would want to carry their ashes with them.

The insecurity of the times is perhaps registered in Eumaeus's life story in the *Odyssey* (15.402ff.). Born a prince, stolen away by pirates while still a little boy, sold to Odysseus's father as a house slave, he lived a comfortable life until at puberty he was sent away from the presence of Odysseus's sister to a hut far out on the property to watch over the swine. More than once the narrator refers to migrant workers, the *thetes*, who have no fixed place and wander from farm to farm in search of work. When Achilles says he would rather be one of the *thetes* on earth than king of the underworld, the poet is voicing a hierarchy in which the *thetes* are the most miserable figures. Their lot was far worse than that of slaves because as the property of no one they had no place, no status in the society. Hesiod's cruel advice in *Works and Days* (601–2), "When you've set your [harvest] all snug inside the house, then let your *thetes* go," is crueler still in the Greek, which says literally "then make your *thetes* houseless"—which is to say, once you have housed your wintertime provender, your food, you have no room for the inconsequential, the human beings who are not of your family, free or slave, so they must go out to make room for the harvest. The rootless *thetes* were without hope in a world in which there was precious little protection outside the extended family group that inhabited a homestead and none beyond the neighborhood community of persons who spoke the same dialect and practiced the same cults. The period of migration and change must have wrought profound psychic damage. Its positive side can be seen in the story of the *Odyssey*, which is about a man who comes from the tradition of the conventional heroic narrative (which the *Iliad* represents) and triumphs over his constantly changing and challenging environment by reinventing himself at every stop.

The *Odyssey* describes people living in small pockets of land—coastal Pylos, Sparta's mountain-enclosed valley, an island like Ithaca—who have some kind of autonomous existence. No larger political unit is presupposed. The narrator of the *Iliad* is vague about the distribution of power in the Achaean camp. Clearly Agamemnon is the leader, but the power of his council of advisers is considerable. Achilles' defection is tolerated, if angrily retaliated against by Agamemnon's taking Briseis from him. Achilles can speak openly against a system that allows Agamemnon a disproportionate share of the plunder from the war. And Odysseus, when rebuked by Agamemnon, replies angrily enough to dispel any notion of absolute power emanating from the king of Mycenae. Yet Agamemnon remains the king. In the *Iliad* he is most commonly defined by the epithet *wanax andron*, "lord of men." On the Linear B tablets the word *wanax* appears, meaning supreme leader. Another word on the tablets, *basileus*, indicates a minor but perhaps kingly or at least very powerful figure. The distinction between the two words is registered in the two poems. The *Iliad* poet is ambiguous about the relative power of Agamemnon and Achilles probably because in the later period no such overlord existed. Power was held locally by the squires of the valleys and coastal plains and islands, men such as Nestor, Menelaus, or Odysseus, as the *Odyssey* described them. In fact, the narrator styles these men as *basileis*. Agamemnon remains *wanax* in the *Iliad*; it may be an anachronism, but the story needs someone with pretensions to absolute power. The later Greeks so little understood the dynamics of Mycenaean power that they invented a myth to account for the contingent of nobles leading their men off to Troy; according to this legend, all the suitors of Helen had to swear an oath to go to the defense of whatever man was finally chosen as her husband if any harm ever came to her. The *Iliad* has nothing like this compact; Nestor tells Achilles that Agamemnon must be obeyed because he is "more kingly," "more powerful." The confusion over the source of Agamemnon's power contributes to the dramatic tension of the *Iliad*. Achilles' rebellion against his overlord is not an absolute act of *lèse majesté*, because the political relationship of the two men is not clear to the narrator. Still, what do we know about the political arrangements of the Mycenaean period? It is strange that the Linear B tablets found at Pylos never mention any place name outside the immediate vicinity of Pylos; what, we may ask, was the relationship of Pylos to Mycenae that the name of the latter is never encountered? Furthermore, in the plain known as the Argolid only a few miles from Mycenae stands the equally fortified citadel of Tiryns. Why, we ask again, was Tiryns built so close to Mycenae, and why fortified?

Despite the uncertain evidence, Agamemnon may be described as some remnant in the poetic tradition of an overlord of the Mycenaean

Empire. His was a hereditary kingship bestowed upon the family by Zeus, verified by the legacy of the royal scepter Agamemnon wields, which, Homer notes, was made by Hephaestus and given to Zeus, who gave it to Hermes, who handed it on to the family of which generations later Agamemnon is heir (*Il.* 1.100ff.). His power seems to be considerable. He can give away a large piece of land containing a number of towns in a part of the Peloponnesus far from Mycenae, hardly under his immediate and personal power. They lie near "sandy" Pylos and thus constitute part of Nestor's domain, yet the old man hears Agamemnon's plan to give them to Achilles without demur. Of course, one could argue that Homer's audience had no particular knowledge of these towns any more than the tradition did; Nestor's silence would be a projection of the ignorance.

Agamemnon's power is not, as we have remarked, absolute. Notions of liberty and balance of power lurk in the action, which may be an inheritance from the social and political arrangements of the migrating, nomadic Indo-European peoples. Surrounding Agamemnon is his retinue. These companions, kings of the major cities throughout Mycenaean Greece, constitute the major characters of the *Iliad*, and Agamemnon does little without consulting them. The Linear B tablets talk of a council of elders to which this group may correspond. These men are responsible to Agamemnon and he to them. His nightly banquets for them are part of the arrangement. This we must remember when reading of the suitors eating Odysseus's provisions; may of them no doubt had the hereditary right to be dining there, though the *Odyssey* poet represses that fact when he wishes to cast the suitors as Odysseus's enemies.

In addition to the council of major heroes there was the army assembly. Its membership was open to any fighting man, but as the *Odyssey* shows, it was also a peacetime civic institution. Any hero could convene it, as Achilles does in the first book of the *Iliad*. Anyone could speak, certainly the nobly born, even the common soldier Thersites. When anarchy grips the assembly after being told by Agamemnon that they may as well go home, it is Odysseus who stops them with an aphorism now grown famous: "We Achaeans can't all be kings here. Many kings is not a good thing. Let there be one ruler, one king, to whom Zeus has given the scepter and the power to judge so that he can make decisions for the people" (2.203ff.).

Yet there is no court after the fashion of Louis XIV or Diocletian. The narrator uses the verb "follow" and its noun "follower" to describe the relationship between Agamemnon and the heroes who surround him as his companions. Each of these principal heroes has his own follower, a companion, sometimes called a servant, although the word *therapon* seems to have a more profound meaning, something more like an alter ego. The relationship of Patroclus and Achilles is the most important example in the poem. Because in fifth-century Athens and other major Greek cities the institution of homosexual love between a man in his late twenties and a boy in his late teens was encouraged, valued, and praised, knowledgeable readers will tend to read that emotion into the relationship of these two. They will be encouraged in that reading by the knowledge that Aeschylus composed a tragic drama (which no longer survives) based on the physical love between Patroclus and Achilles, in a few extant lines of which Achilles fondly remembers Patroclus's thighs.

Nonetheless, it does not seem to be the case that in the *Iliad* their relationship is physical. As the younger of the two, Achilles would be expected by the culture to follow the lead of Patroclus. Indeed, Nestor reminds Patroclus that Peleus, Achilles' father, had advised the two when they set off for Troy that Achilles was the younger and should be guided by Patroclus. Elsewhere, the narrator however, seems to emphasize quite the reverse in their relationship. When they entertain in the absence of servants, Achilles cuts the meat and Patroclus deals out the bread (*Il.* 9.215ff.), certainly gender-specific activities of which the former relates to the out-of-doors and the hunt, the latter to agriculture and the household cookstove. Later, when Patroclus is dead, Achilles laments that his friend is no longer alive to serve him his dinner (19.315ff.). When they go to bed at night, the narrator describes them stretching out in the same room (*Il.* 9.663ff.), each in his own bed, each with a woman by his side, and as the narrator notes, Achilles had given Patroclus the woman who slept by him. Achilles thus furnishes Patroclus with his sexual fulfillment, an arrangement of profound power on the one hand and extreme dependency on the other. When Patroclus entreats Achilles to return to the fight, the latter characterizes his friend as a little girl crying at her mother's apron strings, wanting to be picked up (*Il.* 16.7ff.), a simile that reinforces what the previous scenes have suggested. These images, however, may be the narrator's way of describing the utter psychic intimacy of the two men to prepare his audience for the depth of the depression and the force of the anger by which Achilles is later gripped. Or is it the two sides of the masculine psyche the narrator has chosen to formulate in this fashion, Patroclus the vulnerable male and Achilles the obdurate? Two further images might be said to speak to that interpretation: Achilles grieves for the dead Patroclus like a lion for her lost cub (18.318ff.), and Menelaus a little later bestrides the corpse of Patroclus like a cow with her first calf (19.174f.). However much the term "follower" may designate power relationships, clearly, differing degrees of intimacy and bonding are nuances of the equation.

In contrast to Agamemnon, King Alcinous in the *Odyssey* has very little power. He seems to be no more than first among equals. As he says of the Phaeacian grandees, "There are twelve preeminent lords [*basileis*] among the people and I am the thirteenth" (*Od.* 8.390–91). His daughter, Nausicaa, can say, "I am the daughter of great-hearted Alcinous, from whom comes the Phaeacian strength and power" (*Od.* 6.196f.), but he seems careful to defer to the counselors, the elders of the island, the heads of the first families. When Alcinous entertains Odysseus, he decides to summon a still larger representation of the elderly male aristocrats. Yet he is quite indifferent to the feelings of the people. After giving Odysseus a number of gifts, Alcinous is moved to a new height of generosity and says to the first citizens: "I say, let's each give him a large tripod and a caldron. Then we shall recover the sum for ourselves by collecting it from the people. After all, it's very hard for one man to be generous without reimbursement" (13.13ff.). Although Alcinous seems to care little about the general population, he *does* need them for his generous scheme. Somehow one cannot imagine Agamemnon behaving in the same way. Such thoughts prompt critics to note some fundamental change in the political landscape between the two poems, but perhaps it is mainly a matter of changed perspective. The *Iliad* may seem so much more archaic because the poet is deliberately archaizing, trying to be consistent with the heroic motives that animate the characters of his narrative. The narrator of the *Odyssey* seems to have a more realistic, at times even cynical, understanding of human behavior, more like Hesiod's.

The *Odyssey* narrator creates a marvelous blend of perceptions in describing the royal situation at Scheria. On the one hand, there is a lengthy description of the palace as Odysseus approaches it. Certainly this palace is the most glorious, rich, and important in either of the epics, perhaps, as has been suggested, a reminiscence of Mycenaean days. Its gold and silver alternating with bronze, the intricacy of its decor, the breadth of view and the logic of its plan cause us to fall silent in contemplation much as Homer says Odysseus does. Yet, on the other hand, Homer describes Nausicaa and her father as engaged in the simplest domestic arrangements, she going to the stream to wash the royal clothes, he personally directing a slave to hitch up a wagon for her. Scheria is never-never land, as the narrator presents it; the juxtaposition of the palace description and Nausicaa's laundry expedition makes it so. In a world in which young aristocratic girls go out to wash the clothes, the extraordinary palace is fabulous. In a world where such palaces exist, princesses going a-washing are equally so.

At Ithaca, in the king's absence, Telemachus's position seems anomalous. He is the adolescent son of the king, yet there is no regent holding the throne for him until he attains his majority. The suitors all agree that if Odysseus is dead, the throne will go to whoever marries Penelope; no one ever talks about Telemachus as the prince and heir to the throne. The legend of Oedipus is about a stranger arriving in town whose marriage to the widowed queen makes him the king. Whether these two stories reveal some early Greek arrangement of monarchy or whether the stories themselves make these demands is not clear. The *Odyssey* is the story of a group of men vying for the hand of a woman who are eventually defeated by one of them who then takes her for his own. This particular variant has as the winner a man who happens in fact to be the long-lost husband of the woman. The *Bildungsroman* of Telemachus is really quite a different narrative, so that his presence in the story of the suitors contesting for a woman has to be adjusted to be compatible.

The human landscape of the two poems rarely displays any but aristocratic males. In the *Iliad* on only one occasion does a male commoner speak: Thersites, whose objections to Agamemnon's greed and arrogance are really no different from those of Achilles but whose outburst is met with a stern blow across the shoulders from Odysseus. Thersites weeps a tear, his mates titter, and nothing more is heard from the lower orders throughout the poem. The *Odyssey* has a domestic setting in which, naturally enough, a variety of serving people play their parts. There are farmhands such as Eumaeus the swineherd, and house slaves or servants: Eurycleia the old family nurse and various maids—some hostile, some loyal to the house. Melanthius the goatherd and his sister Melantho, Penelope's maid, are the principal house traitors among the servants, established to balance the extreme loyalty of Eumaeus and Eurycleia and also to make the atmosphere in which Penelope lives and the disguised Odysseus maneuvers all the more sinister and perilous. In Homer's world there are *thetes*, slaves, craftsmen, and the aristocracy. The poet has no word for "the people" as opposed to the aristocracy (*aristoi*, "the best people"); they don't exist for him as a recognized category, as a group with a legitimate claim to his attention or, more to the point, his audience's. The narrator consistently takes the view of the master class, as may be seen from his approving description of Odysseus's cruel treatment of the women servants who slept with the suitors. Narrative approval also reflects the strongly masculine point of view that shapes the narrative. There is naturally no recognition that women are acculturated into compliance, but neither is there sympathy for women who as servants, perhaps slaves, have little defense against the sexual demands of powerful, aristocratic young men.

One must assume that these two poems were created by a long line of male bards, that they were composed for a male audience in a culture that valued the male far more than the female. The *Iliad* takes place in war, the arena in which men have throughout history taken not only center stage but the whole stage, since the suffering of women and children—raped, pillaged, bereft—has never had glamor, at least for the males who were composing the stories of the war. Nonetheless, there are some women in the poem; they seem, not unreasonably, to be stereotypic women, women viewed as men tend to see women of their family, the kinds of stereotypes that generations of poets might work out. Hector's visit to Troy in the sixth book of the *Iliad* gives the poet a chance to introduce his audience to what Hector is fighting for—not values but his possessions: that is to say, his women. His mother, Hecuba, offers him wine for refreshment; his brother's paramour, Helen, encourages him to sit by her for a moment's rest; and finally his wife, Andromache, appears with their son to suggest that he withdraw within the walls and make a defense from a place she has noticed as strategic. To each, Hector's response is to refuse. Note the magical three, as though Hector had to run the enchanting fairytale gauntlet of delaying or ensnaring women before he could be free to go back to the battle to die. His farewell to Andromache in this scene is final; they will not meet again. These three women in a way replicate the women of Gilgamesh: his mother, Ninsun the goddess; Ishtar, who propositions him; and finally Siduri, who advises him to stay behind and live the good life and make babies.

Conventional masculine views of women tend to this tripartite arrangement: the nurturant woman, the sexual partner, and the wife and mother of the dynasty. Notice as well that all the women of the *Iliad* are heavily dependent upon their males. Andromache explains that Achilles killed her entire family and thus Hector is everything to her. Aphrodite's harsh rejoinder to Helen's complaints center on Helen's utter dependence upon her sexual charms at Troy, and thus upon Paris's continuing interest in her. Even Hera is afraid of Zeus's strength and malice. She clings to her role as queen and consort because she has nothing else left; Zeus has long since achieved his dynastic ambitions by impregnating numbers of women. Hera, however, has the only sexual experience described in this poem. Despite the sensual naturalistic setting, so like that of the *Homeric Hymn to Aphrodite*, she wields her sex as a weapon, a means for deceit and control and defiance toward her divine spouse, whose response to her seduction is as pompous as one may imagine of the typical male king. Hera is determined to help the Achaeans, whereas Zeus favors the Trojan cause. She sets out to seduce him with the prospect that he will fall asleep after orgasm. Decked out provocatively, she proves to be instantly attractive to her consort, who proceeds to compare her favorably with a long list of women with whom he has slept (*Il.* 14.315ff.) Zeus's pompous obtuseness equals that of Agamemnon, who complains to Odysseus when they meet in the underworld that Clytemnestra was an accomplice in his murder and that she killed Cassandra, who was at his side (*Od.* 11.421ff.). The narrator makes women speak more from roles than from any developed personality. Thetis, for instance, is always the *mater dolorosa*. Hecuba, when Hector stands before the walls awaiting Achilles' charge, pleads with him to come inside the city, and she bares her breasts in a demonstration of what she or any mother has given her child, her claim to be treated well in her turn in old age. In the moment when Achilles drags Hector's lifeless corpse around the city and Andromache peers down from the walls, her lament springs from her role as mother, not as wife, as she contemplates the future in which her male child will have no father to protect him.

The slave women Chryseis and Briseis are so many possessions to be taken, used, and displayed by their captors or the men who are given them as prizes. Nestor tries to rouse the troops to martial ardor by telling them (*Il.* 2.354) that the Achaeans should not go home until they have each had the chance to rape a Trojan wife; women are no more than objects for Nestor as well. When Agamemnon declares that he wants to take Chryseis home with him, since she is in no way inferior to his wife, Clytemnestra, as a weaver and a bed partner, he depersonalizes both women. Helen is discovered in the *Odyssey* back home again with Menelaus, not unlike a cat that has run away and up a tree and has been retrieved with some effort, brought back, and set on its pillow. Despite the attempts at self-castigation in the *Iliad* by which she insists upon some modicum of adult responsibility (and so gives her adultery dignity), none is allowed her in these two epics. She is simply another possession. Yet notice that Nestor's call for rape is, he says, to avenge Helen's longing to escape and her lamentations (*Il.* 2.356). Male character, male narrator, male audience will not tolerate the notion that she left Sparta because she sexually and emotionally preferred Paris to Menelaus. The *Odyssey* narrator seems to have understood this, however, or at least he allows his Penelope to understand it: she remarks that Helen would never have gone if she had thought the Achaeans would make such a fuss and come after her (*Od.* 23.218ff.)!

Yet the *Odyssey* is remarkable for the number of strong women who fill the narrative. In describing the old slave woman, Eurycleia, the narrator remarks that Odysseus's father, Laertes, bought her but was afraid to sleep with her because of his wife, Anticleia. The poet feels compelled to give this little insight into the domestic relations at Ithaca—so foreign, it seems from our other evidence, to the normal masculine behavior—at the very beginning of the poem (1.430ff.). At Sparta, as Telemachus talks with Menelaus, not yet having identified himself, Helen enters the room and instantly exclaims that he must be the son of Odysseus (4.138ff.). When Nausicaa gives Odysseus advice about how to comport himself in the city, she recommends that he go at once to pay court to her mother, Arete, obviously the power in the palace (6.304f.). Arete's acuity is immediately demonstrated by the speed with which she identifies the palace clothes that Nausicaa has lent the shipwreck (7.237ff.). Even in the underworld Odysseus sees not only the great dead heroes from the *Iliad* saga, not only such major tourist attractions as Sisyphus and Tantalus, but he reviews also in catalogue fashion a band of famous women who appear.

In the nineteenth century Samuel Butler wrote a book titled *The Authoress of the Odyssey* in which he set out to show that the poem was the work of one person (this was back when plural authorship was in style) and that she was a woman, an inhabitant of Trapani, the small island off the coast of western Sicily. His arguments seem silly today, having to do with what a woman would or would not know of the material about which she wrote; still, it is a book not to be missed, if only to encounter a male taking seriously the so-called feminine in the poem. Robert Graves made an amusing fiction from this material, the novel *Homer's Daughter*. Anthropologists have not discovered much epic poetic work that has been in the hands of women; that does not rule out the possibility, but it is difficult to believe that this poem could possibly be the work of a woman. First, Penelope, who is the object of Odysseus's long voyage home, disappears from the narrative after their first night of reunion in bed. Second, a pervading fear, if not loathing, of women runs through the scenes in which they appear in the *Odyssey*. There is also an interesting symmetry with the *Iliad* poem: three women, Calypso, Nausicaa, and Circe, appear in the story to tempt Odysseus to stay or to bar him from journeying further; he must get away from these three in order finally to get home, just as Hector in the sixth book of the *Iliad* has to decline the invitations or entreaties of three women.

The women of the *Odyssey* who most affect Odysseus are Calypso, Circe, and Penelope. Of course, the first two are not nearly as important as Odysseus's wife; still, all three share so many traits that one would not be wrong to say that there is a basic stereotype to which they all belong. All three are women on an island waiting for a man to come by. Calypso, like a spider in a web, wants to detain the man who stumbles into her power. Circe has the power to enchant a man who has sex with her. Even Odysseus, armed with a charm against her seduction, is sufficiently besotted that his crew must make a real effort of persuasion a year later to get him to leave. Penelope, the wife waiting at home for her husband to return from the wars, is frequently juxtaposed with Clytemnestra, who in a similar situation killed her man. Agamemnon, when he speaks with Odysseus in the underworld, insists Penelope will not behave as Clytemnestra did and all wives generally do, thereby establishing a paradigm of wifely behavior, which, though perhaps it causes no suspicion to enter Odysseus's mind, certainly plays to the fears of every male in the poet's audience. The suitors complain that Penelope plays them false declaring she will remarry when she has woven a shroud for her father-in-law, Laertes, while sending them messages of hope by day, unweaving Laertes' shroud at night (2.91ff.). Toward the end of the story, when the narrator is bringing all the elements together, he has Athena inspire Penelope to appear once more before the suitors (18.206ff.). She descends the stairs and looks at them radiantly, thereby exciting them to a new frenzy of desire. At this moment she is certainly not unlike Circe. Yet Penelope dreams (19.536ff.) of an eagle coming to destroy her pet geese, and in the dream she cries for her dead geese. The woman who has been so steadfast these many years, has resisted so courageously the importunities of the lusty suitors downstairs, still has enough sense of the fundamental attraction of their attention to know that she will miss it when they are gone. That is what her dream tells her. Penelope is one of the poem's more complicated figures. By the time Odysseus is finally reunited with her, she has become a complex of expectations built up by Odysseus and the reader through their associations with Calypso and Circe and their knowledge of Clytemnestra.

Homeric women are supposed to be beautiful, good at weaving, loyal to their husbands and households, and chaste. Males are judged by very different standards, since their decisive actions are in another arena. In perilous times and in the absence of organized stable governments, a male must be able to assert his will against other males. Therefore, Homeric man, to be successful, must be a successful fighter before all else. He is judged by his success, not by his intentions. When Agamemnon makes his public apology to Achilles for having taken Briseis away from him, it is how this action affected military strategy that claims his attention. He says that what he did was wrong because by keeping Achilles out of battle, it gave Hector and the Trojans great success. He does not consider himself culpable for having been arrogant or for having hurt a fellow warrior; he suggests that Zeus pushed him to it. But that is no more than the common human inclination to assign frailty to divine will. Paris tells Helen (3.439) that Menelaus won the duel with the help of Athena, when the auditor knows that in the battle just fought no mention was made of Athena's presence. On the other hand, when Patroclus's helmet is knocked off by Apollo, it is the narrator who tells us so. Apollo, of course, is not even the real agent here; as the narrator tells us, it is Zeus who has willed that Hector shall have this helmet. Zeus in turn is only the instrument of fate, which has decreed that at this moment Patroclus shall die.

Two passages, one in the *Iliad* and one in the *Odyssey*, seem to be offering comments on the cause of good and evil in this world which are meant to apply to the entire narrative. In the *Iliad* is Achilles' story of the two jars of Zeus, one filled with evil, the other with good from which Zeus indifferently makes a mix to sprinkle on humans (24.527ff.). In the *Odyssey* is Zeus's complaint that mortals blame the gods for miseries they bring upon themselves (1.32ff.), a quite contrary view suggesting that in the long run the good and prudent man will triumph over adversity, that the universe does not condemn him to random misfortune. Some see these two passages as being in a kind of dialogue with each other and the two poems as displaying conditions for man's behavior which dramatically illustrate the difference between so tragic a poem as the *Iliad* and so comic a story as the *Odyssey*. Others might point out that in the first instance it is a human, Achilles, who is made to try to define the universe, whereas in the second instance it is a god, the very king of the gods, a figure who might, one imagines, speak from the behind the scenes, knowing it all. The very great difference might therefore derive from the difference between what a human or a god would understand about the workings of the cosmos.

The aristocratic males of these two poems are often called "good," "noble," or "best" by the poet, even when (as in the case of the suitors) they are exhibiting apparently destructive or hostile or antisocial behavior. The fact of the matter is that they, like "noble Aegisthus," belong to a class of persons whose inheritance, physical endowments, and capacity for leadership all make them good. These men are generally called "good" because of their class, then specifically called good because of their achievements, which must be in the narrow range of activities designed to promote the success and well-being of the community. In the society portrayed in the Homeric poems, success basically means the successful physical defense of one's home or one's army companions. A good person, then, is a good killer, a ruthless killer, an unsentimental despoiler of anyone or anything that threatens his turf. Good has nothing to do with ethical positions or morality. Furthermore, the good of a person is determined by his fellows. Homeric males do not judge themselves; they are what their peers make of them. This is the mechanism of a society in which self-worth—indeed, the very sense of self—is more often than not fixed by the praise or blame of the society at large. If therefore every man is the invention of the group in which he finds himself, the makers of praise poetry assume an even larger role, even greater importance, in this culture than is generally assigned to them. For it is they who can create for all time the self of any warrior dead or alive, an identity that finally transcends the vagaries of the moment's public esteem or contempt and is not dependent upon success or failure in any specific venture. Through heroic poetry a man can gain permanence, become a person entire through all time. It is perhaps not too much to say that poetry of this sort offers a version of what the Christians had in mind when they invented heaven.

· 3 ·

Poetic Technique

Mother of mine, why do you object to our trusty singer
giving delight in whatever way his mind inspires him?
The poets are not responsible for their subject matter
but Zeus is, who gives to each man what he will.
So don't blame this man for singing the Achaeans' sad fate.
For men are much more going to praise whichever song
comes newest to their ears.

—*Odyssey* 1.346–52

As the reader may now understand, who or how many persons composed the Homeric poems, and how and why, remain utterly elusive questions. The persistent mystery profoundly affects what critics say about the technique of the poetry. What seems a subtle authorial gesture to one is identified as a commonplace mechanical necessity by another. Those who initially solidified and refined the theory of the oral nature of the two poems insisted upon the fact that the Homeric poet must have been illiterate. Their fieldwork with South Slavic oral poetry confirmed them in this view. Jugoslav oral bards were not only illiterate, but when becoming literate—more specifically *when they accepted the concept of a fixed text*—they seemed to lose the skill and the technique for oral poetry. The consequence for Homer was that there prevailed a theory of composition which envisioned generations of oral poets who kept the meter, the diction, the stereotyped characters and typical scenes and commonplace story patterns as so many components in their brains which they brought together extempore, yet studied in some way and certainly recollected from previous practice and rehearsal, to make poems on the order of the two that survive.

That these were far longer than the kind of evening performance apparently performed by the *Odyssey's* Phemius and Demodocus was always a problem. Somehow the theorists had to avoid the notion of a fixed text, whether written or memorized verbatim. They had to imagine that the bards were in the habit of delivering evening performances of the familiar episodes—"Achilles spurns his comrades," for instance, or "Patroclus dies in battle," or "Telemachus goes to visit Sparta," or "the night Odysseus strung the bow"—and that somehow certain poets had the occasion or the idea to bring these episodes together into the great story of "Achilles' wrath and the Trojan war," or "how Odysseus came home," both of which were elaborated on the frame of stereotypic stories of battles, falling cities, fairytale adventures, and homeward-bound voyagers. That these two long narratives seemed to show so much control, organization, and subtle authorial penetration of the story was also bothersome. Such refinements seemed to demand a single author, or at the most two, rather than a tradition that would seem to exercise considerably less control. Strict oralists, as a counterargument, insisted that somehow over time generations of poets either refined the story or carried in their memories what had been perfectly elaborated in an earlier period, to be recollected in the creative act of making out of it what was always something new. Skeptics looked at the examples of indisputably oral poetry from Jugoslavia and Turkey and Africa, judged them inferior poetry, and were not convinced that they provided an insight into or evidence for Homeric versemaking.

More recently, comparativists have focused on cultures in which poets who practice an oral poetic style are also literate. This has freed students of the Homeric poems to imagine a poet or poets who, though deeply immersed in the oral poetic tradition, nonetheless knew how to write well enough and was or were comfortable enough with this new means of communication—not to mention a form of preservation that makes memory obsolete—to use it extensively. The notion is seductive because it allows for a process of literary production with which the critic is familiar. Suddenly the poet or poets and the poems are ours.

In fact, contemporary field experience with oral poets who use writing resolves nothing. It is one thing to know enough or care enough about writing to make notes for a performance; it is another to compose more than fifteen thousand dactylic hexametric lines in writing and still more for two persons, probably, to use this *very new* and thus uncertain technology for two poems that betray a master's sophisticated manipulation of his medium. This master or these masters, we must remember, would also have to struggle with the crude means for writing that prevailed until certainly the end of the sixth century B.C.E., some two hundred years after most persons date the composition of the poems. One could in fact argue that the long poem would become obsolete because the invention of writing *was* so seductive but, at the same time, so unwieldy that this new technology of cultural transmission would limit poets to the creation of short pieces; these alone could be efficiently handled in the new technique.

Because so very little is known about the origin of the Homeric poems, scholars have the license to think what they will. Arguments developed from minimal hard facts quickly enough become articles of faith no different from those of the different sects of a religion. Heresies and orthodoxies abound. In the 1930s the old guard fought a dying battle against the notion that the *Iliad* and the *Odyssey* were two integral poems, composed by a single consciousness which was called the oral poetic tradition. Among American scholars at the moment, and to an extent among those British who can drop their Romantic preoccupation with an individual creative genius, the orthodox belief is that the poems were in origin oral, but the heresy of a *literate* oral poet—once thought no less fanciful than a unicorn—is rapidly moving to orthodoxy. These controversies may strike the casual reader of the Homeric poems as so much tiresome caviling. Theories do, however, determine the way one reads a text. If present-day scholars have the license to think what they will, it must probably follow that present-day readers of the poems are absolutely free to interpret as they choose without fear that there are contextual or historical facts that would or ought to inhibit them.

It is ironic that in the nineteenth century, before the oral theory had been elaborated, most Homeric scholars dealt with the problem of the composition of these two poems in a preliterate culture by imagining that when literacy arrived men stitched together episodes that had been handed down as remembered verbatim. Scholarly enterprise was directed to searching out the flaws of imperfect stitching that betrayed the beginning and end of "genuine" episodes. *Their* analogue was no Jugoslav *guslar* (as the oral poets of Jugoslavia are called) but rather the great psychological, realistic novels of the nineteenth century. Since realism of the sort found in those pages is utterly removed from what the Homeric poets are about, that scholarly enterprise not only was doomed to failure but generated a lot of laughs along the way from later generations who realized the anachronism of it all. Of course, he who laughs at his predecessors is tomorrow's butt, as we all know but forget. Contemporary scholars who spurn the notion of the oral poet recollecting in performance the vast array of words, formulas, half-lines, narrative turns, scenes, characters, story lines that are the matrix of his every performance choose to read the *Iliad* and *Odyssey* as, once again, nineteenth-century novels, in which scenes are psychologically motivated and characters have depth, change, react and interact after the fashion of so many Emma Bovarys, Aloysha Karamazovs, Isabel Archers, and Count Vronskys.

Consider, for instance, the later episodes of the *Odyssey* in which Odysseus disguised as a beggar enters the palace and finally has an audience with Penelope. The beggar tells her that Odysseus is close at hand; Theoclymenus, a man who has journeyed to Ithaca with her son, prophesies that Odysseus will soon wreak vengeance on the suitors; Penelope interprets her dream in which an eagle kills her pet geese as a sign of Odysseus's return. In this context she decides suddenly to hold the contest of the stringing of the bow, announcing that whoever manages to do so will win her hand in marriage. Readers of nineteenth-century novels are stunned by this turn of events because there is no psychological preparation for the decision. Desperate means have to be employed, therefore: the argument that Penelope has penetrated the disguise of the beggar. Marvelously subtle readings of her dialogue with the disguised Odysseus in Book 19 sustain this notion. One cannot, of course, absolutely deny this reading of the passage; it is also attractive to those who would strengthen the roles of women in these poems, since it shows a feminist's Penelope who takes more authority for the working out of her own life. But for the believer in another kind of poet, the idea of a knowing Penelope is not only absurd but seems to be essentially no more than a vulgar appropriation of another culture's artifact for assimilation into one's own. The poet is either a performer for an audience of auditors for whom extreme verbal subtlety of this kind is impossible to put over, or he is some kind of early writer dealing with procedures of writing that must give him constant difficulty finding his place in the text and to whom such extreme verbal subtlety would not occur.

It is better to understand that the poet is putting his narrative together out of story structures. One of them is the princess who is won by the underdog Prince Charming in disguise in a contest with all her suitors. Another is the beleaguered wife or sweetheart, long separated from her husband or sweetheart, who has kept her chastity through one travail after another, and is rescued just in the nick of time by husband or sweetheart, who suddenly arrives on the scene to save her from the villain. Homer's audience, fully habituated to these story structures, knows from the narrator that Odysseus is at hand, that Athena has encouraged Penelope to appear before the suitors one more time, that the suitors have reviled, insulted, and humiliated Odysseus-in-disguise to the breaking point. The story has gone on long enough, and it has nowhere else to go. Everyone knows this, and it is time for the finale. Penelope calls for the contest. In this view, Penelope and the audience are equally complicit with the narrator in advancing the plot.

There are no subtly realized characters in early Greek literature. There is minimal belief in the psychological development of events. Stock stories, stereotypic characters, typical scenes, formulaic descriptions of human action are all ingredients of a world view in which everything is idealized and generalized, on the one hand, and which, on the other, engenders and insists upon a constantly ironical viewpoint. One has only to consider the extreme difference between the recognition scenes in Aeschylus's *Libation Bearers* and Euripides' *Electra* to see the difference between a view of the universe in which things fall into place and one in which human beings are in control of their decisions. In Aeschylus the recognition scene is an extension of the Homeric manner of presentation, whereas in Euripides it looks forward to the novel.

Critics who would subvert the Homeric narrative to find novelistic readings are perfectly free to do so, of course, but they are denying the uniqueness of ancient epic narrative. If Homer had wanted his audience to understand that Penelope was aware, even dimly, that the disguised beggar was Odysseus, he would have said so. The oral poet always helps his audience to an understanding of the story. That is the very essence of the oral manner, which is manifest in line after line of these remarkable and, true enough, immensely mysterious poems. Those who know the surviving artifacts of archaic Greece will ponder the so-called archaic smile of the sculptured figures and consider how the poet or poets of these poems would so smile in the presence of earnest contemporary theorists of Homeric epic. And yet, some will say, let the archaic statues smile their smile; let them condescend as they will. The contemporary reader of these poems knows what the archaic Greeks do not, is sophisticated as they are not. For the contemporary reader has two thousand years of a European cultural experience to read into these two poems, to give them depths, resonances, and subtexts beyond the wildest imaginings of archaic audiences. Even if contemporary readers try to jettison this baggage so as to approach the poems without preconception, there will always lurk the probably perfectly sound suspicion that they cannot.

We can get some idea of the circumstances in which the bard performed from the *Odyssey* scenes in which Phemius and Demodocus perform—assuming, of course, that the narrator was being at least somewhat true to his own experience. He seems to be listened to in relative quiet, since Homer describes the loud noise that starts up when the poet leaves off singing. The occasion for singing is after dinner in the same room where the banquet takes place. The bard is preceded or followed by a dance performance. These facts establish that however rapt the audience may be, the conditions for reception are not those of the twentieth-century concert hall, into which the bourgeoisie have transferred a kind of holy silence from their previous attachment to religion. Indeed, the narrator describes Telemachus and Athena carrying on a conversation somewhat to the side of the room in which Phemius is performing for the suitors.

Demodocus's audience could call out for a favorite story, or perhaps an episode of some greater saga, as Odysseus does when he calls for the story of the Trojan Horse. These were evening's entertainments. It has been calculated from timing modern Cypriote poets that it would require 26.9 hours to recite the *Iliad* and 20.7 hours to recite the *Odyssey*—festival conditions, perhaps, or at least a series of evenings. Moderns think of each of the two poems as divided into twenty-four "books" (the ancient Greek word for papyrus roll is *biblion*, translated "book"; hence that usage instead of "chapters"). Both narratives fall into more natural divisions occasioned by the narrator's mentioning nightfall when the principal characters proceed to fall asleep. Other natural divisions are those in which the locale changes significantly: when Telemachus leaves Pylos, for instance, and goes to Sparta. The ancients had names for many of these episodes: the Nekyia is Odysseus's descent into the underworld in the so-called eleventh book of the *Odyssey*; the Embassy, when three of Achilles' comrades vainly attempt to persuade him to return to the fight, fills the ninth book of the *Iliad*. Some critics argue that the present book divisions are the legacy of very early times, representing so many performance scripts; each book of the *Iliad* is more or less an hour's performance, about the same running time as a tragic drama. Others point out that obviously the poems when written down had to be divided to accommodate the physical limitations of the papyrus roll; the division into twenty-four books is artificial, suggesting the mind of an organizing librarian more than of someone interested in performance. Any number of instances where the divisions are problematic support the latter view. First of all, the books of the *Odyssey* seem really too short to represent performances. Further, where there is continuous flow of narrative, no sensible performance division seems possible. For example, the *aristeia* of Diomedes, which begins with the fifth book of the *Iliad*, comes to a close in the sixth after Hector's visit to Troy has been motivated; the weaving of these two quite distinct episodes is seamless. The neat twenty-four divisions are artificial, probably made as an accommodation for storing the text on papyrus rolls in the Library at Alexandria. However convenient it is to be able to refer to the narrative as it appears in these divisions, the reader must not be seduced into believing that they represent any aesthetic decision on the part of the narrator. Episodes, yes; book divisions, no. It has been said, for instance, that Hector is the only figure to be mentioned in every book of the *Iliad*. As a crude indication of his ubiquity in the poem, that is a worthwhile formulation, but it does encourage the unwary to think that the poet has made Hector a part, no matter how small, of every scene.

To speak of the poet and what he does is difficult when the poetry seems to be so traditional. The narrator is equally elusive. Both poems begin with a call to the Muse for the story, the *Odyssey* poet saying "Sing for me about the man . . ." Thereafter the narrator disappears, returning only very occasionally to complain of the effort of memory. Before the Catalogue of Ships—a particularly treacherous piece of memory work, it would seem, since it is mostly proper nouns—he summons the Muse again to give him special help: "I couldn't relate all that crowd or name their names, not if I had ten tongues, ten mouths, and a voice that wouldn't break down, and a heart of bronze, unless the Muses, daughters of aegis-bearing Zeus, were to remind me who they were who came to Troy" (*Il.* 2.48ff.). And once when he starts to describe a battle, he seems to grumble. After beginning in a conventional fashion with "Some were carrying on the fight at one gate and some at others," the kind of line that is often prelude to a list of names, he breaks off: "It would be very hard for me to narrate all these things, as though I were some kind of god" (*Il.* 12.175–76).

Sometimes his call to the Muse seems not to betoken a problem with memory so much as to signal an important turn of events. In Book Eleven, for instance, when Agamemnon is presented in a small star turn and this *aristeia* ends quite abruptly with his being wounded (for reasons important to the direction of the narrative), the narrator calls upon the Muse (11.218); this gives grandeur to Agamemnon's battle scene but also signals the great turn of the tide as the Achaeans begin to lose. In the fourteenth book the narrator calls upon the Muse to help him with the names (14.508), and there follows a truncated catalogue of victors and victims which could hardly have put sufficient strain on memory to necessitate summoning Muses. The call, how-ever, gives force, severity, and greatness to this little list of deaths so as to motivate Zeus's anger when he discovers how the battle has gone while he slept. The Muse is called again when the narrator commences the description of the long-awaited Trojan fire attack on the ships (16.112). This call marks a truly serious turn in the events of the story. The narrator not only mentions the fire but also notes that Hector inactivates Ajax, who slips away from the battle while Achilles, who suddenly realizes the gravity of the situation, tells the Achaeans to arm.

The narrator breaks the third-person plane of the narrative very infrequently to address a character directly, as for instance in the moments preceding the death of Patroclus: "Three times thereafter he [Patroclus] made a charge, like swift Ares, shouting out fearsomely. Three times he slew nine men. But then when he rushed out the fourth time like a kind of god, then, O Patroclus, the end of your life showed forth." (*Il.* 16.784ff.). The moment is tragic indeed, and the culmination of events and emotions of many preceding scenes. The reader shares with the narrator the desire to break through the frame of the narrative, to call out, to warn, to sorrow for the young man doomed—no different from Zeus's son Sarpedon, so recently dead (16.481ff.), over whom the king of the gods on his Olympian throne anguished and for whom he could do nothing. But it is odd that the two to whom the *Iliad* narrator calls out are Patroclus, the minor figure, and Menelaus, the definitely inferior warrior and man, and odder still that he calls out three times to Patroclus. Oddest of all is the *Odyssey* poet's habit of calling out in the same fashion, "O, swineherd Eumaeus," rather more frequently than Patroclus and Menelaus are so dignified. One critic has suggested that perhaps the *Iliad* poet had a soft spot in his heart for these two; how much greater must be the *Odyssey* poet's affection for Eumaeus! Or should we call it the *Odyssey* poet's intention to mock the *Iliad*'s heroic pomposities? Upon reflection one must concede that the use seems to be indiscriminate. Those who insist upon a kind of authorial control will cavil. Let them therefore sigh as they will at the apostrophes to Patroclus in the sixteenth book. Trite as it may be as a reason, these apostrophes could be simply a convenience to which the narrator yields or submits in the tiring process of turning out line after line of narrative. Any narrator who wields such a demanding and rigid technique as the traditional formulary style must occasionally fall victim to that technique.

There seems to be similar indiscrimination in choosing between two metrically identical formulas such as "ox-eyed lady Hera" and "Hera of the white arms." Statistical studies show that the poet has a tendency to cluster either one of them, as though having thought of the one, he used it over again several times before it slipped from his brain. The same is true of other phrases that are used suddenly, repeated a number of times in a short space, then dropped for the rest of the poem. The selection of one or the other of the formulary doublets cannot be laid to aesthetics, story line, or any other reason of composition or exposition. It seems to be whatever came to mind.

One can easily multiply irrational irruptions in the narrative. There are contradictions, for instance. The beggar whose nickname is Irus was named Arnaeus by his "lady mother" (*Od.* 18.5), says the narrator (who does not seem to have his tongue in his cheek), who elsewhere uses this commonplace expression for an aristocratic mother. Penelope holds the keys in her "big, thick hand" (*Od.* 21.6). The narrator says Antilochus has swift horses; his father Nestor remarks on how slow they are (*Il.* 23.304). When Priam sets out to fetch his son's body, Idaeus goes first, driving the mules hitched to a cart; Priam follows, both of them grieving mightily, but, the narrator says, Priam lays on the whip, implying some real speed. Apollo knocks off Patroclus's helmet, tears away his shield, rips his corselet; the narrator calls him "naked" (*Il.* 16.815), and Patroclus in death responds to Hector's taunt saying, "It was Zeus and Apollo who did me in when they stripped the arms from my shoulders"—yet almost immediately thereafter (17.125) the narrator describes Hector stripping Patroclus of his armor. Achilles laments that he is fated to die at Troy "far from my mother and father," when, of course, his goddess mother, Thetis, is forever hovering around the scene.

These passages are troublesome only to a reader who has the time to pause, speculate, reread. For the habitué of oral poetry, Achilles says what every soldier at Troy says; Hector does what every warrior does after killing someone; Priam despite his age, despite the slower mules preceding him, drives his horses as every gentleman of his class is described as doing; the horses of any hero such as Antilochus will be called swift; any hand that can hold a bunch of metal keys is the stout hand of an athletic male hero warrior; every mother is a lady. The narrator unconsciously creates the generalized, idealized scene in his narrative—no doubt a convention that arose from its very great convenience. As a convention, its incongruence with the specific will not be noticed. As a matter of aesthetics and description, it reveals what early Greek art also demonstrates: the capacity for viewing things separately. The archaic statue was carved laterally and frontally, and these two planes were not necessarily blended into a wraparound. Similarly, what is generally true is allowed to exist side by side with what is particularly true in the situation of this Trojan War. These two planes of reality have an equal claim upon the narrator and his audience.

At times the *Iliad* narrator seems to use such juxtaposition for great effect. The characterization of Hector is a case in point. Just as Patroclus is outfitted in Achilles' armor, which is too grand for him, so the narrator outfits Hector in descriptive formulas that conflict with the behavior given him. The formal descriptions of Hector, however, are exactly the kinds of conventional views of hero warriors which one would expect to be applied to the man who not only appears everywhere in this poem but kills more named and unnamed figures than anyone else, and who is described from time to time as fighting brilliantly (e.g., 8.437–71; 13.136–54). Yet when the principal Achaeans are wounded, it is not Hector who does it; and more often than not he shrinks, retreats, has to be encouraged, displays all the acts and attitudes of a fearful man (e.g., 5.470–92; 11.163–64; 11.357–60; 13.193–94; 14.435–39). The Achaeans talk about him, however, as though he truly is the main menace of the Trojan forces. Diomedes treats him as a great hero when Hector enters battle against him (5.596–606). The Achaeans are said to lack the courage to face Hector (7.92–93); even Achilles is said to fear him (7.113–14).

This could be another instance of the poet using the traditional language of heroism to describe the man, his entry into battle, and all the other occasions when his superficial heroism is to be noted. It would be easier that way. But since this dichotomy is so persistent in the poem, one might better say that here the narrator portrays the man divided against himself. In *The Naked and the Dead* his fictional account of World War II, Norman Mailer describes a GI who leaps up as though fearless in the face of enemy fire because in fact he has shat in his pants from fear. We might call him the modern equivalent of Hector, who is what all heroes must be—brave, overwhelming, terrorizing, and yet cringing, fleeing, and cowering as all men are, if only in their hearts. Another common critical position maintaining that the narrator wishes to present a conflicted Hector rests on his remark to Andromache when he justifies returning to battle and spurning her desire to see him stay safe in the city: "I have learned to be noble" (6.444). *He is acculturated into being a warrior*, we might say of one who does not have his heart in it.

The monologue the narrator gives Hector in the twenty-second book as Achilles charges him is possibly a better index of his state of mind. It is the speech of a man possessed by fear, whose terror makes him feverish enough to imagine anything, even going up to Achilles and giving Helen and everything else back. Yet at this moment Hector also coolly understands the impossibility of such a thing and views himself ironically: how can he "go up and bill and coo like some girl with her swain?" (22.128). The man who contemplates his mistakes, whose concern for reputation has left him out before the walls in this fatal encounter, is not craven. The irony that animates his remarks to Andromache in Book Six is present also in this monologue. But like everything else in the scene—the running around the walls, the imprecations of father and mother, the lamentation of the wife, the movement of the scales held up by Zeus—Hector's response to Achilles' charge is a cliché. It does not gain its validity by coming from the mouth of a specially realized human being; it is the cliché of a cornered and doomed man. As such, it fits into the scene as a thoroughly idiosyncratic speech, true to some special Hector, would not. Achilles, we must remember, is told by his father to be the best in battle. He, too, had to learn. Men may be strong, they may be powerful, but all of them (except the psychopaths) have to learn to be killer warriors.

Characterization, then, is minimal in either poem. As previously mentioned, the women of the *Odyssey* share traits that make them sometimes seem to be a composite of male notions of woman: for instance, Circe and Calypso singing in their houses as men approach, the Sirens singing, Penelope weaving as Circe and Calypso do, Penelope's grief for her loneliness, Calypso's anger at contemplating her loneliness, Penelope's sexual encouragement of the suitors, Circe's invitation to her bedchamber, Helen and Arete sitting beside spouses who are their intellectual inferiors, Circe and Calypso dominating the males who come their way, Nausicaa controling the encounter on the beach. Each woman reveals qualities that link her to another; none shows particularities that give her individuality; Homer does not describe personalities that inspire action.

Likewise, the Achaean warriors before the walls of Troy replicate each other. Whatever individuality they have comes mostly from emphases. Idomeneus, for instance, the man from Crete, is generally lumped with the other *aristoi*—the best men, as Homer calls them— in lines that are clearly formulaic, often repeated, meant to give some personality to the phrase "best men" by naming a few of them. The narrator refers to him as being like a boar in his strength; Agamemnon is lavish in his praise when he encounters him while reviewing the troops; Helen tells Priam that Idomeneus was a guest in Menelaus's house in the old days; he fights and kills in the battle, urges Nestor to take the wounded medicine man, Machaon, out of danger. These quite ordinary and conventional references are slightly augmented by the narrator's remarking that Idomeneus called for the charge in battle, "greying though he was" (*Il.* 13.361). His age intrudes again a hundred or so lines later when in an encounter with Aeneas in battle Idomeneus calls for help, remarking that because he is not in the flower of youth like Aeneas, the going will be rough (13.484). And the narrator has this characteristic sufficiently in mind that even after some six thousand more lines he has Ajax, son of Oïleus, make a sarcastic reference to Idomeneus's age in the scene of the athletic contests (23.476). Yet it is clearly not a feature that gives Idomeneus distinctive behavior throughout the poem, or more to the point, it is not a feature that the narrator renders into something by which to shape the man as he appears in the narrative. Essentially, Idomeneus behaves like anyone else.

Diomedes has the particular feature of being very frequently described with reference to his father, Tydeus. Reviewing his troops, Agamemnon rebukes Diomedes for delaying a forward march; he brings up the valor of Tydeus as a contrast, describing a time he visited Mycenae and a subsequent valorous attack and route of a band of Cadmeians (*Il.* 4.370–400). While Diomedes rests briefly from the ardors of his imposing *aristeia*, the goddess Athena rebukes him for doing so, reminding him of the valor of his father by mentioning the same fight with the Cadmeians (5.800–813). When Diomedes sets out on the nighttime expedition with Odysseus in Book Ten, he calls out to Athena for her support, asking her to remember the aid she rendered Tydeus in that very same incident involving the Cadmeians (10.284–94). In the hours when the battle is going very much against the Achaeans, and Agamemnon in despair asks for better counsel than he himself can offer, Diomedes speaks up, first justifying his right to be heard by reciting his lineage: "You can't very well claim that my inheritance is that of a coward and a weakling and dishonor my words" (14.110–32).

Since Diomedes enters the narrative often enough without an extended reference to Tydeus, however, one cannot say that the association is automatic. But the linkage may in fact instruct the characterization of Diomedes. Consider that he, unlike Odysseus, tolerates Agamemnon's unjustified rebuke as the outburst of an overburdened authority figure (Book Four); he rescues old Nestor, an obvious father figure, in battle (Book Eight), tolerates Nestor's kicking him awake (Book Ten), and is mentioned by Nestor as being like a son to him (Book Nine); and when told by Apollo to desist from fighting, he immediately does so (Book Five). These are the acts of a son, or at least one might say that Diomedes behaves toward these three authorities as toward a father. Perhaps the persistent association with Tydeus is the source for this aspect of his character. Certainly the narrator uses Diomedes' obedience in the narrative to effect. When Diomedes tries three times to assault and pass by Apollo in order to strike Aeneas, the god at the fourth assault warns him to stop, and he does (*Il.* 5.436–43); this is in symmetrical opposition to Patroclus, who in the sixteenth book three times disobeys Achilles' injunction not to launch an assault on Troy, and the fatal results of the fourth assault (16.786f.). With this maneuver the narrator sets the Diomedes personality in symmetrical opposition as well to the Achilles personality, Patroclus's willfulness and ambition being an extension of it in this instance.

At the start of the *Iliad*, when several figures who will play major roles in the ensuing narrative make their appearance, Achilles and Agamemnon are scarcely described, the one called "shining," and the other "leader or men." On the theory that these are important figures in a saga tradition, the narrator perhaps does not need to say more, although he does not scruple to include a good deal of other information that one might imagine his auditor to know. Formally, however, there is no real identification. Old Nestor is the first character for whom the poet stops the forward flow of action to offer description: "Then between them there rose up sweet-speaking Nestor, the clear-voiced speaker of the men of Pylos, whose voice poured forth from his tongue sweeter than honey. Two generations of men had he seen go to their graves, his agemates and their sons, in sacred Pylos, and over the third he was ruler" (*Il.* 1.247–52). Since identification is so random in the poem, one is inclined to think that the description serves other narrative purposes. Here it has the effect of retarding the intensity and speed of the angry quarrel that Nestor is breaking into, preparing a shift in the auditor's mental gears to allow for the speech that follows, a rather more thoughtful and analytical piece. The characterization furthermore invests the speech itself with qualities that its formulaic language will not: that is, sweetness (in the sense of political gentleness, tact) and dispassionate aloofness.

A similar strategy of narrative seems to govern details entered for a minor figure in the *Odyssey*. It is noteworthy that Penelope's suitors are very sketchily delineated, as are the men of *Odysseus's* crew. The suitors are not familiar figures of saga, we assume; so little identification is given that two, Antinous and Eurymachus, are suddenly set apart by so innocuous a phrase as "leaders of the suitors, who were by far best in terms of prowess" (*Od.* 4.629). But when Lord Aegyptius rises to speak in the assembly called by Telemachus, he is more fully portrayed. This is a man who will not appear again in the entire poem, yet the narrator can say:

> Among them the hero Aegyptius began to speak, a man who was bent with age, who had seen everything. One of his sons had gone off to Ilium, the land rich in horses, with godlike Odysseus in the hollow ships, Antiphus, the fighter; him the wild Cyclops killed in his hollowed-out cave, he made him the last for his meal. Three others still lived for him, one, Eurynomus, gone to join the suitors, two at hand doing their father's farm work. But him, Antiphous, he could not forget, grieving and crying over him, and now, shedding a tear for him, he spoke amongst them and gave this public speech. [*Od.* 2.15–24]

In effect, this presentation of Aegyptius describes the situation at Ithaca, as well as the general condition of "homecoming" as it relates to Ithaca. He has lost one son to the Trojan War whose homecoming he may despair of but does not know yet will never be; he has lost one son to the outrageous behavior of the suitors, just as today a parent speaks of a teenaged son who runs with a "wild crowd." Two are home doing their work, reflecting the stability and normality that is so threatened by the war, the wanderings, and the palace irregularity. Much of the emotional intensity of the speeches that follow stems from this passage. Yet little has been learned about the father himself. One could, of course, argue that there is nothing else to know about Lord Aegyptius; he exists as an instrument of dynasty in this story of sons finding fathers and fathers returning to sons; there is only the surface person, the reflection of an environment, rather than a persona that is somehow the outer manifestation of an inner self. In other words, the narrator is not trying to locate a psychology in Lord Aegyptius.

Sometimes action rather than description forms the figure. Such is the case with Patroclus: he is never described and in his first appearance in the ninth book of the *Iliad*, the scene of the Embassy, never utters a word, but he begins to take shape in his serving the bread, in his sleeping in Achilles' tent with the woman given him by his friend, in Achilles' likening him to a little girl crying at his mother's apron strings, and so on. That he does not speak and that he has a complementary role in serving the food and sharing the tent make him appear all the more as Achilles' alter ego, his surrogate figure. Thus, when Patroclus dons the armor to which he is finally ill suited, one can read this as the complement of inevitable death standing beside eternal hope. These are the components of human expectation, which knows the truth of mortality but acts on the assumption of immortality. It is by the very narrative contrivance of the person of Patroclus that his death is made to resonate all the more in Achilles' heart.

The most successful physical description of the two poems is the celebrated oblique portrait of Helen as she appears on the walls to the old men of Troy in the third book of the *Iliad*. Men's sexual appetites being various, no two would likely settle upon an identical description of the world's most beautiful woman, so Homer leaves the matter to each auditor or reader. But he guides our imagination by describing the effect she produces on the old men of Troy. They have in turn just been described by their quavering, high-pitched voices—like the sound of cicadas, says the narrator. Disembodied, they arouse themselves so far as to agree that no one can blame the Achaeians and Trojans for fighting over such a beautiful woman; so aroused are they at the sight of her that they can in that moment accept the death of their progeny and the collapse of their entire world. Helen has never been nor will ever be more formidably beautiful.

The epithets the narrator attaches to the characters, as noted in Chapter 1, tend to be minimally descriptive, but sometimes they come alive in the narrative. Achilles is defined in three different metrical situations as swift of foot, and in the final encounter with Hector as they race around the walls—the one desperately fleeing, the other pursuing and gradually overtaking—Achilles' swiftness of foot is, indeed, realized. Hector is usually described by the epithet "having a shining helmet," which of course does not really illuminate him, but perhaps the narrator extends it into the story in the brief vignette of his last meeting with his wife and baby son: when Hector held out his hands to embrace the baby, "the boy shrank back . . . terrified as he saw the bronze and the crest with its horsehair nodding dreadfully, as it seemed to him, from the peak of the helmet" (*Il.* 6.467ff.). The father takes off the helmet, embraces his son, utters a wildly ironic and tragic wish for the boy's future career as a warrior, and puts the helmet on again.

Achilles is not so much individualized in the narrative as made the complete realization of the heroic stereotype. Diomedes, Idomeneus, Ajax, all the more active fighting men in the narrative, stand in a hierarchy of excellence and power, live for glory and find it in killing. Perhaps because they are depicted in the situation of a protracted war, little else matters to them. Achilles is really no different; he is only more so, we might say. Nestor and Agamemnon's exchange when the argument between the latter and Achilles rages is indicative (1.247ff.). Stop this extreme aggression against a king, the old man advises Achilles, since kings to whom Zeus has given glory never ever share in the same honor as the rest of men. If you are stronger, it's because you've got a divine mother, but Agamemnon is in some way greater because he rules over more men. So stop your anger. Agamemnon responds that Nestor has said it all just as it needed to be said, and then angrily observes that Achilles wants to be superior to everyone, to be more powerful, to give the orders, to rule. Agamemnon's observation should lead us not to imagine that Achilles has some special arrogance, some *characteristic* need to control, but to understand rather that the narrator singles out in him what is basic to all these ambitious, competitive heroes. He is the stereotype come alive, as it were, rather than a singular, individualized figure.

Odysseus is the most complicated, least stereotypic figure in either poem, although he may be the projection of a myth stereotype, the trickster figure best realized in the Norse god Loki as he is described in the poem *Lokisanna*. When Helen is identifying the heroes whom Priam points out on the battlefield, the identification of Odysseus is extended. Priam asks, "Who is that man shorter by a head than Agamemnon, though broad in the shoulders and the chest? . . . He seems like a thick-fleeced ram." Helen's reply contains the particularizing features that dominate the Odysseus of the *Odyssey*; she calls him "a man who knows both all kinds of tricks and plenty of ideas" (3.202). The narrator then has a prince of Troy, Antenor, amplify the description with an anecdote in which Odysseus is said to be shorter also than Menelaus but commanding respect while seated. Antenor remembers that Odysseus, when standing to speak, gave the impression of a surly man, a know-nothing, eyes on the ground, stupid, until he opened his mouth; then he dazzled, was unsurpassed, and all who had beheld the physical appearance were amazed at the man who spoke.

Here is the essence of the *Odyssey* character, the duplicitous, intelligent, seductive speaker whose appearance always belies his extraordinary strengths, whether it be as a dubious prospect in athletic games at Scheria or as the man in beggar's disguise sitting humbly in the great hall at Ithaca. Odysseus does not resemble a hero, and in a culture in which outward self is the essential self, he is thus some kind of outsider. James Joyce reflects this when he makes Bloom, his latter-day Odysseus, a Jew in Catholic Dublin. The emphasis upon Odysseus's considerable speaking talent and his negligible physical attributes points to the ephemeral and utterly changeable personality he has the power to create, as opposed to the strength of the other warriors, which is, like the bodies in which it resides, constant. Yet the narrator of the *Odyssey*, while on the one hand creating a character who reinvents himself each time he is asked to identify himself, has on the other hand made a monolith, just as Achilles' persona is limited to an enraged man. For Odysseus is first and foremost a man of fiction or deception—say it how you will—who at the very end of the poem, when absolutely no need remains, lies, cruelly and with forethought and deliberation, to his aged and vulnerable father. This scene is

probably in origin the outcome of the oral poetic narrative technique—
that is, the generalizing formula overtakes the particular moment—
yet Odysseus's hesitation at lying reflects the narrator's command of
the formula; in that sense the deceiving of his father is finally a statement about character as well. Odysseus's physical appearance and
reliance on words make him something other than the stereotypic
warrior. For this reason, if for no other, he is immediately a fuller,
more particularized character in the context of these two poems where
physical violence and the power of brute strength are constantly and
almost exclusively valorized.

Neither narrative requires many characters who activate the story
line. Chryses wants his daughter home, and Athena wants her favorite home. Agamemnon reacts to this, and Achilles responds; both
act out of selfishness, so there is no clash of personalities. Hector, a
secondary figure, is bound by duty and a sense of shame (although
these may be the same thing) and sometimes acts out of the enthusiasm of battle. In the *Odyssey* everyone is a passive partner first to
Athena, who gets things going, then to Telemachus, who acts on her
instructions, then to Odysseus, who acts upon a vast assortment of
other persons. The *characters* of none of these people effectively cause
the action.

Poets who must recollect and create a poetic narrative in performance are helped by using typical scenes that are repeated exactly
or with modifications throughout both narratives. The *Odyssey* is
distinguished by the number of times the narrator describes his
characters engaged in eating, as one might imagine in a poem
devoted to the theme of survival. The banquet scene is common;
there are two typical patterns. One appears six times, indicating the
beginning of the feasting rather then the entire affair: "A serving
girl brought water for washing the hands in a beautiful golden
pitcher which she poured into a silver basin, so they could wash.
Then she pulled up a polished table beside them. And an honored
housekeeper brought in and set before them bread, and any number
of good things to eat, liberally dishing out from what she had with
her." The other is used three times without an absolute line-for-
line fidelity: "The heralds poured out for them water upon their
hands, while young men filled the bowls with drink up to the brim,
and then served some to everyone, first pouring into the goblets a
few drops for the libation. Now when they had made a libation
and had drunk to their heart's content, then . . . " This second pas-

sage describes the last moments of a banquet; the participants are only drinking and making libations, but this formula can also describe the eating of food. It seems that the poet had two stock descriptions, one for beginning and one for ending a meal, but was free to use the second for a drinking scene only.

Throughout the poem, when he uses the passage first quoted, he shows that he is continually aware of its several elements. In making imaginative use of the formulaic lines he shows also that the description, however often repeated, is not at all mechanical for him. In the seventeenth book, for instance, about 150 lines beyond the description of Telemachus's first meal at home after returning from Sparta (in which, of course, every element of the dining sequence is included), the goatherd Melanthios comes in late for dinner, after the others have already started. The poet therefore says (the italicized part is the repeated typical element): "Then the workers set by him a piece of meat, *and an honored housekeeper brought in and set before him bread to eat*" (*Od.* 17.258ff.). The description is made to fit the occasion: Melanthios arrives too late to wash his hands at table; he is not a guest or honored person (nor is there time), so no table is drawn over to him. That the food is set down in a businesslike manner is made obvious by the omission of the usual line—following the italicized one above—that stresses the liberality of the household.

The first meal in the *Odyssey* is the most extended. Telemachus and his guest, the disguised Athena, sit down to eat. The serving girl brings on the water for hand washing. Then the poet extends the description: "And a carver lifted up and set by them a wooden platter of all kinds of meat, and next to them he set golden goblets, while a herald went about always ready to pour wine for them" (*Od.* 1.141ff.). Now enter the suitors, and the poet brings in the other typical description, this time adding a number of lines that have to do with eating (the italicized lines are again the repeated ones from the typical scene):

Heralds poured out for them water upon their hands, while female servants piled up bread in baskets. *Then the young men filled the bowls with drink up to the brim.* And they stretched out their hands to the food lying there awaiting them. *But when they had set aside their desire for food and drink* [a phrase equivalent in general signification to "now when they had made a libation and had drunk to their heart's content" but different, of course, verbally and metrically], the suitors began to think of other things, of singing and dancing. [1.146ff.]

The banquet has begun and ended in this scene for two sets of people. The typical language has been used and at times amplified. No similar passage is so extended. Perhaps the poet of the *Odyssey*, clearly in control of the technique of repetition, wants to create an unusually full description for the first meal in order to set the ritual mood of banqueting peculiar to the *Odyssey*; throughout the narrative material comfort and human relations, as they are realized through social convention, are celebrated elaborately in ways that sometimes remind one of a novel of manners. Perhaps also the arrival of the suitors provides the clue for interpretation: the quality of service, the elegance and richness of the house are set against the corrupt and boorish men who are feasting. In so doing they are wasting Odysseus's substance, the very stuff that animates the entire description— bread, meat, silver and golden serving ware, polished tables, and wine. The banquet is an important motif with or without the language of the typical scene. It is where Telemachus learns about the more sophisticated world; it is where his father impresses his Phaeacian hosts; it is at the banquet table that the suitors congregate for their last and fatal get-together. At lines 279–80 in Book Twenty the narrator shows them cooking up the meat; they are still at their feast when Odysseus strings the bow, then turns and shoots Antinous, who is just in the act of lifting a goblet of wine to his lips (22.8–12).

Four times in the *Iliad* warriors arming for battle are described in repeated language, yet these typical scenes function well in the context where the narrator has situated them. The parallelism in the language is very close: in each episode the warrior dons in order his greaves, breastplate, sword, shield (which must come before the helmet because the shoulder straps would not go over its plume—traditional formulaic language can be surprisingly exact at times), helmet, and spear. The sparse, mechanical quality of what is almost a list is sometimes amplified by descriptive detail that helps to materialize the items. The arming of Agamemnon (11.15–55) has the most detail, so expansive that the poet seems to have lost himself in the richness of it all. One has trouble visualizing what is being described, yet the passage does what it must: it makes Agamemnon's entry into battle splendid and signals that his finest hour in battle is at hand. Nothing he does thereafter substantiates the sensation, but the full arming sequence has been sufficient. Since even Homer cannot credibly magnify Agamemnon's feats of arms, he achieves the necessary grandeur required for the "lord of men," this lonely splendor of eminence, in a mosaic review of his equipment. The formulaic arming sequence has a life of its own, as one can see when Paris (3.328–38), as the typical scene demands, picks up his sword (although in battle he does not use it, even when Menelaus attacks him with a sword) and his long thrusting spear (although the narrator then has him start the duel with a throwing spear). Likewise, Hephaestus makes Achilles some special "tin" greaves, but when he arms, again in this typical list (19.364–424), no mention is made of them. The poet is not totally a slave to his formulas, however; when Patroclus arms himself with these items from the list (16.130–54), the narrator notes that he does not take up Achilles' spear, which Achilles alone could handle—an obvious foreshadowing of the inadequate surrogate's coming death.

The narrator is judiciously sparing in his uses of this arming sequence. Far more numerous are the occasions when he omits it as a hero is girding up for battle. He first gives the arming sequence to Paris as he is about to duel Menelaus for the possession of Helen in Book Three. This event, momentous in the long ten-year story of the Trojan war, has been converted to nothing more than an inconsequential suggestion in the present narrative. Serving other narrative goals, the duel advances nothing in the story. The arming sequence, however, sets the stage very importantly for the duel; although like many stage settings it promises far more than will be delivered, the disparity between promise and delivery does not matter in oral performance, where the audience cannot check back. The next arming sequence the narrator gives to Agamemnon (11.16–44), whose entry into battle signals the start of a grand tide of defeat for the Achaeans. Agamemnon's fighting is in fact a very abbreviated *aristeia*, quickly terminated as he falls back wounded; again the arming sequence gives weight and substance to what is otherwise a relatively slight event. The reason for the remaining two instances is self-evident: Patroclus's fatal entry into battle (16.131–54) and Achilles' entry into his great *aristeia*, which culminates in the death of Hector (19.369–91).

The omissions are equally susceptible to interpretation. Of Ajax, for instance, as he prepares for his duel with Hector, the narrator says only, "Meanwhile Ajax armed himself in shining bronze. Then when he got his body up in shining armour . . ." (7.206–7). Perhaps the narrator was concerned to distinguish between this duel and that of Paris and Menelaus; there are parallels, but this duel matters to the narrative. Before it is stopped, Hector is on the verge of losing;

when shortly thereafter the Trojan prince Antenor proposes returning Helen, this stratagem seems to be motivated by a subtext of defeat logically extending from Hector's poor performance. But Paris refuses, and the war continues (although to the degree that all the earlier episodes of the *Iliad* resonate with the events of the first days of the war, one could say "and the war commences"). This duel therefore is crucial to both the surface story and the subtext of the plot, as the duel in Book Three is not. One could argue that the earlier duel needs to be dressed in significance, however spurious, while this duel does not. Repeating the arming sequence would only emphasize a parallelism that is neither needed nor real.

One may object that such interpretations are all dependent upon the notion of the poet, poets, or tradition as self-conscious or far too controlling in narrative. Consider that it is Ajax who is passed over so quickly in the passage quoted above. Observant readers of the poem will note that Ajax, who will be one of the major figures in the *Iliad*, is almost dismissed in the Catalogue's listing of contingents and that when Helen is giving a kind of mini-catalogue of players on the field of Troy for Priam's benefit, she identifies Ajax but then, without the slightest anecdotal material, passes on to Idomeneus. Here again the narrator mentions that Ajax is girding up, then immediately takes him out to the battlefield without any embellishment. It is as though the poet has an *instinctive* minimalist response to the thought of Ajax, and the absence of the arming sequence is altogether mechanical, rather than being the least bit designed.

In Diomedes' *aristeia* the gods come out to play as well; there is a parody of the arming sequence (5.733–47) as Athene puts on her battle gear. The poet uses much the same language and keeps the six-part description: Athene slips off her gown, puts on a chiton, takes up the aegis, puts on a helmet, mounts the chariot, and grasps a spear. The narrator takes the form partly in fun, partly in earnest. The coming battle is dignified when one of the principal Olympian martial figures prepares to enter the field like a heroic general. But in a battle where one god is wounded and whimpers and another falls flat on his face, the presence of deities can by their very disparity and distance from the human condition be absurd. Variation of the typical arming scene reinforces that notion.

Another mock arming sequence occurs when Hera prepares to seduce Zeus in the fourteenth book. In effect, she is getting all dressed up for her tryst, but her hostility and cold deceit make the passage more like a scene of girding up. Even without verbal parallels, the sense of the list, the rhythm of it, makes the reader imagine that the poet is self-consciously manipulating his form. After washing and anointing herself, Hera dresses in an ambrosial gown, pins it with a golden brooch, encircles her waist with a belt, puts on earrings, covers her face with a fresh veil, and puts sandals on her feet. There is the six-part arrangement of gown, brooch, belt, earrings, veil, and san-dals—the weapons of women in their sexual enchantment of men. The entire account luxuriously drawn out is a very funny counterpoint to the heroics of the typical arming scenes.

The arming sequence is essentially a list of what a warrior puts on in order to go to battle. Lists are common in most early epics through-out the world. The Alexandrian scholars who studied the Homeric poems called passages in which items are enumerated or listed, obe-dient to a metrical scheme and poetic usage, by the name "catalogue" (literally, "the telling of things in order"). The subjects for catalogues seem to be the same the world over: ships, troops, a queen's suitors, illustrious visitors, those who have fallen in battle, places visited, and so on. A catalogue is first and foremost informational; moderns some-times imagine that if prose had been highly developed in this early period, the material of catalogues would not be found in dactylic hexameters. Yet students of oral poetry in modern times have re-corded the intense enthusiasm that animates an audience as they greet a catalogue during recitation, and even modern literate poets have remarked on the virtues of similar passages in twentieth-century poetry. Catalogues are to be found in prose as well: for instance, the place names in Marcel Proust's *A la recherche de temps perdu,* John Dos Passos's *U.S.A.*, and Vladimir Nabokov's *Lolita* (in the passages de-scribing Humbert Humbert's wild flights across the United States). The hexameter line is a great help in remembering catalogues, of course, and thus the information that they contain. The catalogues in Homer, however, seem to help the narrative rather than impart information. One must turn to Hesiod's *Theogony* to find a poet who is a master of the informative catalogue.

In performance, a catalogue is a *tour de force,* it makes great demands upon memory because it is essentially composed of proper names that will not fit easily or quickly into the dactylic hexametric line. Some oralists who consider that the poets created afresh each time through improvisation in recollection will grant that the catalogues were perhaps memorized verbatim and passed from poem to poem.

So it is that the Catalogue of Ships in the second book of the *Iliad* is considered by some scholars to be a Mycenaean relic because it preserves the geography of Mycenaean times, naming places which in later times were either no longer inhabited or no longer powerful. Others argue that it seems to represent a voyage along the coast of Greece because the order of place names corresponds to a logical circuit of much of the known Greek world. Critics of the poem will note that as a list of the *dramatis personae* of the *Iliad*, the Catalogue is certainly deficient, because it omits some who matter to the narrative and features others who are not part of it. It may therefore be considered a piece memorized verbatim by the poet, who enjoys the shouts and applause as he steers his way through the tricky metrical obstacles of proper nouns but who also wants to remind his audience more or less of the group who appear in his poem and, at the same time, establish the architecture of a very long poem by giving it a monumental gateway. Of these motives, surely the last is the most important.

The structure of the Catalogue of Ships is essentially a series of blocks of information: name of the hero (or heroes), his geographical origin, often an anecdote relating to him or his homeland, then the number of ships accompanying him to Troy. The same pattern appears in other demonstrable catalogues, such as the group of women who appear to Odysseus in the underworld (11.225ff.) and the contingent of Myrmidons going into battle with Patroclus (16.168): that is, names, accompanying (usually biographical) detail, and finally some notice of the relevance of the item to the dramatic moment. Elsewhere there are groups of names, such as the list of Nereids who come with Thetis to join Achilles in his grief at the death of Patroclus, but these have none of the concomitant detail that the Catalogue of Ships displays. Students of oral epic in other cultures have noticed that catalogues can be treated in an accordionlike fashion: that is, they can be reduced to bare lists of names, or they can be enlarged to include considerable ancillary information. Beyond this, the poet seems at times to be playing with the form, making up names to create a list. In the *Odyssey* there is a series of names all of which come from nautical occupations (8.111ff.). They seem to have been created and assembled as a play on words rather than to represent a carefully memorized traditional list.

Homer, as we have said, uses the Catalogue of Ships for purposes other than purveying information. The same may be said of the other catalogues in the two poems. For instance, in the third book of the *Iliad* when Priam asks Helen about the Achaean heroes assembled on the plain below, the formulaic question "Who is he . . . ?" together with its response is a common frame for a catalogue. Here, however, Homer does not try to complete the form. Helen's description of Agamemnon is formally cataloguelike, that of Odysseus is enlarged and made dramatic; then, after the brief reference to Ajax and an anecdote about Idomeneus, neither of which is elicited by a question from Priam, the form is dropped. Obviously, Homer had something else than a list in mind, although the structure suited his purpose and got him into it, perhaps, at the start.

The catalogue form seems to underlie the scene at the close of the fourth book when Agamemnon reviews his troops, passing by and speaking with the leaders of the contingents. Essentially, Agamemnon approaches each chieftain separately, names him with the formulas of patronymic and epithet, and encourages him to battle. There is a response, equally formal, and Agamemnon moves on to the next leader. There is something about the essential isolation of each encounter that reminds one of the separate items of a catalogue. Again the scene at the beginning of the tenth book of the *Iliad*, when the Achaian leaders are awakened serially and identified formally, resembles the catalogue structure much dramatized and embellished. Some scholars have calculated that if the *Iliad* were delivered as a solid piece of narrative, its recitation spread over days, the second day would commence with Book Ten, and so the catalogue would be an appropriate reminder of some of the principals in the narrative as well as a suitable suggestion of commencement.

The battle narratives in the *Iliad* seem to be what one might call catalogues in a state of transition. Consider two passages (5.37–83; 6.5–65) that resemble rather closely the structure of the Catalogue of Ships. They are composed of essentially separate blocks of information: the names of the victor and the victim in each encounter, often an anecdote relating to either of them, then a realistic description of the fatal wounding and/or the throes of death. Original catalogues in Mycenaean epic very likely commemorated the noble dead of every military engagement, as Irish catalogues of the thirteenth and fourteenth century do. These lists in meter giving name, biographical remarks, and a notice of the hero's valor in dying in battle were absorbed in the course of time into a saga tradition. They lost their historicity, becoming instead a technique of narrative and a source of names and facts, and were gradually transformed into a formulaic element that provides the fiction and fabric of battle but scarcely a record of any past event involving recognizable or known personnel. That these battle narratives became a texture rather than a list of particulars seems obvious from the fact that eight heroes are killed twice and three heroes are killed thrice, and always by celebrities: Cromios is killed by Diomedes, Odysseus, and Teucer; Melanippus by Teucer, Menelaus, and Patroclus; Thoon by Diomedes, Odysseus, and Antilochus.

The battle narrative, which the Greeks called *androktasia*, "man-killing," tends to strike modern readers as boring, if only because they don't know any of the persons killed or wounded; furthermore, there is not much contemporary taste for the poetry of proper names. Then, too, there is the contemporary disinclination to attend too closely to the details of physical mayhem. On the other hand, twen-tieth-century filmed brutality and sadistic violence display reaches of the imagination that Homer cannot begin to match; this perhaps is proof of the notion that readers take in the words they read and make them their own by imagining, whereas filmgoers and television watchers are simply passive spectators of something that finally and forever remains on the screen, not in the brain. Contemporary readers tend to skip over the battle scenes in the *Iliad*, however, and this is a mistake, since in doing so they miss a considerable part of the poem's story. The battle narrative is not simply a recital of traditional saga names, nor is it the poet's bow in the direction of an insensitive, bloodthirsty majority of his audience. The *Iliad* is as much about war as it is about Achilles, and the battle narratives develop an important philosophical and psychological frame for the whole poem.

What personalizes the battle narratives or *androktasiai* are the small anecdotal descriptions of the men in combat. The major themes of these anecdotes are the status and wealth of the man, the circum-stances of his birth, his place of origin, the circumstances of his mar-riage, and prophecies about him—in sum, all the enduring things of consequence in the human lot—except, curiously enough, children, who rarely occur to the narrator. Among the participants in this story only the very old and Andromache, of course, who is the *Iliad*'s stereotypic mother, seem to show any concern for children, a re-minder of the curious limbo of age into which the heroes have been cast. Their accomplishments and certain chronological considerations would put most of them in their thirties, when children would be the natural primary concern of any male bent on creating a dynasty. Yet many of the attitudes, values, points of view shared by the Achaean warriors seem to spring from an adolescent male's psychology. Certainly this seems so vis-à-vis the comparable mentalities to be found in the *Odyssey*, which definitely belong to older men.

The miniature stories set into the *androktasiai* develop a kind of melancholic vision of the wastage of war, which serves as a counterpoint to the glory and vigor created by the descriptions of armor and the act of killing. Some of these anecdotes are very similar to the pattern in the Catalogue of Ships:

> Then Aeneas killed two of the best men among the Achaeans, the sons of Diocles, Crethon and Orsilochus. Now their father lived in well-built Phere, a very rich man, of a family sprung from the Alpheius River that flows in a wide stream through the land of Pylians. This man begat Orsilochus to be lord over many men. And Orsilochus begat greathearted Diocles, from whom came the twin boys Crethon and Orsilochus, both of them well skilled in all manner of warfare. In the prime of their young manhood they followed along with Agamemnon in the black ships to Ilium famous for its horses. And now the end of life which is death covered them over. [*Il.* 5.541ff.]

On other occasions the genealogy stays with the circumstances of birth and conception. The pastoral mood of creativity in nature contrasts sharply with the violence of death:

> There Telemonian Ajax hit Anthemion's [literally "blossomy"] son, the blooming young Simoeisius, whom once upon a time his mother bore, when she had come down from Mount Ida to the banks of the Simois River, since she had followed after her parents to look over the herds. That's why they called him Simoeisius. But he never paid his dear parents back for raising him; his life turned out to be very short for him, as he was struck down by the spear of greathearted Ajax. [*Il.* 4.473ff.]

Or again:

> [Euryalus] went after Aesepus and Pedasus, whom once upon a time a spring water nymph named Abarbarea bore to blameless Boukolion [literally "cattle herder"]. Boukolion was the eldest son of the eminent Laomedon, though his mother bore him a bastard. He in turn while shepherding lay in love with the nymph who conceived and bore two

sons. And the son of Mekisteus caused their strength and their glistening limbs to give out, and he stripped the armor from their shoulders. [*Il.* 6.21ff.]

Some anecdotes bring out the abnormality of war, a kind of welcome antidote to the commonplace equation of heroics with martial prowess. The idea of another time and place, where a productive life is carried on, is in the story of a grand host who used to receive passers-by but who now on the field of Troy has no one to help him. There is also the man who leaves behind a beautiful bride of high station and great accomplishments as he dies on the field.

Many anecdotes concentrate upon the sad inevitability of fate: for instance, the prophet who knew he would die if he came to Troy nevertheless does come and does die; the prophet father who foresees his sons' doom vainly tries to prevent their coming. The same inexorable pattern appears in the common story of the man who, having murdered a blood relative, flees to a foreign king and enters his service, only to die on the field at Troy. Most heartrending perhaps is the story of the young man who, caught once and ransomed to freedom, is caught again and killed. Finally there is the chilling loneliness of death in a strange land: "and he himself collapsed prone . . . far away from fertile Larisa" (*Il.* 17.300–301).

This somber thread woven through the brilliant tapestry of heroic courage and grandeur on the field of battle makes these scenes a continual reminder of the other side to the celebration of death. Together with many of the similes they bring a kind of perverse relief into the *androktasiai*. The intrusion of such woe into the ritualized grandeur of the battle narrative has the same quality as the growing dawning in Achilles' mind of what it is to be mortal. But the reader remembers especially the waste of it all.

The anecdotal material in the *androktasiai* leads the audience very temporarily away from the grim business of killing, which otherwise is the foreground. Throughout both narratives there often occur passages that take the audience away from the foreground action for an even longer time by offering a relatively extended view of action and places unconnected to the scene at Troy. The perceived lack of connection has led critics to refer to them as digressions, although it is not at all clear that this is what they are. Their very ubiquity in the text suggests that together they form another viewpoint to set beside those traditionally identified in the poems: that is, the divine, the

heroic, and the simile world. Thus, they do not appear to be interruptions in the story but rather another level of the same story. A
narrative logic of their own seems to distance them from the story
from which they depart, but since they are so numerous, one has to
assume a convention in which alternative story lines and points of
view are equal and simultaneous in the telling of the so-called main
story. There is a theory that each long digression underscores the
importance of the action immediately subsequent to it. But such a
theory assumes that an audience will tolerate a story told not for its
own sake but for the emphasis it gives to the events of the main story.
This seems unlikely. Rather, it is one of the peculiar delights of Homeric narrative that it is so rich, so immediate, so insistent—all of
which is to say that the so-called digressions, like other centrifugal
elements of the epic, are integral and equally important; they simply
extend the field of action.

Some would call many of these passages paradigms, since it seems
clear that they are presented by a speaker in the poem as an example
of behavior to follow. Such, certainly, is the story of Niobe, which
Achilles introduces to encourage the grief-stricken Priam to eat
(24.602ff.) Critics note that the narrator seems to have emphasized or
introduced details—her eating, and her children lying unburied because the townspeople have been turned to stone—not known in
other versions of this myth. The traditional Niobe story seems to be
that when she boasted of bearing more children than Leto, Apollo
and Artemis killed her twelve children and turned her to stone. The
narrator modifies the traditional story to make a suitable paradigm
for Priam at this moment. Such also seems to be the case with the
longer Meleager story, which Phoenix tells to Achilles as an example
of destructive intransigence (9.529ff.). As is true of the Niobe story,
the sketchy nature of what is told implies that the audience knows
the tale, but the divergence from what scholars think to be the traditional version as well as the confusion within the story as Phoenix
tells it suggests that the narrator moves details about to suit his own
narrative goals. One could argue that the aesthetic value of these
secondary story lines lies partly in their plasticity, that they do not
need to hew to a well-defined story line because they do not constitute
the principal action of the narrative. Aeschylus seems to have constructed his choral odes using these paradigm passages or digressions
as examples. Certainly the first great choruses of the *Agamemnon* resemble such pieces as the Meleager story or the reminiscences of

Nestor, both of which have an idea (rather than a story line) to which bits and pieces of a story attach as though to a magnet.

The story of Meleager, as Phoenix begins it, has the Curetes and the Aetolians fighting around the city of Calydon, the Aetolians defending it, the Curetes besieging it. He gives the background—the boar hunt, the quarrel—and then tells how as long as Meleager was in the fight the Curetes would not leave their city walls, but when he stayed in his bedchamber because of his anger at his mother—and here Phoenix proceeds to give a vivid account of that anger—then the city fathers, his family, his friends, and finally his wife beg him to return to the fight. The material is so dislocated that it is hard to make out the story line exactly, and it does not make sense at all that the Curetes, who are at first said to be attacking the city of Calydon, are later said to be so fearful of Meleager that they would not leave their city walls, as though Meleager and his band were besieging the Curetes. But in another way it all makes sense because Meleager is meant to parallel Achilles, and therefore some reference to the opposing band's previous fear and sudden courage is necessary. The longish description of the mother's anger at Meleager, which is not worked into the story, is nonetheless a superb portrait of destructive rage within the family and reminiscent of Phoenix's story of his own mother's angry behavior a few hundred lines earlier, all of which works well in an episode given over to a man's destructive and self-destructive anger. And of course the figures who supplicate Meleager replicate the men who entreat Achilles: Odysseus is represented by the city fathers: Phoenix, the family; Ajax, the friends; and Patroclus, Meleager's wife, when he begs Achilles to return to the fight in Book Sixteen.

Nestor delivers the longest of all his reminiscences in a speech of nearly 150 lines (*Il.* 11.655–802) to Patroclus, who has dropped by to find out about the wounded Machaon, whom Achilles saw being carried out of battle by Nestor. The old man is in the habit of reminding his companions of his youthful glory whenever the chance allows him. It is typical of enfeebled old men who need to demonstrate prowess in so competitive a society; it is also the bid for authority from someone who alone knows the past in a society without written record. The *Odyssey* poet plays to this tendency of Nestor's in a wonderful moment when Telemachus, eager to return to Ithaca, declines to make a stop at Nestor's palace because "the old man is so hospitable he would certainly keep me there," by which remark his audience understands the polite young fellow's reluctance at getting stuck with another long-winded tale of days gone by. To Patroclus, Nestor describes a battle of his youth in which his father did not want him to participate, since he was the only son left alive after Hercules had killed the rest. It is the story of a young man's first real adventure with battle and his joy at the success of it. The narrative of the *Iliad* is on so gigantic a scale that it is aesthetically pleasing to have something tighter from time to time, something with a beginning, middle, and end, set out for the audience to grasp. Beyond that the story is charming in itself; one is reminded of Tolstoy's Count Nicholas Rostov, whose first experience of battle is a mixture of terror and exhilaration. Nestor's story functions also as a paradigm without Nestor's intending it to do so. Patroclus is a character new to the story when the audience meets him in the Embassy scene. Achilles will not let him go to fight; the narrator has not let him appear in battle. He is thus like the young Nestor whom his father Neleus keeps from battle. As Nestor describes the thrill of the fight and somewhat later encourages Patroclus to suggest to Achilles that he let him go to fight in his place, the audience will transfer Nestor's youthful excitement of his taste of battle into the breast of the as yet (at least in this narrative) untried Patroclus. Achilles' likening Patroclus to a child who wants something from its mother proceeds from the notion of Nestor's wanting to fight and his father's preventing him.

In the *Odyssey* Menelaus tells Telemachus about his experience of Proteus, the Egyptian old man of the sea (4.347–587), a very long tale set within the episode of Telemachus's visit to Sparta, which itself totals only about six hundred lines. This tale is again interesting in the telling, but more than that, it contains stories of the homecoming of several Achaean heroes which amplifiy the general theme of homecoming that informs the *Odyssey* story. Its centerpiece, however, is Menelaus's encounter with Proteus. He is told by Eidothea, Proteus's daughter, how to approach the father and get instructions for his voyage home. Proteus will speak the truth only when he has been grasped and held and kept from changing his shape, exactly as in the American English expression one "pins down" a less than truthful speaker. The story is also strikingly revealing of the main character of this narrative, Odysseus, who behaves as Proteus does until Penelope corners him. Eidothea's words about the homeward voyage are exactly repeated in Circe's instruction to Odysseus to visit Tiresias in the underworld. Both Proteus and Tiresias prophesy the end: for

Menelaus, life eternal in the Elysian Fields; for Odysseus, an easy death after a quiet old age. The story Menelaus tells, therefore, like the Meleager story, is a rehearsal of events in the main story. As becomes clear, rehearsal is one of the ways in which narrator and audience are helped to hold the story in their heads as each event is played out. For the narrator it is a chance to try out material that will be used in the main story later on; for the audience it is a chance to get a grasp on a narrative line before it becomes crucial to their understanding of the main story.

One might call the extended similes—comparisons of some length—of these two poems minor digressions themselves, since the point of comparison is always minimal, and the simile description takes on a life of its own, as demonstrated in Chapter 1. The extended simile, a hallmark of literary epic, found again and again in Virgil and Tasso and Milton, is a direct inheritance from the Homeric poems. But extended similes are unusual in oral epic poetry reported from other cultures; nowhere but in the *Iliad* and the *Odyssey* are they found in such number or so skillfully contrived. Since oral epic poetry the world over shares so many features, the uniqueness of the Homeric simile as a feature peculiar to the Greek tradition is remarkable.

There has been scholarly argument over the place of similes in the grand scheme of evolution imagined for Greek epic. The human world they sometimes describe displays customs and artifacts that anthropologists and archaeologists contend belong to a period toward the end of the epic tradition rather than to Mycenaean times. Further, many of the words and grammatical forms that appear in similes seem to be datable to a later development of the Greek language. And whereas repetition is often a criterion of an early date, since the more common a phrase or motif is the more obviously it seems to be worked into the very fabric of oral epic poetry, there are only eight repeated similes in the whole of the two poems. On the other hand, the phraseology of the similes observes all the other mechanics of oral formular poetry: the traditional metrical positioning of words, commonplaces of meter, the repetition of theme, formulaic phrases, and so on. For this reason, and because they work so well in the poetry, and, perhaps most important, because a number of them seem to have developed out of one theme—the comparison of human action to a lion's movements—they are probably the work of some time and many minds. That they are so frequent in battle narrative, which itself seems to be an inheritance from the early epic tradition, adds to the supposition that the extended simile had been employed for a long time—though one might want to argue that however long the technique had been in place, the similes became a more important feature of the narrative toward the end of the period of epic poetic evolution.

The *Iliad* is filled with similes, nearly two hundred long ones and about thirty short ones. The *Odyssey* has only about forty long and fifteen short similes. The great majority in the *Iliad* (about three-fourths) occur in battle narratives. Since the *Odyssey* has few battles and considerable dialogue, in which similes are almost never found, the smaller number appears reasonable. The simplest and—by now— shopworn explanation for the heavy concentration of similes in battle narratives is that these passages need something to relieve the tedium they engender. This seems a dubious proposition. In what theory of literature can we accommodate the view that poets spin out lengthy passages that they know will bore the audiences? Arguing from the ancient poet's supposed obligation to his tradition won't help either; there is too much obvious poetic rehandling of the material to let stand the belief that the poet felt any reverence for its absolute historicity. Battle narratives fill the *Iliad* because the poet liked them, and the audience liked them, too. It is very likely exactly the combination of descriptions of death, melancholy histories of the combatants, names, and geographical allusions, *laced with similes*, that made for the pleasure. Similes do not appear in dialogue, so none appears in the episodes that fill the first and sixth books of the *Iliad*, two very talky passages. The focus is always on action in epic, and in these books the action is redefined by the emotional and intellectual reaction of the speakers. Where there is little speaking, as in battle narrative, similes supply a reconsidered point of view.

Similes that make numerous points of comparison, such as the one comparing Paris to a horse let loose from its stable, are rare in the poems. The simile comparing the bloodied thigh of Menelaus to the staining of an ivory cheekpiece is the more common sort. Most likely, simple little comparisons such as "he went along as the night" (said of Apollo) or "she rose like a mist" (said of Thetis) were gradually extended by phrases each redefining the preceding one; this seems to be the underlying poetic manner of creation in these narratives. The following simile is translated as literally as the difference between the Greek and English languages will permit in order to preserve the word order. The poet states his thesis immediately (the joy of welcoming the moribund father back to life), then proceeds to reveal the dramatic potential behind the original statement:

> As when to his children appears their father's life as something joyfully to be welcomed back, when he is lying in sickness, suffering strong pains, wasting away for a long time, and a malevolent spirit was hanging on to him, but then the gods freed him from this evil, to the children's joy, so did the land and the trees strike Odysseus as something sweet to see again. [*Od.* 5.394ff.]

Although the style encourages the poet to leave the original point of comparison, often the secondary elements of the simile reflect the elements of the plot as a whole. For instance, in the one just quoted the malevolent spirit can be equated with Poseidon, who is the main obstacle to Odysseus's return, and the gods who finally free the man of his sickness can be read as the consensus of the Olympian council in agreeing that Odysseus should get home. The children's joy at having their father restored would reflect the yearning of Odysseus's family and household at Ithaca.

Closely spaced similes often seem to reflect one another. In the first real battle scene of the *Iliad* there are three similes in a short space (4.422–56). Each relates to a specific moment, yet all three are unified. In the first, as the armies are coming together, the Achaeans are compared to resounding waves breaking on a beach. Homer is true to the fact that they are an invading army, beached on a shore, and attacking a city. In the second, the Trojans are compared to sheep waiting to be milked, bleating when they hear the sound of their lambs. The Trojans are throughout the *Iliad* portrayed as defenders of their city and their families (principally through the character of Hector), to which the sheep crying for their lambs correspond. The sound of bleating implies weakness when set against the sound of crashing waves: the sheep are penned in, subject to a shepherd's whim; the waves are free forces crashing upon the beach. The effect is much like that of the opening to the third book, where the narrator compares the Trojan approach to the clamor of birds and then adds the chilling remark that the Achaeans came on in silence, which somehow makes the Trojans seem frivolous and excitable. The third simile in this passage moves the reader away from the immediate scene to a kind of poetic high, describing the battle as a clashing of storm-filled rivers, heard from afar by a shepherd. By bringing together the shepherd and the furious water, the poet has united the first two similes, helping to give the simile world a real coherence and consistency. The known and partially visualized simile world becomes another dimension of the entire narrative scene. Similes that project the reader to what we are calling a poetic high function as establishing shots do in film. The narrator is fond of such views, whether creating them through similes or through description of the approach, for instance, to Calypso's house or King Alcinous's palace.

In the fifth book of the *Iliad* when Diomedes takes the field, he is compared at length to a winter torrent that sweeps away everything in its path (5.87ff.). As the battle progresses, Diomedes triumphs but is finally stopped by the sight of Ares, the god of war, fighting at the side of Hector. In his hesitation he is compared to a man who halts in dismay at the prospect of crossing a storm-swollen river (5.597ff.). The poet thus implies that the thrust of the battle, which is the energy of the rushing water in both similes, has been taken from Diomedes. The comparison is reinforced when, toward the close of the episode, Ares in leaving the battle is likened to black storm clouds (5.864ff.), the source, as we all know, of those sudden rains that produce rapid torrents.

The world described in the similes is more homely than the heroic or aristocratic situation of the main stories. Farm people and their occupations, little people caught up in the necessary details of daily existence, form a world more like that which Hesiod describes in his *Works and Days*. Despite the fact that Hesiod is also a poet of the tradition, one senses that he is describing the world of the eighth and seventh centuries. Homeric similes, therefore, are perhaps the ground line that makes perspective for the poet's audience. Composed of a divine world, a heroic world, and a simile world—or the eternal and changeless world, the "once upon a time" world of heroic deeds, and the contemporary world of quotidian events—the Homeric narrative displays an extraordinarily ecumenical view of things, which in turn has remained a hallmark of epic poetry.

A great number of the similes describe the world of nature, particularly in the battle sequences: for example, a tree is felled with a great crash or, more commonly, a beast of prey, a lion or a wolf attacks or makes off with a sheep or other domestic animal. The simile of the predator in all its variations recapitulates the archetypal confrontation of an invading army and a beleaguered city population. Because it describes a situation from the natural world, the comparison reiterates the natural rhythm of death and survival that underlies the elaborate heroic war ritual. These predator similes provide a desperate view of human life in which the strong always prey on the weak and there is no room for the emotion of pity, compassion, or ruth. No wonder Hector realizes the absurdity of trying to negotiate with Achilles. The fighting man is either lion or sheep, slaughterer or slaughtered. No other dimension is allowed in a male's life.

The significant aspect of the Homeric similes is that they work through suggestion rather than statement, which is the normal Homeric mode of exposition. Ordinary epic usage is direct; scenes and attitudes are fully described. But the similes have an economy of language after the fashion of lyric poetry. More is demanded of the narrator's audience.

Consider the scene when King Alcinous feasts Odysseus for the last time at Scheria, and the guest waits for nightfall to be taken home. After several lines describing a lavish banquet scene, Homer notes that Odysseus turns his head toward the setting sun "as a man yearns for his supper for whom the whole day long the oxen have been drawing the plow" (*Od.* 13.31–32). Obviously, the supper is Ithaca, and the day's labor is ten years of wandering. Ironically, however, the Phaeacian surfeit of plenty produces hunger in a man who, by nature, moves on and lives off his wits and a lean belly. Rest and recreation at Scheria has produced only fatigue—the fatigue of impatience at delay, as well as the fatigue of manipulating a strange environment. The simile illuminates the complexity of Odysseus's personality.

The similes show a poet who is exercising close control over his material. Such control, subtly extending into minutiae, somehow seems contrary to the manner of the practitioner of the formula, the traditional theme, and the mechanical response. The relationship between similes and the remainder of the narrative will always be enigmatic; but in the similes more than anywhere else in the two poems, one senses the personal quality of poetic creation.

The similes are one means by which the narrator brings into the foreground for closer inspection a detail or moment of the myriad facets of his complex narrative. A modern critic reared on film narrative can only marvel at the mysterious fact that Homer has almost made a screen play. In his *Iliad* narrative one senses the panning shots, the close-ups, the medium shots, the establishment shots, and so on. The Homeric poets have a sense of foreground and background, high and low, which helps to give these two narratives their reassuring solidity. There are other methods of foregrounding: for instance, during the conversation between Diomedes and Glaucus (6.119ff.) time seems to stand still; a brief encounter is removed from the melee of the ongoing battle exactly as close-ups in films sometimes have no background and time is stopped. Likewise, during Achilles' mad battle sequence, his *aristeia,* no other warriors appear to kill their opponents. In a kind of slow-motion, surreal dream sequence Achilles is all alone on the field at Troy, killing, killing, killing.

The critic who singles out one or another aspect of either poem will search as well for the means whereby the narrators could keep such gigantic plots in place in their brains while they extemporized through recollection, as one imagines them to have done. The narrative of these poems is put together in an appositional style, as one thing begets another. Consider the opening lines of the *Iliad: Sing of the wrath* (then "wrath" is defined), *the wrath which destroys* (then "destroys" is defined), *which brought myriad woes upon the Achaeans* (then "woes" is defined), *many souls of heroes it sent into Hades* (which calls for differentiation), *but their bodies it left for pickings* (and then a summation, which is to say, a redefinition of the several items), *and the will of Zeus was accomplished.* This is the way of any good storyteller, forging ahead, resting and redefining, and forging ahead again.

What seems the most important structure of narrative in both poems, however, is the technique of storytelling known as ring composition: narration that returns to the point from which it begins. A poet who is firmly committed to this pattern knows that whatever he begins with is where he will end, that he has his conclusion in his premise. Anyone who has ever attempted narrative will know what a valuable tool this can be. It is to be found everywhere in both poems. For instance, Achilles begins the Niobe paradigm (*Il.* 24.602–3) with "Even Niobe with the beautiful hair remembered to eat, at the time her twelve children were killed in the palace" and ends (24.613) with "And so she remembered to eat." Another example, showing how a larger narrative is structured in ring composition, is the exchange between Odysseus and his mother Anticleia in the underworld (*Od.* 11.170–203). He asks her first how she died, next how his father and son are faring, and then whether his wife has remained faithful or remarried; in response his mother speaks first of Penelope, then of Telemachus and Laertes, and finally of her own death.

Ring composition seems to form the entire narrative of the *Iliad*, or so numbers of critics have tried to establish. Readers who review the proposed symmetries and compare them with the text may find the scheme absurdly simplistic; nonetheless, there definitely is a kind of mirror symmetry to the narrative, even if it does not necessarily work out in the details. Ring composition has long been observed to account for the almost symmetrical reversal of action to be found in the first and twenty-fourth books of the *Iliad*. Observe that item one in the first book is symmetrically opposed to item six in the twenty-fourth book, item two of the first to item five in the twenty-fourth, and so on.

Book One

1. Apollo brings a plague, and as a result the Achaians bury many dead.
2. Agamemnon and Achilles quarrel, and Briseis is taken away.
3. Thetis and Achilles speak, and she goes to speak with Zeus.
4. Odysseus goes to the island of Chrysa to give back Chryseis.
5. Thetis and Zeus speak, and he agrees to her plea to help angry Achilles.
6. The gods quarrel.

Book Twenty-Four

1. The gods quarrel.
2. Thetis and Zeus speak, and she is told to ask Achilles to relinquish the body (hence to subdue his anger).
3. Thetis comes from Zeus with a message, and she and Achilles speak.
4. Priam goes to Achilles' camp to get back the body of his son, Hector.
5. Priam and Achilles settle their differences; Achilles returns the body of Hector.
6. The women of Troy lament, and the funeral of Hector takes place.

It would be an absurdity to push the correspondences, but there is no denying a general sense of mirror structure. Consider, for instance, the Book Six episode in which Hector visits the city: the narrator's introduction to the alternative theme of the death of a city or civilization is paralleled in Book Eighteen by the depiction on the shield of the ideal city and its occupations. And the third book's episode of Helen and Priam on the walls as Paris and Menelaus fight below is paralleled in the twenty-second book by the cruelly ironical scene of Priam and Hecuba watching from the walls while below in the plain their son flees Achilles and later, with Andromache, as her husband's body is dragged about the city. The power for signification in this technique seems endless and constantly fruitful, although it is also the case that some of the correspondences are wildly subjective.

The careful reader who observes the techniques of narration to be found in the two poems may conclude that the poet of the *Odyssey* has a firmer grip on his story than the poet of the *Iliad*. Needless to say, such a judgment or, better yet, intuition is perhaps irresponsibly subjective. Yet one cannot help but read a kind of authorial judgment into Achilles' jars of Zeus speech at the close of the *Iliad* and Zeus's observations upon the folly of humankind at the opening of the *Odyssey*. Without question there are large questions of theodicy being addressed and resolved in each instance. Yet one might say that Zeus is the grand narrator. The reader senses that the narrator of the *Iliad* has less control, is more the creature of his own oral narrative poetic devices than the poet of the *Odyssey*, who is very much in control, is shaping a narrative that is economical and tight. It is as though the narrator of the *Iliad* were sprinkling his audience with a bit from one jar and then a bit of mixture from the two jars, as though there were not immediately apparent some grand plan. The narrator of the *Odyssey*, however, insists upon control and responsibility, and he has even introduced one of his characters into the narrative as a narrator of the story himself. Accountability is very important to the Zeus of the *Odyssey*, and the same control grips its narrator; the *Iliad* poet is perhaps more willing to set the scales for his narrative and let destiny or the oral poetic technique work them.

· 4 ·

The *Iliad*

Cattle and fine flocks may be had for the stealing,
tripods are easily come by, even horses' tawny manes.
But a man's life is not to be snatched back again
nor captured when once it has fled the barrier of his teeth.

—*Iliad* 9.406–9

The *Iliad* sometimes seems to have developed like churned butter, bits and pieces sticking together until a perceptible amount, clearly butter and no longer cream, clings to the paddle. By simple accretion, new words and phrases explain or define more fully what has gone before. In this sense, over fifteen thousand lines of hexameter verse become the spontaneous amplification and redefinition of the poem's initial word, "wrath." This theory of composition does not necessarily require a poet with a strong sense of unity; certainly the *Iliad* does not have a tight plot. The episodic quality of the narrative bothers some, although one could argue that "real life" itself can be read as so many random happenings, which the Homeric poet mirrors. More to the point, a narrative style of this sort bears marked affinities with the way any raconteur overheard on elevator, subway, or bus tells his or her story. Achilles' absence from Books Two through Eight seems to some to require explanation, yet the *Odyssey* poet also leaves his main character out of the first four books. The phenomenon may represent a commonplace predilection or an instance of influence or the mark of some narrative genius whom we will reluctantly posit as the man who gave shape to these two poems. Readers of the *Iliad* should probably resist the impulse to look for signs of the kind of overarching and all-inclusive unity that is expected to inform most literary pieces. The aesthetics of the Greek archaic age are not, it seems, so dependent upon unity. A devotion to order, an insistence upon cause and effect, often moves the contemporary critic to seek patterns, connections, and correspondences in even the smallest places. The problem is somewhat analogous to that of the nineteenth-century art critic who understands and accepts the exact representation of trees in the background of Italian Quattrocento paintings (scaled naturally for perspective) but cannot accept the convention of the French Impressionists who turn these trees into blobs of color, shadow, and light—even though the latter technique is far more realistic because it brings out the truly blurred and synthetic view of distant objects that humans have. In the same way the sometimes unsubstantial linkage between events in Homer's narrative represents more honestly the generally inexplicable train of human affairs. The theory of cause and effect is, after all, just another narrative scheme, nothing more. Homer's episodes sometimes tell the story, sometimes comment on the story, sometimes offer alternatives. The sequence of events nevertheless remains the basic skeleton of the story.

One may object to this notion by pointing out that the seemingly spontaneous and meandering talk of the patient in psychotherapy tends to return to the point from which it began at the end of the hour and that the therapist is able to establish extraordinary connections between all the things that have been said. There is, many will argue, a pattern in all speech. And others will argue that patterns are no more than what the beholder, hearer, or reader recognizes.

The narrative seems to be shaped most of all through the mirror symmetry of ring composition. Yet the reader must exercise utmost discretion in identifying the symmetrically arranged passages. Chapter 3 noted the mirror parallels between the first and twenty-fourth books, but they are often only very approximate. For instance, the few lines (1.43–52) describing the plague that decimates the Achaian forces, ending with the terse notice "the place was thick with pyres of the dead, burning continuously," hardly correspond to the lamentation over the corpse of Hector and the preparations for his funeral. It is perfectly reasonable to imagine that the narrator has the hint of both passages registering in his brain with equal intensity and that the hint activates the hexametric expression of the scene. But the scenes are of considerably different aesthetic quality, if only by virtue of their difference in size. One must not confuse the technique with the manifestation of it.

Ring composition provides a sense of foreshadowing and retrospection often enough in the more than fifteen thousand lines of this poem, yet there are other points of reference within the plot—more deliberate interventions of the narrator, one might imagine. Such, as Chapter 1 argued, is the function of the repeated similes. Or, for another instance, when in the sixth book Hector says farewell to Andromache and prays for his son's future, it is the last time they meet; she will see him again as Achilles drags his corpse below the walls of Troy, and then it is that she cries out in lamentation for her son's future orphanage. In Book Seven Nestor suggests that the Achaeans build a wall around their ships, and the battle in Book Twelve centers on the fight at the wall. In the ninth book Achilles refuses to return to fight but modifies his refusal by saying he will fight when Hector sets his ships on fire; it is when he sees this happening at the beginning of Book Sixteen that Achilles tells Patroclus to gird up for battle. When Achilles sends Patroclus out to learn who has been wounded, the narrator far more pointedly than usual remarks (11.604), "And that was the beginning of evil for him," a long-range forecast of the death of Patroclus thousands of lines later in Book Sixteen. Odysseus tells Achilles in the nineteenth book that fighting men have to eat rather than grieve, a lesson Achilles has absorbed by the twenty-fourth, when he urges the grieving Priam to eat.

The basic plot of the *Iliad* is that of a man who pulls out of his fighting unit, which then suffers a series of setbacks so increasingly severe that they affect the very fellow who originally backed out; he returns and wins the victory. It is a plot grown ubiquitous over the centuries, not least in second-rate American movies of the 1930s where the high school or college football hero has a falling-out with the coach, his teammates, or his girlfriend and sulks in the locker room or his dorm until some kind of crisis motivates a reconciliation that brings him back on the field to make the winning touchdown.

The Homeric *Iliad* seems to be a complicated version of the commonplace narrative account of heroic military exploits found around the world. The peculiar feature of the ancient Greek form of this story is the hero's rejection of the structure and values of the world of warrior-heroes: Achilles does not just walk out in anger at Agamemnon; he first criticizes the hierarchical system that has created the relationship between him and his overlord. Some literary historians would like to believe that this represents a time when the social order was in disarray. It is more to the point that the narrator needs to show a man whose understanding of events is sufficiently profound as to make his alienation equally profound and decisive. Some things humankind will rail against but finally cannot change. The *Iliad* is also remarkable for the narrator's development of the Trojan side of the story. As has been observed, it is the introduction of the story of a doomed city, a doomed people, and by extension a doomed civilization that makes for the deeply tragic tone of the narrative. There is tragedy, of course, in Achilles' desperate situation, confronted as he is with the utter nothingness of life, as he reveals in his responses to the Embassy in the ninth book. The anguish of his vision, however, is an augmentation and deepening of the tragic sense of things inherent in the previous scenes of Troy in the third and sixth books, showing persons who act out their lives in the dead calm of the center of a collossal hurricane of action that has been set in motion, from which there is no reprieve and against which there is no remedy.

The *Iliad* is true to—if it did not in fact inspire—Aristotle's dictum that a successful narrative must have a beginning, a middle, and an end. Books One through Eight constitute the beginning, Nine through Seventeen the middle, and Eighteen through Twenty-Four the end. Each section is roughly the same length, the first being nearly five thousand lines, the second somewhat over six thousand, and the last a little over four thousand. As was said earlier, the narrative is continuous. The division into what we would call chapters and the ancients called books often falls loosely into natural separations or lulls— the obvious demarcations of episodes established by the fall of night, the arrival of dawn, or a dramatic change of scene—but one must avoid thinking of each book as an aesthetic construct with the sharply defined edges of a modern short story or chapter in a modern book.

The story commences with the quarrel between Agamemnon and Achilles, which results in Achilles' withdrawing from battle and his mother's gaining the consent of Zeus to favor the Trojans and let the Achaeans lose for a while to show them what they are missing. These facts motivate the action until Patroclus enters the battle and is killed in the sixteenth book and the Achaeans fight for and retrieve his corpse in the seventeenth. Thereafter Achilles reenters the battle, his anger at Agamemnon now supplanted by a giant wrath turned against the Trojans who killed Patroclus, particularly Hector. He fights viciously until he has killed the slayer of Patroclus; then his situation is regularized with the rest of the troops as he acts as master of ceremonies at Patroclus's funeral games, and human decorum is re-established when he returns to Priam the body of his son Hector.

As discussed in Chapter 3, the poet manages to introduce almost everything of consequence into this story. The events depicted cover slightly more than fifty days in a ten-year war, yet the panoramic sweep of events from the origin of the expedition to the death of Achilles register in the hearer's or reader's mind as he or she moves through the story. Particularly in the opening books the narrator provides what in later narratives will be called flashbacks. After getting the plot under way in the first book's description of the quarrel and Thetis's appeal to Zeus, he describes in the second book a dream sent to Agamemnon by Zeus which encourages him to send his men out to battle and thus to their destruction, since Zeus is determined that the tide of battle shall go for the Trojans. But in a strange reversal, Agamemnon determines to test his troops by telling them that they have the option of heading for home. It is an odd passage, since after the dream instructions have been repeated three times—an unusually emphatic narrative gesture—Agamemnon quickly and lamely mentions his plan of testing the troops, and Nestor, whom the narrator uses as the figure in reply (all speeches in this kind of oral society must inevitably have a reply), says nothing about it.

Critics note that there is no motivation for Agamemnon's decision; they often fault the Homeric narrator for failing to observe the norms of human psychology. Psychological motivation, however, though a hallmark of the nineteenth-century novel, is not necessarily a reasonable vantage from which to address an archaic-age narrative of human events. Realism, it has been remarked, is a people's way of exercising control over nature by recreating it slavishly enough so as to make it their own. The same might be said about psychological motivation. In a democratic society the projection of psychological states upon one's fellows is a way of controlling them to the extent of making them one's peers. In aristocratic cultures, by contrast, one does not know, cannot know, the reasons for the behavior of one's betters; hence, they act without reason. This could be said of the autocratic Agamemnon: he suddenly chooses to test his troops, and neither the narrator nor Nestor is privy to his reasons for this tactic; both remain silent.

If one imagines that the *Iliad*, as we have it, represents a far more ambitious narrative than the usual productions, then one can consider that the story traditionally proceeded from Zeus's promise to Thetis, to his sending a dream to Agamemnon to get the troops on the field of battle, to a scene of carnage for the Achaeans and glory for the Trojans, to a scene of the supplication of Achilles. Into this scheme of events the narrator has intruded with his grand series of flashbacks, and he motivates the interruption with the brilliant and sudden idea of having Agamemnon test the troops. This allows for a scene of anarchy as the men rush pell-mell to the ships. Once order is restored, Nestor encourages a general review of the troops to reestablish the hierarchy of the army command. In this way the poet motivates the long passage called the Catalogue of Ships, which functions as a kind of review of the troops who are stationed before the walls of Troy in this tenth year of the war. Various omissions and inclusions of personnel may offend or puzzle the studious reader, but the audience of an oral performance will certainly not notice. They will rather hear this as the panoramic beginning of a great narrative of events in this war; and very likely there will resonate subliminally within the auditor a memory of a narrative account of the beginning of the Trojan War itself. The Catalogue is preceded by a remarkable collection of five similes describing the troops pouring out of their tents to the place of assembly (2.455–83); these constitute a brilliant device to remind the audience of the mammoth human scale of this enterprise as well as to give movement and variegation to the ensuing Catalogue, which, like any list, is absolutely static. The Catalogue is a natural corollary to the preceding scene of the men in mass flight to the beach, for the episode of the second book has to do with the inherent anarchy of an army of men and the controls over them. Once the men are under control, the story can truly begin; likewise, once the narrator subdues, orders the disparate and unconsidered data of "reality," he has organized them into a poem.

The poet has thus diverted the narrative stream into an entirely different channel. Achilles' anger, Thetis's request, Zeus's consent are all forgotten for the moment. From a review of the troops the narrator proceeds to a sketch of the Trojans and Achaeans drawn up for battle so that he can introduce a duel between Paris and Menelaos, the two men whose argument over a woman has made this war happen, as well as depict the unfortunate woman's captive situation. At the same time he presents another kind of catalogue passage as Helen identifies the major Achaean figures by name after Priam has described them physically. If the Catalogue of Ships is some kind of index of geography and power, this mini-catalogue functions as a brief introduction to the principal Achaeans of this story in terms of their looks. Having the duel interrupted by Aphrodite, who snatches Paris from the field (otherwise, his story would be over before it began), allows the narrator to begin once again. He does so with another review of the troops, this one Agamemnon's walk past one leader after another. Again the review is not at all complete, but the words that Agamemnon and his colleagues exchange function as a kind of mini-catalogue of their personal intimacy. For instance, he addresses Idomeneus with lavish warmth; this is someone with whom he clearly enjoys passing time. He mistakenly rebukes Odysseus for lagging behind, and that saucy, tough gentleman replies angrily in self-defense; one senses that they mutually tolerate each other and no more. By contrast, when Agamemnon makes the same mistake with Diomedes, whose henchman Sthenelus replies in kind, Diomedes tolerantly, soothingly, deferentially explains away Agamemnon's ill temper: it's just the natural nervous tension of the man at the top.

Diomedes' deference to Agamemnon is the narrator's gambit for identifying Diomedes not only as the exact opposite of Achilles in his posture before his noble lord but as the model, the stereotype, against which Achilles may be measured. Just as the oral poet uses the rehearsal of a scene to make it still more accessible the second time around, or as the *Odyssey* poet presents the most elaborately formulaic construct of a banquet the first time a scene of eating is demanded, one against which all other banquet scenes can be measured, so the *Iliad* poet presents the stereotypic warrior fully, in the round, as it were, so there will be no mistaking what Achilles has forsaken or rejected by going off to his tent. But he shows Diomedes yet again deferential to authority when he obeys the god Apollo's command to desist from fighting against the gods. To put it in commonplace Greek terms from a slightly later time, Diomedes knows the limits or, as they said it, "nothing too much." And limits are what the *Iliad* is all about.

The narrator now abruptly intervenes again to have Helenus suggest to his brother Hector that he go back to Troy and tell their mother to join with the other women to propitiate the goddess Athena so as to bring the Trojans victory. The narrator has his reasons, it seems, for a more or less arbitrary direction which needs to be carried out by someone as important to the field of battle and as inconsequential to the successful transport of the message as Hector. He means to show Hector in the context of the civilized life he is defending, a world in which there are temples, statues of deities, ritual processions, mothers who offer their sons wine, houses, families, moments of repose, wives and babies, polite discourse, conjugal affection. It is a world in which a husband and wife can laugh at the sight of their infant son startled and frightened by his daddy's war helmet. That is, indeed, the only warm laughter in this otherwise entirely grim, humorless, cold poem. Their little scene evidently meant so much to the ancients that they called the sixth book "The Get-Together of Hector and Andromache."

The narrator returns to a duel again in the seventh book, this time between Ajax and Hector, two men of valor. It is another contest of force, done in close-up, and again it is stopped without issue, since otherwise a decisive closure to the story would come much too soon. The poet's story rides upon a nexus of events that might be labeled wife is abducted, abductor is challenged, abductor refuses to return wife, abductor and husband fight a duel, abductor is killed, wife is returned. The Trojan War is the duel between husband and abductor writ large, translated to the contest between the abductor's family, city, and retainers, and the cuckold's supporters and their retainers. But the narrator can bring up these microcosmic events as well, as with the duel between Paris and Menelaos in the third book. Here in the seventh he fashions another version of such a duel, using other heroes for other narrative ends, but follows it with the abductor Paris's refusal to return the wife. So the story of the war proper can now begin: battle as it concerns Achilles, Patroclus, and Hector. Book Eight advances the Trojan cause as Zeus agreed at the very beginning. The story is back on track, and the first part of the narrative has been completed.

In Book Nine the narrator brings Achilles back into the plot to repeat the intransigence that sent him forth at the time of his quarrel with Agamemnon. This time the scene is pregnant with Achilles' self-knowledge and with the foreboding conjured up by his three refusals to fight. In Book Three the narrator began to situate the tragedy of the Trojans in Paris's reply to his brother Hector's condemnation of his sexual irresponsibility:. "Brother, you're certainly right to take me to task so . . . but don't bring up to me the gifts of golden Aphrodite. The glorious gifts of the gods are not to be cast away, whatever they may happen to give. No one, on the other hand, would willingly take them" (3.64–66). The narrator returned to the Trojan tragedy in the sixth book when he had Helen remark, "Perhaps Zeus set this doom upon Paris and me, so that we would be subjects of song for later generations" (6.357–58), and Hector say to Andromache that he knows Troy will be destroyed and its inhabitants killed or enslaved. Now the ninth book begins to limn the tragedy of Achilles. By having Achilles refuse *three* times, the narrator endows his refusal with the fatality of fairytale action; at the same time as Achilles edges toward staying in Troy, he implies his submission to death, accepting thus the immanent truth of human life. Just so, Paris, Helen, and Hector are made to acknowledge in one way or another the tragic amber of fate into which they have become fixed to all eternity.

With everything in place the story unfolds as it must. The middle section is a tale of epic war. The battle for the wall built around the Achaean fleet forms an action in which most of the major heroes get the chance to show their prowess in a series of *aristeiai*. The narrator as well gets his chance to use the formulas for siege fighting; no doubt what inspired him to have Nestor suggest building the wall was the need to vary the language of war fought on the plain. Books Ten through Twenty-One are the least read of the poem, but those who read the *Iliad* only for the tragedy of Achilles and Hector miss the sadness, the nostalgia, and most of all the physical mayhem. Readers who skip the great *androktasiai*, the battle narratives, are being sentimental. Zeus may say to Ares, "Most hateful of the gods are you to me, for you love discord, war, and battles" (5.890–91), but the similes proclaim that killing is natural; the full details of maiming and killing, so often presented in the very well-rehearsed formulas, attest to the general interest in these scenes among Homer's audience. It must be remembered that the *Iliad* narrator describes a world in which rape, pillage, despoliation, destruction, and killing are more or less commonplace. Anyone engaged in brutal acts needs that certain *distance* which art provides; no doubt oral epic martial poetry provided both glory and comforting distance, just as televised scenes of American destruction of Third World sites play as so many fascinating games of Nintendo. The conventions of made-for-television crime movies and of computer games blend to provide a distance very much like that of formulaic dactylic hexametric phraseology. Because it is described in *poetry*, critics often find it easy enough to overlook the barbarity of the Achaean and Trojan men. But however much Diomedes, for example, may be justified for reasons of strategy in slitting Dolon's throat after promising him his life, however much the narrator may suggest that Dolon is an undesirable wretch, this is not the action of the drawing room. The essential quality of heroism, *arete*, is real enough, but so is brutality in this poem. While nineteenth- and early twentieth-century scholars, particularly Germans, fastened on the former, the late twentieth-century audience can scarcely get past the latter.

The killing goes on through the retreat of the wounded Achaean leaders, through the entrance of Patroclus into battle in the sixteenth book as he kills Zeus's son Sarpedon and is himself killed by Hector, through the fight that rages over his body, into the long episode filling the twentieth, twenty-first, and twenty-second books when Achilles returns to the fray, raging, raging, madly killing everyone who crosses his path, filling the Scamander River to the choking with corpses, until finally he rushes at Hector, awaiting him all alone before the walls of Troy.

In Book Nineteen Achilles and Agamemnon make up their differences and in the Book Twenty-three the Achaean high command honors the funeral of Patroclus with a series of athletic contests that reconfirm the solidarity of this masculine society. In the twenty-fourth book Achilles gives back the body of Hector, Priam returns home with it, and the women of Troy lament their fallen protector. The poem is over; fifty-three days have passed, a brief moment in the ten-year war fought at Troy.

The action with which this poem begins is a quarrel between Agamemnon and Achilles. It is a quarrel over a woman but lacks the erotic element with which posterity has endowed Menelaus's quarrel with Paris. Briseis has been given to Achilles by the army assembly as his share of plunder following the pillage of some nearby locale. The captive woman represents an object of great value; she is a sign of the high esteem accorded to Achilles, the army assembly's acknowledgment of his great worth and superiority on the field of battle. Agamemnon has been given Chriseis, but when her father, the priest of Apollo, successfully invokes the god to force the Achaeans to give her back, Agamemnon cannot endure being left without external honors until the next division of the spoils once again confirms his position of superiority to all other Achaean men at Troy. This is his reason for taking Briseis for himself. Readers who consider such concerns too trivial and primitive may consult the pages of the *New York Times* for the many accounts of figures in any presidential administration in

Washington who will not countenance being left off Air Force One, who cannot endure using any lesser vehicle than a limousine, who must have White House staff accompany them even to the five-and-dime store. The same goes for Hollywood personalities and their compulsive need for preferential treatment, often written into their contracts with the studios.

The society Homer describes is one in which males place an absolute premium on their public reputation. Hector, for instance, will not stay within the walls as his wife suggests, because he would feel shame in front of the rest of the Trojans. And when he confronts the last and fatal charge of Achilles, he laments the fact that he cannot withdraw within the walls; to do so would prove his companion and adviser Pulydamas right and embarrass him. The narrator describes a man who will literally die, go to his death, in order to maintain what contemporary Italians call *la bella figura*. The Sumerian king, Gilgamesh, is described in the narrative of his adventures as preoccupied with his posthumous fame. It seems to be ubiquitous in early war narratives, this masculine need for renown. The Achaean heroes of the *Iliad* are constantly concerned with the glory, the honor attached to their names. Diomedes is forever being told of the glory of his father, Tydeus, or he himself is boasting of him. One must also note that there is no instance in this poem in which one male praises another for any ethical position he assumes, for any act of generosity, kindness, benevolence, or other socially positive and humanly ethical behavior. Briseis says Patroclus was nice to her; Helen says Hector was nice to her. Males may treat kindly such inconsequential figures as their womenfolk (while they feel free to use, as they will, the captive women), but in their conduct toward other men it is always the lion against the sheep or deer, as the similes indicate. Homeric society is ruthlessly competitive; every hero is utterly self-interested, if not truly narcissistic, as the term is used by psychologists. A male lives for glory, for the honor extended him by the group, since it is the only way in which he is validated. Just as no figure in this poem holds interior conversations, meditations, ruminations, so no figure looks within for some affirmation of his worth. Everything is external.

This being the case, Agamemnon rightly enough is paralyzed at the thought of losing his prize of honor, the priest's daughter. Needless to say, in the course of ten years he and Achilles have received any number of such prizes, oversize rewards for their share of the fighting or the direction of the action. Their tents, we may assume, by this time are bulging, but no matter; the loss of the meanest amount will make them lose face. What is more, when Achilles suggests that Agamemnon, his acknowledged leader, return Chryseis, he is asking that *his overlord* give up one of the distinguishing marks of his superiority. And Achilles makes this suggestion—in an assembly he himself has called—before the entire army, those "other people" who confer status and recognition. Thus the anger that flares up within the two men is so deep, so abiding, because their very being is threatened by the fearful prospect of losing a public mark of honor.

When Agamemnon demands another such symbol, another prize of honor, if he is to give up Chryseis, Achilles' reply (1.149ff.) is a wild, strange rejection of the transaction and compact that hold this male military society together. He questions Agamemnon's right to a greater share in the plunder on the grounds that he seems always to lag behind when battle comes; Achilles suggests that his own greater effort in war should be better recompensed. It is a revolutionary speaking, demanding that the fixed institutions of society be revalued for their true worth to that society. The fundamental impulse to heroic action, glory, is set aside and the heroic ideal collapses as Achilles realistically talks of profit and fear as the motives for war. In this strong and abrasive speech Achilles begins to reject the heroic world; as a way of life, as a convention, it is suddenly making demands upon him that he cannot tolerate. He cannot endure to serve a dishonorable man who in a sense threatens to emasculate him.

Agamemnon's answer to Achilles is equally devastating but for the man himself, not the society in which he lives; his answer cuts Achilles out of the social fabric. "Go," he says, "there are others who will honor me, especially Zeus" (1.173), thereby reminding Achilles of the ultimate source of his power. A little later, he makes the truly humiliating remark "I won't give a thought to you." Homeric heroes, like movie stars, can endure anything but being ignored. The glory syndrome demands constant recognition, approbation, and, in fact, applause. Achilles is effaced, the more so because Agamemnon arbitrarily and haughtily then chooses to seize Achilles' concubine, Briseis, as recompense. It is a deadly game of musical chairs. Achilles is ready to kill for his, but just at that moment Athena comes in the form of common sense to tell him to put up his sword, that he will get three times the gifts later. There is no appeal here to abstract principles of right and wrong, good and bad; rather, Athena's appearance manifests aristocratic right instinct. Agamemnon strains the heroic code too far when he demands a new concubine as formal insignia of his superiority at a time when no new prizes are available. By determining to take one from an inferior he dangerously forces a realistic appraisal of his worth, at the same time demanding that the others recognize their own inferiority. Stupidly having gone this far he has no choice but to go all the way. Achilles, like any privileged person suddenly shut out, is forced to reconsider the conventions that form his life. When he talks to Agamemnon bluntly, disregarding the heroic commitment, disregarding his social function and position, he retreats from his society to take refuge in what is left, his individuality. The psychological truth of the anguish of this retreat resides in the old adage "we each of us die alone." Thus is the personal tragedy of Achilles launched in this poem.

Thetis, his mother, to whom Achilles now complains, raises yet another important theme of this narrative: "my son," she describes him here and repeatedly, "who is fated to die so young." Thetis is a goddess, as such, immortal. It is she, we are told in other accounts, who was fated to bear a child by Zeus who would be strong enough to overthrow his father, but Zeus, learning of this in time, married her instead to the mortal man Peleus, by whom she bore Achilles. We have no way of knowing for sure whether the *Iliad* narrator or his audience knew this story. If so, it makes the situation of both Achilles and Thetis more poignant. Instead of that brief moment of sexual glory in the bed of Zeus whom, in any case, she would continue to see whenever she went to Olympus, Thetis has as spouse a senile, failing old man with whom she cannot bear to spend time. Instead of a son strong enough to overthrow his father and raise her to who knows what heights of grandeur, she has a son who will, like any other mortal, die, who is capable even of growing old, senile, and feeble like his father. Achilles, who might have been a god, a celebrity in the firmament of Olympus, is instead a young man making his way in an unappreciative world. Even if the poet does not know that story, he nevertheless has Thetis display a full complement of parental disappointment, as well as wifely regret. That this situation resonates with the ego-investment problems of any parent in a competitive society is amusing but normal. These poems would not have remained so popular with the successive generations of humankind who find and read them the world over if their stories did not appeal to the very elemental qualities that animate us all.

More specifically, the references to Achilles' early death set the dimensions of his own tragedy as it is played out in the poem. The stereotypic warrior-hero is a physically powerful, highly intelligent, daring young man who is defined by his capacity for conquest on the field of battle. These qualities when exercised to their fullest bring on his greatest triumphs, reinforcing his right to be regarded as a warrior-hero. But the potential for tragedy lies in this formulation as well, since the fullest exercise of these qualities occurs when the young man battles his most formidable adversary in that moment of exquisite concentration before he himself is killed. Death is therefore the measure and the potential for any true hero: his glory comes from his death. If, indeed, these poems owe much to early praise poems chanted over the shrine or grave of a local hero renowned for protecting the neighborhood, even dying for it, then the very medium itself demands that death be the definition of the principal characters.

In the ninth book when Odysseus, Phoenix, and Ajax come to Achilles to ask him to return to the fight, he refuses their pleas for various reasons. The first speaker is Odysseus, who brings Agamemnon's offer of amends in the form of a handsome array of gifts that will thoroughly reestablish in the eyes of all the paramount value of Achilles to the Achaean enterprise. Achilles rejects this offer. Instead he talks about death: "The man who does much and the man who tried not at all, both must die" (9.320). Having renounced the convention of the Achaean heroic world, he finds himself naked before the elemental truth of his own mortality. The futility that death imposes has come to him. One says "has come" because there seems to have been a deepening in Achilles' thinking, derived, it can be imagined, from spending the time alone, away from his normal daily occupation, inactive in his tent. Yet it is not so much a change of perception as the unveiling of yet a deeper level of understanding residing in the stereotypic male breast. If we think of Longinus's notion of the *Iliad* as a product of Homer's youth, then we might add "the *young* male breast," since it seems true enough that doleful thoughts of mortality preoccupy young males, who statistically tend to take their own lives rather more often than other groups, at least in the contemporary world.

Achilles' grim rejection of his society can be measured against the typical world view of a young male warrior which the *Iliad* narrator puts into the mouth of Sarpedon. He speaks to his friend Glaucus in a series of rhetorical questions. Why is it, he asks, that the Lycians give us the finest wines, the finest meats, the best pieces of land, orchards, vineyards, and fields for wheat? His answer is, to urge us both on to fight. The Lycians can say, he points out, that not for nothing do they honor and reward us, since we fight in the forefront of the Lycians. "You know," he adds, "if we could live forever, immortal and ageless, then I would not be in the forefront of the Lycians, I would not urge you back into battle, where men win their glory. But since a thousand deaths surround us at every turn, and no man can turn them away, we may as well fight and win for ourselves glory or make glory possible for some other" (12.310–28).

The narrator chooses to dramatize Achilles' new understanding by having him declare that his mother had told him he had the choice of living a long life in tranquil obscurity at home in Phthia or dying gloriously on the field of battle. The attentive reader might object that Thetis, constantly bemoaning her son's brief stay upon this earth, seems to have forgotten making this prophecy of choice; another attentive reader might counter that Athena's argument for Achilles not killing Agamemnon rests on the great number of gifts he will receive later on—which would be of little consequence to him if he is to be, as his mother contends, so short-lived. The fact of the matter is, of course, that the narrator plays with both options, essentially mirroring both the human instinct for a long full life, without which one would scarcely be able to live from day to day, and the certain knowledge of one's corporeal demise. Achilles will deny the war, he says, reject the scene at Troy and sail home, for the meaning of existence is in existing. The lines quoted at the opening of this chapter underscore this recognition. Prizes such as Odysseus is now proposing are all very well, but human life, Achilles suddenly sees, can be defined and grasped only in the living of it. No metaphysical superstructure, no system, no rationale can make it more meaningful. He will withdraw completely from a system in which he as a young male warrior-hero can be defined only in terms of death.

This, as the psychologists define it, is the fugue stage. Achilles' thoughts of flight are all part of his struggle against having to yield. If there is any one suspenseful idea in the *Iliad* story, it must be, "Will Achilles finally yield and accept what must be?" Students of the human experience of confronting terminal illness reveal that there are common psychological states through which a terminally ill person passes, from denial to negotiation to rage to depression to acceptance and tranquility. Achilles goes through much the same series of emotional states, as though the *Iliad* were the grand psychodrama of the acceptance of death.

Yielding, in any case, is another central theme of the story. Nestor introduces the idea when he tries to mediate the quarrel between Agamemnon and Achilles. "Yield to my persuasion," he says, "for it is better to yield" (1.274). Nestor urges Agamemnon, however great he may be, to relinquish his claims to Briseis. He admonishes Achilles not to contend with a king, "since the sceptered king to whom Zeus has given glory does not ever hold equal honor." Although Achilles is physically more powerful and the son of a goddess, Agamemnon is the greater, Nestor observes, because he rules over more men. Nestor's vagueness reflects what is assumed to be a political truth. As discussed in Chapter 2, the poet has inherited in the poetry a situation of kingship and vassalage that does not correspond to the time of the creation of the poem, when the Mycenaean Empire was long since gone. The vagueness serves the narrative, however. The relationship between Agamemnon and Achilles is fluid, the tension always unresolved, but somehow Agamemnon has a power that cannot be challenged; it is yet enough abstracted and void of detail to slip easily into symbol for that vague, ill-seen, yet inexorable force in life against which man's will always fights.

The notion of yielding is dramatically replayed in Agamemnon's brutal taking of Briseis from Achilles' tent, then by the quarrel between Zeus and Hera when she shrinks from his threat of physical violence, and then by Odysseus's treatment of Thersites, the one ordinary person to speak up in the entire poem. He rails against Agamemnon's greed and ineptitude in almost the very same words as Achilles has used; for his efforts he is beaten by Odysseus, and his mates snicker nervously as "he [sits] down, afraid, in pain, looking helpless, and he wipe[s] away a big tear" (2.268–69). Thersites' complaints are voiced after the men have been let loose by Agamemnon and anarchy prevails in the pell-mell rush to the ships. The Catalogue that follows is an instance of form being the content of the narrative. The rigidity of listing is the actual drama of action in the story as it imposes its own order, or seems to, upon a narrative otherwise far freer in its construction and direction.

In the pivotal episode of the ninth book, old Phoenix, the second speaker to appeal to Achilles, mimics the behavior of Nestor in his speeches. He recounts episodes from his earlier days and gives advice based on that authority. His speech is largely devoted to yielding, picking up where Nestor left off in the first book. Phoenix remarks to Achilles that even the gods yield to errant humans who pacify them with sacrifices. He then describes the psychology of asking for forgiveness, as quoted in Chapter 1, arguing that the man who will not bend to such persuasion will suffer for it thereafter. Phoenix speaks to no avail; Achilles remains obdurate in his rejection of the Achaean entreaties.

But, as the narrator shows, Achilles does indeed finally learn to yield. The preparation is in a speech of Odysseus in the nineteenth book. When Achilles, griefstricken and mad with rage, wants to return to the fight immediately after his formal reconciliation with Agamemnon before the assembled troops, Odysseus argues for eating a meal beforehand. Men cannot fight on an empty stomach; death is so pervasive that it must not take precedence over the will to eat and live. A hungry belly is one of the insistent signs of humankind's animality, humankind's obedience to the material truth of their stay on this earth. Just as a body must have air to breathe and food to eat, must take rest for the night, so it will someday cease to function and will die. In the Epic of Gilgamesh, the king of Uruk wishes to attain immortality. His chance comes to him while visiting Utnapishtim; he need only stay awake for the length of seven days. He cannot, of course; each time he tries, he nods off—another sign of humankind's necessary obedience to the animal truth of the body, which, just as it sleeps, will someday rot and decay. Achilles too learns this lesson; in the twenty-fourth book when Priam sits desolate before him in his grief over the death of his son Hector, Achilles is able to counsel the old king to eat. It is the master stroke of the narrator to have devised this scene, to have provided so oblique and moving a way to show that Achilles has finally not only given up his great anger at the inevitability of yielding but has softened and mellowed into an acceptance of what must be.

Hera's fight with Zeus in the first book is not only a part of the yielding theme but also a hilarious parody of the human scene that has just taken place. As such, the divine counterpart is a puzzling moment of comedy. What are the gods in the *Iliad?* From what religious experience do they derive? Critics of the poem have sometimes argued that the narrator treats the gods so irreverently because this is court poetry created for an audience of sophisticates who no longer accept the excessively anthropomorphized deities of Homer. Or they argue that the Ionic origins of the poem, manifest in the Ionic coloration of its language, point to a part of the Greek world where very early on philosophical ideas took root that were inimical to the notion of anthropomorphized gods. Powerful versified objections to such a notion appear in the fragments of the work of Xenophanes of Colophon, who was born and grew to manhood in Ionia in the last half of the sixth century B.C.E. He may have been part of a trend to which the narrator responded by making his gods objects of fun.

Cult in Greece was a strictly local affair in origin. Deities of the neighborhood were propitiated for whatever the inhabitants of the area needed. It is thought that the long gestation period for the *Iliad* and *Odyssey* was a time in which the poets who created the tradition rid the stories of material that was too topical or local to make sense to the poems' expanding audience. In this view, the local cults continued as religious centers, but the gods of the poems became more and more homogenized and less cult-related figures. As such, these Homeric gods would on the one hand be seriously transcendent figures, such as Zeus is from time to time, as when in the twenty-second book he holds up the scales and the souls of Achilles and Hector are weighed. On the other hand, they would be figures who had lost the efficacy of those deities normally propitiated for immediate favors, such as crops, babies, and rain. The skillful poets of the tradition could bring them into the narrative and treat them from both perspectives.

Even as objects of fun, however, the deities serve a serious purpose in the *Iliad* narrative. In the first book Agamemnon quarrels with Achilles, and Nestor attempts to mediate. The rupture cannot be mended, however; Achilles stalks off in anger, and Agamemnon takes Briseis. At the close of the first book Zeus, who has promised Thetis and her son to favor the Trojans, returns to his house on Mount Olympus. The narrator describes an entrance befitting the king of the gods, but follows with a marital squabble in which Hera quarrels with him as any human wife might in a culture where a wife is dependent upon her husband; the dependency will make her especially fearful and angry when she discovers that he has been doing favors for a former sweetheart down the block. Zeus shuts Hera up with threats of violence; she responds in fear, sitting down and holding her tongue. All the gods in Zeus's house are troubled, says the narrator, until Hephaestus offers his mother a goblet of wine and words of consolation. She smiles and takes the goblet, and he begins to pour for the others. "Then," says the narrator, "uncontrollable laughter arose among the immortal gods to see Hephaestus bustling about the palace" (1.509–600). In this parodic scene Zeus plays Agamemnon to Hera's Achilles to Hephaestus's Nestor. In a culture that values youthful physical vigor Nestor has the handicap of enfeebling old age. The aging warriors justify their place in the councils of the fighting men by their knowledge of days long gone and the memory of their youthful exploits of strength. We may read into the equation of Hephaestus with Nestor a gentle hint that the old gentleman from Pylos, though earnest and sincere in his efforts at peacemaking, may be a little wordy, perhaps boring, although lovable and maybe even laughable. Hephaestus is crippled and earnest; this naturally produces unquenchable laughter among the so very grand beauties of the divine kingdom. Unlike the terrestrial quarrel, the Olympian one is resolved in food, wine, song, and laughter.

The narrator turns again to a comic parody of human action in the fifth book's *aristeia*. Diomedes wounds Aphrodite, who whimpers and returns to her mother and father. Athena pushes Sthenelus out of Diomedes' chariot and takes up the reins herself; when Diomedes casts a spear at Ares, Athena leans on it so that it penetrates deep into Ares' skin. He too becomes an object of fun as he returns complaining to the Olympian home of his father, Zeus. Once again in the battle episode of the twentieth, twenty-first, and twenty-second books there occurs a scene of the gods themselves at war (21.385–513). This has been prepared for by the first seventy-four lines of Book Twenty, in which an assemblage of gods solemnly proceeds down to the terrestrial battle. As is so often the case in this poem, the action of war takes place on the divine level, the heroic level, and the simile level. The high seriousness of this introduction of the gods into the terrestrial scene is undercut by the later passage in which Athena knocks Ares to the ground and then takes on Aphrodite, who has come to his aid, while Hera takes Artemis's bow and arrows and beats her about the face and shoulders with them. And when Artemis goes to Zeus to complain, he can but laugh softly at her.

That the divine figures mimic human action suggests, first, that the narrator has designed them to undercut the seriousness of human affairs, to remind the audience that all action seen from the right perspective can become ridiculous or absurd (just as the sex act so often appears to be in pornographic films). But given the tragic intensity of human action in this poem, it is perhaps better to consider, second, that the divine parody of human events is in place to suggest the utter unimportance of choice or emotion among divinities, who do not die. It is mortality that defines humankind, and mortality that gives human actions definition. Agamemnon and Achilles quarrel over the emblems of their honor because honor is all they can use to sustain a decent sense of self in the vast emptiness of their shared knowledge of their ultimate doom. Humankind moves inexorably toward death. In that sense human action has consequences that stay in place. Achilles' remark that life cannot be recovered once it has "fled the barrier of your teeth" is pregnant with this sense. But divine action in a world that exists forever, among people who will not age or change and certainly will never die, is endless and repeated and continuous and forever the same. It has no issue, it does not matter, its actors are inconsequential. It is death and death alone that gives dignity to human beings. That is the other side of the great anguish that moves Achilles and Hector and everyone else in this narrative. It is one of the great discoveries of the Greeks, one to which they return again and again throughout the sixth and fifth centuries. It is the aristocratic view of things that the proletariat's yearning for an afterlife destroyed in the centuries during which the Christian religion was imposed upon the ancient pagan world.

The gods are more or less inconsequential to the action—spectators, as has been pointed out—of the theater played out on the field at Troy. Fate intervenes as the force that moves the scales of doom for the souls of Hector and Achilles. But sometimes doom is represented through the medium of narrative reminiscent of fairytale. When, for instance, Hector, visits Troy in the sixth book, it is three women who attempt to keep him within the walls. He resists the lure of a mother's nurture, a beautiful woman's invitation of company, and a wife's promise of safety (Odysseus might be said to face a similar triad in Calypso, Nausicaa, and Circe). Elsewhere, Hector must confront the wise counselor, a commonplace feature of traditional tales. In this instance it is Pulydamas, whose good advice he twice accepts (12.60–80; 13.725–48), both times with praise for the man, and twice rejects (12.210–50; 18.249–309), the first time with an angry denunciation of the omens upon which Pulydamas has relied, the second in a fatal outburst against the advice to go within the walls.

The narrator uses this second instance to say far more, however. He remarks that Pulydamas, born on the same night as Hector, was "better at speaking, while the other was better with his spear"

(18.252); in other words, he is one of those alter ego figures the narrator fashions to accommodate the kind of soul-searching that later writers manage in an interior monologue. Here Hector the thinker knows it is better to stay within the walls, but Hector the body, the man of action, complains that he cannot endure being cooped up inside the city any longer. Self-destructive impulse wins over analysis. Later (22.99–110), Hector is too embarrassed to admit his mistake and withdraw within the city to escape Achilles. Thus are glory-seeking heroes victims of their audience in a shame culture, in which behavior is dictated by the praise or blame that the group gives to each person. Nothing better delineates the inherent tragedy of Hector's behavior than the juxtaposition in Book Six of his speech to Andromache (quoted in Chapter 1)—which is marked by his clear-eyed vision of the fall of Troy, the death of the Trojan warriors, and his wife led into slavery—and the prayer to Zeus that follows it, in which Hector prays that his son will be a great warrior: "Let him kill his man, bring home the bloody plunder, and make his mother happy" (6.480–81). Hector, the stereotypic conflicted figure (as noted in Chapter 3), is surely the direct ancestor of Tolstoy's Prince Andrew Bolkónski, as well as of Ashley Wilkes in *Gone with the Wind*.

When Patroclus is told by Achilles in the sixteenth book to drive the Trojans away from the ships but not to launch an attack that will lead to the walls of Troy (16.89f), it is like the injunction of the Fairy Godmother to Cinderella, who like Patroclus is heedless of the command. Three times, the narrator says, Patroclus charged the Trojans, "then on the fourth . . . the end of his life appeared" (16.784–87). The same fatal nexus structures Achilles' three denials to the appeals of Odysseus, Phoenix, and Ajax, combined with his granting the fourth, the appeal of Patroclus at the beginning of Book Sixteen; the initial fatal consequence is Patroclus' death, motivating in turn Achilles' subsequent return to battle, which is prelude—as both the audience and Achilles know—to his own death. The ninth book's episode is very precisely and obviously structured on the fairy-tale's fatal triad of repetitions, just as in the sixth book Achilles' principal rival, Hector, has heard and denied a similar triad of requests—in his case, to stay away from the fighting. Book Nine is remarkable as well for other elements of stylization: the near allegorization of the speakers, for instance, and the symmetry of both their speeches and the replies. Some scholars in bygone eras insisted that this stylized, contrived episode was so unlike the narrative quality of the rest of the poem as to be either therefore very late or altogether interpolated, depending upon their theory of the creation of the poem. We can argue, however, that the extreme importance of this scene to the story requires this kind of fierce narrative concentration to which, one assumes, an audience would respond.

The almost allegorical speakers are Odysseus representing the army authority, Phoenix, the authority of family, and Ajax, the ethical or emotional demand of Achilles' comrades in the field. The plea of each is met by a reasoned and rhetorically well-developed reply from Achilles. The parallel with fifth-century Athenian tragedy is unmistakable: speakers in tragedy tend to present positions that are answered by another position rather than engaging in what passes for stylized conversation. Consider Antigone and Creon debating the issue of family or civic loyalty in Sophocles' play, or Jocasta arguing against oracles and Creon defending a life of noninvolvement in *Oedipus the King*.

The narrator frames the episode of the Embassy with speeches by Diomedes that reveal an attitude, as one might expect, quite opposite to that of Achilles. Agamemnon is so distraught at the beginning of the episode that he is willing to evacuate the Trojan beachhead and sail home. Diomedes curtly dismisses the idea, rather sarcastically suggesting that Agamemnon may go if he chooses but that the others will stay on, steadfast in their purpose. The previous long battle scene, the *aristeia* of the fifth book, has shown that the war belongs, in a sense, to Diomedes. This gives him the authority to speak out. When the three come back bearing the bad news that Achilles has rejected their pleas, it is Diomedes again who dismisses Achilles, injecting hope and courage into the general dejection. Diomedes' *aristeia* reveals the stereotypic warrior-hero in action and a measure from which Achilles has departed. In the adventure that fills the tenth book the narrator has followed up the decisive Embassy scene of the ninth with another kind of reflection on Achilles' defection. Diomedes and Odysseus go out at night to reconnoiter. Again Diomedes is central to the episode, providing yet another alternative to Achilles' behavior. The tenth book has always seemed peculiar to scholars because it does not fit in any way into the overarching narrative scheme; nothing in this nighttime adventure advances the plot or refers to anything else in the poem. It does, however, dramatize the *cooperation* of two men, something rare enough in this story of competitive loners. The concerted effort, the almost intuitive togetherness of Diomedes and Odysseus, speaks to Achilles' specific rejection of Ajax, who had urged the plight of his fellow soldiers.

Despite the fact that the speech of each of the three visitors suggests the kind of personalization of an abstract idea that is allegory, the narrator also keeps up a psychological interaction that insists upon the humanity of all four figures. Odysseus, for instance, begins to speak after intercepting a nod from Ajax to Phoenix. The oldest man should have begun, and Ajax is the kind of conventional figure who would defer to a hierarchy of age. But the narrator will want Odysseus to begin because in setting up allegories or near-allegories he will make the plea of society precede that of the family. The nod and its interception can be richly interpreted to say something as well about human intercourse. Odysseus knows that Phoenix as stereotypic old man will be garrulous, and as surrogate family will practice emotional blackmail. Odysseus, control freak that he is, wants persuasive argument and legalities neatly established.

His speech is masterful. It is unemotional at the beginning. He speaks, for instance, of ships destroyed, not men killed, in describing the plight of the Achaeans. He appeals to Achilles' vanity in remarking upon Hector's newfound success in battle. He is practical in reminding Achilles that what he fails to do now cannot be rectified later. There is a marvelous little hint of what these warrior-heroes must have been like in the reminder from Odysseus that Achilles' father, Peleus, had told his son that his strength would come from the gods but that it would be his responsibility to keep his anger in check, not to get into trouble with the army. These words help the reader to imagine Achilles correctly as a physically huge, overly muscular, overly powerful young man, self-obsessed and narcissistic. Thus, like all the other young warriors of this story, he is indifferent to or ignorant of the feelings of others; he reacts or overreacts in an infantile fashion and with his strength and temper can be a real menace to group activity. It is easy to forget that these aristocratic young males—the heroes of our Western world—were trained to encourage and refine their natural aggression and instinct for violence. Whatever virtue attaches to these attributes, their exaggeration can be a genuine plight for the young men themselves.

Father Peleus had good reason to remind his son to watch himself when he was with his peers—advice, Odysseus says, that Achilles has forgotten. The ancient Greek notion of moral responsibility did not allow for the kind of active transgression of known law which

Christians call "sin." Achilles' behavior here comes from his failing to remember, or overlooking while considering other matters—in sum, it is a kind of error, nothing more. It is important to keep this in mind; his later rage and grief at the death of Patroclus are sometimes considered to be the outward expression of his inward guilt at having caused the other's death, but this seems unlikely. Rather, it is his own identification with that death, a narcissistic appreciation of its application to his own mortality, which causes his extreme reaction.

Having coolly indicated the present disaster as well as Hector's newfound stardom, warned of a future rapidly becoming irreversible, and reminded Achilles of his father's advice on the dangers inherent in group activity, Odysseus continues by listing the gifts that Agamemnon is offering. And if this handsome restitution of Achilles' heroic identity and place in the hierarchy is not enough, if this glory will not satisfy, Odysseus alludes to the enthusiastic reaction to be expected from the army upon his return. The speech is properly manipulative, as one would expect from a speaker of Odysseus's quality.

Achilles recognizes it as such in his reply: "One ought to speak out without inhibition, Odysseus. . . . You don't have to sweet talk me, one after another, since hateful to me as the gates of Hades is the speaker who keeps one thing in his heart and says another" (9.309–13). He rejects Agamemnon's offerings and threatens to go home to Phthia and a comfortable old age. Achilles can attempt manipulation as well. His threat of leaving is an even more extravagant denial of the heroic stereotype than any of his previous gestures. It matches his unlikely capitulation to the rhetorical flourish of declaring that he loves Briseis as any man will love his wife.

> Why are the Achaeans fighting the Trojans?
> Why has Agamemnon led the army he collected hither?
> For the sake of Helen and her beautiful hair, right?
> Well, are the sons of Atreus the only men who love
> wives? Fact is, any good man and true loves,
> loves his wife and cares for her, and so do I,
> even if she is a slave, love her with all my heart.
>
> [9.337–43]

The notion that either Menelaus or Agamemnon loves Helen or Clytemnestra rather than treasuring her as a prized possession is, of course, ludicrous. That Achilles loves anyone other than himself, or maybe Patroclus a little bit, is surely obvious to all the men gathered together in this parley. The narrator means Achilles' defiant rhetorical questions and flamboyant declaration to be just that. They are a prelude to his revelation that he has the choice of an obscure long life or glory in an early death. For a warrior-hero like Achilles this is, of course, no choice at all—a fact in itself guaranteed to provoke rage. Achilles ends his reply to Odysseus with a tellingly childlike gesture: he invites old man Phoenix, the surrogate father, to spend the night and return the following day with him to Phthia. Stooping again as in the self-pitying reference to his love for Briseis, this time to a contest of loyalties from nursery days, Achilles means to win a moral victory of sorts by getting someone from the other camp to come over to his side. Phoenix comes, of course, but only out of love.

The old man begins by reminding Achilles of his love and devotion to him as an infant and of the curse that kept him from having a family of his own, all of which establishes the warmest emotional credentials for the advice he gives the lad. Yield, my boy, yield as even the gods yield, counsels this surrogate father. Yield now before it is too late; learn from Meleager. Phoenix devises a penetrating psychological insight of the emotion of asking forgiveness and uses the paradigm of Meleager's wrath as instruction for Achilles' own obduracy. Achilles is clearly emotionally devastated, as the narrator indicates by having him reply, "Don't mix up my heart with your crying and carrying on" (9.612). Mixed up he is, too: to Phoenix's final "you won't get the same honor, if you come back to the battle too late," he first responds vehemently if altogether confusedly with another of those rhetorical flourishes: "What need have I of honor? I have a feeling I'll get all the honor I need as my lot from Zeus, which will keep me here by the curved ships as long as there is breath in me." Then, catching himself up moments later, he concludes: "Let the others take back my message; you stay here and sleep on a nice soft bed. Then tomorrow we'll make up our minds about whether to go on home or to stay."

Ajax, who speaks last, understands little, but he knows about friendship. Achilles, he says, has forgotten the friendship of his comrades, who have honored him above everyone; he is hard, relentless. Anyone else takes recompense, even for the murder of a relative. Achilles lost a girl; Agamemnon offers seven. What's his problem? Be more gracious, he urges Achilles: "We are guests in your house. ... We just want to be your friends and to be loved in return." The emotional intensity of the speeches has increased from the abstracted list of Odysseus to the fatherly emotive yet didactic speech of Phoenix to these words from the heart about friendship, caring, and letting go of revenge; Ajax brings out all the love that fighting men have for one another, an appeal so emotional, so honest and direct, that it cannot be met.

Achilles' reply is again lame. He concludes his brief answer to Ajax by declaring that he will not return to the fight until Hector has brought the battle so close that Achilles' own ships are in danger of fire. The narrator has managed to show that Achilles keeps his obstinance, his intransigence, intact throughout the assault from three men who have each found a distinct stance and vantage from which to touch Achilles' vulnerabilities. Yet curiously enough, with each reply Achilles moves from the determination to go home to the assumption of staying. This seems not so much a psychological reversal as an expression of the tragic truth of this poem: Achilles may imagine himself free to act as he chooses; he will be angry, assert himself, make new choices; but in fact, the way for him has been prepared since the beginning of time. Despite his talk of choices, he will die here at Troy. There is an important element of traditional stories often forgotten by readers of fiction of aggressive originality: the audience of a traditional story knows how it will end. The teller of a traditional story knows with his audience that the story will move in a certain direction; he also knows that his audience will not tolerate narrative deviance. It is not too much to say that the audience invests even the characters with the same knowledge, they have been in the story so many times. Thus when Hector says to Andromache, "I know in my heart that Troy will someday fall," he *does* know; it has happened to him and her and the city so often in the telling of the tale. Likewise, Achilles may talk of going home, but as the conclusions of his replies demonstrate, he moves ever closer to the tragic truth of his life. This almost subliminal message makes the episode among the saddest in the poem. The young man talks of choice when none is really available.

The quarrel between Agamemnon and Achilles has two results. First, it causes a major dislocation in the Achaean forces, a disunity that brings about a setback for the Achaeans. The poet has given this greater depth by attributing the turnabout to the plan of Zeus in response to Thetis, but the Achaean reversal is a realistic outcome of Achilles' withdrawal, together with his army of Myrmidons, from the

battlefield. The second result of the quarrel is the dislocation in equi-
librium of the angered, isolated Achilles. As a hero, as a young man,
as a human being, Achilles has defied the natural order of things.
When he opposes the rhythm of existence, he is a puny opponent
for a great cosmic force. He is a kind of Thersites battling, shouting,
arguing against his betters. As Thersites is struck a harsh blow from
Odysseus and made to understand his place, so Achilles will inevitably suffer the effects of the natural order's reassertion of itself in
the face of his disavowal; he will be deeply injured when his surrogate
dies in battle. The narrative from Books Eleven through Seventeen
brings us the consequences of the quarrel as they arise separately and
as they come together. The Greeks are driven back; Patroclus is finally
killed.

Entertainment even of the most trivial kind satisfies some social
goals; society would not otherwise permit its existence. In the period
in which the Homeric poems took shape the medium of communication was controlled by the bards who created such poems and the
aristocracy who tolerated or encouraged their performance and who
supported the poets. What, then, was the social value of the *Iliad*? It
must be the case that in a world in which plunder was a source of
revenue, cities—or where cities did not exist, the aristocratic class of
the countryside—had real reason to fear their neighbors. The warrior
in such a situation was absolutely vital to the community. Yet fighting
is always dangerous, and young men are not keen to die. Poetry such
as the *Iliad* glamorized the battlefield by emphasizing the glory that
such work confers. Apart from the exercise of political power with
the trappings of office, males had little else than poetry of this sort
to give expression to their insatiable quest for posthumous fame. It
will always be the case that a woman who can experience giving birth
and see the fruit of her womb lying in her lap will be more immediately
assured of her place in the endless succession of being than a male,
whose pitifully evanescent ejaculation is hardly the equivalent. Perhaps it is for this reason that males, as literature around the world
attests, constantly crave immortality.

In addition to the idea of glory that was made a significant part of
the military enterprise, the oral narrative technique sent a powerful
subliminal message to the young men of the community. The *Iliad*
narrator describes Diomedes in the fifth and sixth books as the central
figure in a fighting scene. Battle narrative contains the most common
phrases and repeated elements of the entire poem. Diomedes is thus

as stereotypic as anything in the story. As suggested earlier, the narrator positions the *aristeia* of Diomedes as he does in order to suggest the kind of person and behavior that Achilles has repudiated by withdrawing to his tent. When Achilles returns to the fight, the narrator can suggest that he is furious to avenge the death of Patroclus, but it is also the case that he is once again donning not only the weapons of war but the language in which he will be given the fullest expression. Achilles may reject Agamemnon's gifts; he may claim that material possessions are meaningless compared with the life force, which is gone for good once it leaves the body. Yet material possessions are, like the language of the poem, tangible representations of the only reality that Achilles and his fellow warriors know. Achilles cannot exist in any other description. There are no formulas for Ferdinand the Bull sniffing the flowers on the hillside but only for the bull charging the matador in the arena. What is more, the ring composition of narrative brings Achilles back into the fight as a mirror opposite to Diomedes in the earlier passage. Achilles finds the place assigned to him by Zeus or destiny, the greater narrator, just as this same agency has created the formulas in which he can be described and in which, therefore, he will find his identity. Nothing is more formidable than the image of Achilles once again falling into place in the grand scheme of things. He himself knows it, as one feels in the mordant speech he makes to Lycaon, the son of Priam, whom he is about to kill:

> But, my friend, you die, too; now why carry on so?
> Patroclus also died, and he was a far better man than you.
> Can't you see how tall and handsome I am? The son, am I,
> of a good father, and a goddess mother gave me birth.
> Just the same, you know, death and a powerful fate
> wait for me.
>
> [21.106ff.]

Traditional formulaic poetry is relentless in its demands upon the poet, who must struggle for whatever morsels of originality it will grant him; upon the audience, who must attend so carefully that they become enslaved to the cadences; upon the characters, who will be rendered up in a diction that forces them into patterns where the will cannot wrench them free. No wonder Achilles can speak to Priam of the jars of Zeus, that the characters talk of destiny, that the ancient

Greeks had so well-developed a capacity for tragic irony. The poem is a story of yielding; its creation is equally an act of acquiescence.

But the tragedy will always belong most to the Trojans, if only because they are shown to have no real illusions, beginning with Paris's remark to Hector about the gifts of the gods (3.64ff.). This exchange is followed somewhat later in the first scene of Troy by a remarkable struggle between Helen and Aphrodite (3.389ff.). Helen's divine patron, acting more the bawd than the goddess, orders her to go to Paris, who lies in bed awaiting her after having been snatched from the battle by Aphrodite. Helen, wearied of being a sexual servant and disgusted with Paris, curses the goddess and tells her to find another victim. Aprhodite, whose disguise as an old woman Helen has easily penetrated, reveals her true self and in a mean show of authority reminds Helen that the only protection a woman who has gone outside of marriage and family has to protect her is her physical beauty. Paris and Helen, prisoners of their destructive beauty and sexuality, are the narrator's way of getting at the sorrow of Troy. Hector too has no illusions when he reminds his wife that he knows Troy is doomed but determines nonetheless to return to the battle. It is not that he is too stupid to get out a cart and take Andromache and the child and move to another country. It is rather that he is a formulaic figure in a traditional story, locked into a situation that he has rehearsed many times and from which the narrator alone has provided an exit. His occasional angry rejection of Pulydamas's good advice is also not so much careless thinking as it is the self-delusion that necessarily comes to one who must at all other times look so unblinkingly at his own self-destruction. Self-delusion in Greek tragedy, just as for Hector, is the little vacation from awareness that provides a moment of false refreshment for the desperate soul.

Hector's visit to the city in the sixth book is balanced in the style of ring composition with a description in the eighteenth book of a new shield which Thetis has commissioned from Hephaestus to replace the one taken in battle when Patroclus is slain. The ancients were fond of what they called *ekphrasis*, the verbal rendering of a material work of art. The description of this shield, however, is unusual because the decoration seems to be more abstract, more symbolic, than what might be expected on an individual piece. It makes sense that the narrator would make it so; the shield description provides the opportunity to give expression to what city life is and therefore what it is that the Trojans are defending and will lose in Hector's death. As Hector dies before the walls shortly thereafter, his mother and father and his widow looking on in horror, a city will be crashing down to ruin as well. The audience of the *Iliad* will have already imagined the many facets of that city's life from the description of the cities on the shield.

In his description (18.478ff.) the narrator manages to include most of the basic antitheses in the human situation: the permanent and the fleeting, the beautiful and the ugly, the serene and the excited, the ideal and the real, war and peace, the finite world and the infinite heaven. He begins with the shield's rim, depicting the encircling river called Ocean that stands next to the universe, then moves down to the specifics of two cities, one at peace, one at war. In the former there is a scene of marriage, symbol of union and conciliation, celebrated in music and dancing; there is also depicted the reconciliation of a quarrel through judgment and good speaking. In the latter a slaughter by ambush takes place; Hate, Confusion, and Death are the leaders, the very antithesis of the civilized arts—music, dancing, and oratory—through which in the first city order and continuity exist. Order continues to be celebrated in a scene of plowing by rows where the plowman receives wine, the rich harvest of fertile fields, as the reward for the sweat of his labor. Workers are depicted laboring in unison, in rhythm, a king watching over them. Each does his appointed task; hierarchy prevails. The reward is a fertile harvest. The poet shows grapes ripe for the plucking, young people at hand who are singing. Order, fertility, the arts of civilization, the dignity of work, the classes of society are all praised and represented in the city. It is one of the few instances in the *Iliad* where the entire spectrum of human society is acknowledged. Then occurs a refrain of the ambush, now conceived in nature's terms: lions attack the herds and the sheep. The lion image recalls the common battle similes, a brief hint of the world of war behind this *ekphrasis*. The description then closes with dancing; creative joy is its final element.

Like the scenes on the shield, the episode of Hector's pursuit and death at the hands of Achilles in Book Twenty-two has no spatial reality; it is surrealistic like a dream, or the nightmare it is for participants and onlookers alike; there is no true distance between the onrushing Achilles, Hector waiting on the plain before the wall, Priam and Hecuba up on the ramparts, and the awestruck crowd of Achaean warriors. As the two heroes race around the walls, the narrator lets us look on from a distance and then brings us up close in the manner of the contemporary zoom lens. Like a Greek vase painting, where each element is given equal spatial expression, the episode has little perspective. Achilles charging, Priam calling, Hector waiting, the two men running, the spectators crowding the city's turrets, the Achaean army watching in silence—all are immediately present. It is action stopped in time in the surreal fashion of a dream, as is the narrator's description of the actual pursuit by Achilles of Hector:

> There they ran, the one fleeing, the other in pursuit.
> A noble man fled in front, but a far greater man pursued him,
> swiftly, since they were not contesting for a piece of hide,
> nor for a sacrificial animal,
> which are prizes for men who are swift of foot;
> no, they ran for the soul of Hector, the tamer of horses.
>
> [22.157ff.]

The episode opens and closes with speeches of bereavement, the two worst kinds to a Greek mind: the aged parent bereft of children for support, and the young son bereft of his father. Hecuba calls out to Hector, begging him to stay within the walls, baring her breasts to remind him of his debt to her; Priam cries out, too, begging Hector not to desert them, not to allow his father to become the meat of dogs, an ugly old naked corpse on the field. Andromache at the end cries out for her child, who will beg for food at the men's common mess and in every other way go without a father's care.

Achilles can speak to Priam of the jars of Zeus and counsel eating as the only remedy. The Trojan perspective is different. After Andromache has lamented the fate of her son, looking down on her husband's corpse as it is dragged around the walls, she ends her dirge with this reflection on human waste:

> But in the halls lies clothing, you know, delicate and fair,
> made by women's hands. But I shall burn these, all of them, you know,
> in the burning fire, since they won't be of any use to you,
> because you won't lie in them,
> but they were to be an honor from the Trojan men and women.
>
> [22.510ff.]

· 5 ·

The *Odyssey*

You stubborn man, full of so many plans, deceits,
not even in your own land have you any intention
of stopping your cheating, your lying words,
which you know you love from the bottom of your heart.
                    —Athena to Odysseus, *Odyssey* 13.293–95

The *Odyssey* seems to be quite different from the *Iliad*. The difference, however, is not in the mechanics of style; its creator knows the same techniques of oral poetic composition, the same metrics, the same formulaic construction, the same reliance on typical scenes and stereotypic characters. If the diction seems at times different, that is no more than one would expect from different times, a different poet or group of poets, and, of course, a very different story. It is remarkable that these poems can be so very unlike one another and yet so very similar. The ancients considered them to be the works of the same man, the "divine poet," and for centuries that was the received opinion, but twentieth-century scholars are more inclined to view them as the work of two poets or poetic traditions. Computerized studies of the language tend to support this view: they show trends and linguistic habits peculiar to each poem which suggest that the *Iliad* is earlier than the *Odyssey* in some kind of oral poetic linguistic evolution. But clearly the oral poetic technique held this poet tightly in its grasp; the opening invocation to the Muse is very real, for the Muse of epic formulary style does possess the poet.

While the story of the *Iliad* proceeds without any sensible interruption, the *Odyssey* narrative might be said to separate into three distinct parts. The first four books, commonly called the Telemachia, describe the conflict of Odysseus's son Telemachus with his mother's suitors, his general impotence, and then his travels to the mainland of the Peloponnesus in search of information about his father. The narration of Odysseus's travels fills the next eight books; one might further divide this second section into the narrator's third-person account of the hero's journey from Ogygia, the island home of Calypso, to Scheria, where he encounters the Phaeacians (Books Five through Eight), and Odysseus's first-person story of his travels before he arrives at Scheria (Books Nine through Twelve). The thirteenth book takes Odysseus from Scheria back to his own island of Ithaca, and the balance of the poem is the story of his reintegration into the life there, first disguised as a beggar and then, having killed his wife's suitors, revealed as the king, father, and husband he is. The poem closes with a series of scenes in which several loose ends are tied up, a narrative maneuver that has raised doubts since Hellenistic times as to whether "our" *Odyssey* poet is actually responsible for them. As with so much else in the criticism of either poem, the reader is more or less free to decide, since there are no authoritative indications in the text or in history.

The sense that these divisions are significant is reinforced by noting that the stories in each section seem to have distinct coloration. The first part tells the adventures of Telemachus; the second part describes Odysseus in what we might call Wonderland; the third is devoted to Odysseus's struggle to regain power in his home and kingdom. The first part uses considerable material from heroic epic narrative, from saga; the second appears to depend a good deal on folklore and fairytale; the third seems to some critics a kind of social, domestic story or a kind of prototype of romance.

The narrative of the *Odyssey* is also set within three or four distinct temporal frames. Before getting Odysseus to the island of Ithaca, where his story then moves forward with linear predictability, the narrator shuffles planes of time in an interesting manner. The poem commences with a council of the gods discussing its hero's fate. They arrange that Athena will prod Telemachus at Ithaca, and Hermes will speak to Calypso on Ogygia. Athena accomplishes her task in the first book, the consequences of which fill the next three. The simultaneous and parallel action of Hermes' visit to Calypso is not woven into the scenes of Athena's visit to Ithaca or its sequence in some version of "meanwhile"; rather it is treated sequentially. The scene of the council of the gods is introduced again, and the repetition of narrative in the council signals that parallel action is being undertaken, but at the same time the structure of the entire narrative is given new shape. The second scene of the council allows for a new beginning, as it were, to be given to the direction of the narrative. And, in fact, as the poet now turns to Odysseus, the poem does in that sense begin again. In this way the poet also lets the Telemachia stand as a kind of rehearsal of the Odyssey travel stories, rehearsal being a favorite technique of the Homeric poet or poets.

These two simultaneous yet sequential narratives are separated by a strange little bridge, a passage difficult to account for because it seems so unusual. This very small episode (4.625–847) describes Penelope's suitors as they plot against Telemachus. It requires an abrupt switch in locale from Sparta to Ithaca, from Menelaus's dining room, where another banquet is being set up, to the exercise field before the palace of Odysseus, where the suitors learn that Telemachus has gone to the mainland. The temporal and local planes merge with the narrator's "meanwhile," but the episode belongs neither to the book it is in nor to the one that follows. The Hellenistic librarians who presumably divided these poems into books clearly did not know what to do with the passage either. It is not long enough to fill its own book; the episodes of the *Odyssey*, though shorter as a rule than those of the *Iliad* and far more sharply defined, run from 350 to 650 lines. This passage is put into the book that contains the Sparta scene, and it is partly this juxtaposition that makes the passage remarkable. Further, however, it is crucial because it describes a plot that functions as the well-known narrator's "hook" to hold the audience in the story. Furious that he has escaped their grasp, the suitors decide to set out in a ship and ambush Telemachus upon his return. The ante is raised yet another round from where it stood after Athena's suspense-laden advice in the first book. One might say that the narrator is very courageous in making this abrupt transition that departs so violently from conventional narrative; indeed, he repeats the maneuver, shifting a scene abruptly from Telemachus's homeward voyage to Eumaeus's hut (15.299ff.).

The second section, which details Odysseus's adventures on Ogygia, in a sea storm, and at Scheria, also shows an adventurous use of time. The scene at Scheria is enlarged by Odysseus's great first-person narrative (books nine through twelve) describing his adventures. The narrator has gotten Odysseus from Ogygia to Scheria on a temporal plane that is simply time prior to the narrator's present. Then, when Odysseus takes over, the action moves to time that is past for Odysseus in his present moment of narration, which is, of course, already time prior for the narrator. This and the change from the third-person narration of the narrator to the first-person narration of Odysseus mark the travel stories as a separate section of the poem. The transition to the third section is dramatized by movement as the Phaeacians take Odysseus by boat from Scheria to Ithaca. As transition, it is made emphatic by the fact that Odysseus is asleep. Just as Hermes flies over the earth from Olympus to Ogygia, a transition into the never-never land of the travels, so the sleeping hero passes without consciousness from unreality to reality. The separation is made both more abrupt and complete by the narrator's story of the Phaeacian boat and crew being turned to stone as they approach home. The Phaeacian king, Alcinous, upon seeing this, determines that they will never transport strangers again. In other words, the exotic and fabulous Phaeacians will never appear in the normal world again. That they are outside of time, too, is suggested by the transformation to stone, an event in which time stops forever.

The temporal limbo into which the Phaeacians are thus dropped calls to mind the commonplace fairytale introduction "once upon a time." It seems fair to say that the Phaeacians are a narrator's fantasy run riot. The narrator describes how they moved away from where the menacing Cyclops lived—already a fairytale land, one might say— to a place "far from men who eat [or work for their] bread" (6.8), again somewhere definitely beyond ordinary human experience. And then their king describes the Phaeacians as men who are indifferent boxers and wrestlers but good at running races and sailing, who care most about banquets, music, dancing, changes of clothing, hot baths, and good beds (8.246–49). Set against the values advanced by the *Iliad's* major characters, not to mention the spareness of Odysseus's life, the Phaeacian scene has all the frightening, magical, seductive charm that sybaritic Big Sur exercises on puritan self-denying psyches from rural New Hampshire. Furthermore, a witch who can turn men into swine, a goddess who transforms men into beggars or obscures people and places so that they cannot be seen or are unrecognizable, giants who eat human beings, enchanted lands and peoples such as the Lotus Eaters, singing women who can lure men to their destruction—these are story motifs from the kind of narrative that comparativists identify as fairytale or, more technically, by the German term *Märchen*. The basic plot of the *Odyssey* is the story of a man who endures loneliness, friendlessness, deprivation until he has the chance to identify himself by performing what those about him who sneer and jeer cannot. All the while he is helped by a mature woman who has supernatural powers. Odysseus, we may say, is playing Cinderella to Athene's fairy godmother. Stringing the bow is like trying on the glass slipper, the suitors are the sneering stepsisters, Penelope is the prince.

Odysseus himself is, as critics note, a strange kind of warrior-hero. He is described by Helen (*Od.* 4.244–47), for instance, as having entered Troy in the disguise of a beggar, even cutting his body so as to have the bruise marks and lacerations of such a person. In the latter half of the poem, once he is back at Ithaca, he is again disguised as a beggar and suffers innumerable insults in that condition. These circumstances seem to mark Odysseus as someone special. One can judge only from the principal figures of the two poems, yet it seems fair to say that it is hard to imagine Agamemnon or Achilles or Diomedes or any other of the major figures of the *Iliad* enduring such physical insults. Their princely sense of decorum—or, more to the point, the narrator's—does not permit it. In a culture that determines a man's worth and status by externals, in which the *Iliad* narrator can lavish such disgusting description upon the non-aristocratic Thersites, Odysseus is someone special; consider, as well, how Antenor describes him to Priam as an unprepossessing, relatively short, surly-looking fellow. In addition, he is at one and the same time a hero of the Trojan saga and someone who consorts with witches and giants and is the subject of mysterious transformations.

Odysseus is already a maverick in the *Iliad*. Agamemnon fairly snaps at him when he passes in review among his fellow captains, and Odysseus angrily replies. Achilles reminds him that he prefers to tell the truth as it comes to him spontaneously, an implied if not an overt rebuke. But then, Odysseus is a thinking man, clearly enough, with all the odium that will attach to such a person from men whose lives depend upon instinctive physical behavior. He is given to intelligent analyses as when he quiets the runaway troops in the second book, for instance, or argues for Achilles' return in the ninth, or expatiates on the necessity of eating while grieving in the nineteenth. His considerably advanced awareness of the human lot often verges on cynicism; the narrator recounts his driving his chariot straight on past Diomedes, who is signaling for help as he flounders at rescuing old Nestor from battle.

"Hateful as the gates of hell to me," says Achilles to Odysseus, "is the man who says one thing, and hides another in his heart" (*Il.* 9.312f.). Throughout the *Odyssey* its principal character lies. Never a straightforward person, he is cunning and always suspicious. In the one instance when he identifies himself readily, boasting to the giant whom he has blinded, he is injured for it (*Od.* 9.504ff.): the giant gets his father Poseidon to wreak vengeance upon the hapless man. Odysseus does not make that mistake again; he gives a false identification even to his old and helpless father, Laertes, when they are finally reunited. Deception is a theme, of course, connected with this character. Some critics consider it to be much more a matter of formula than of deliberate cruelty; it comes with the character whenever he meets someone new. That formulation, however, seems simplistic, since it is also the manifestation of a basic character type. That Odysseus trusts no one, the narrator consistently implies, is his greatest strength. His instinct for trickery might in someone younger suggest a mischievous prankster. Folktales around the world know such a character as the Wily Lad. The Norse god Loki is one example; the Bavarian Tyl Eulenspiegel is another. Sly baby Hermes, who tricks pompous Apollo in the Homeric *Hymn to Hermes,* is probably a Greek version of the same. Certainly Odysseus is a figure from the saga tradition—he is a warrior and leader—yet there are enough folk elements in this poem to endorse the notion that the portrait of the heroic Odysseus has been touched up with character traits from a source other than saga. At times he is presented as, or considers himself to be, a runt or a victim, very much the underdog of folktales. What has happened in the tradition from which this poem springs is that generations of narrators mingled characteristics of figures from two very different narrative traditions; this makes Odysseus a complex human being, enlarged and deepened, compared with the one-dimensional men of the *Iliad.* Since the narrative turns so very much on the question of identity, the character complication serves the story.

Not only the figure of Odysseus but a great deal of the narrative derives from the saga tradition. One story theme to which the narrator makes constant reference is the *nostos,* the Greek word for "return." Evidence suggests that there were any number of poems describing the adventure of return for each of the major heroes of the Trojan War: some were blown off course and had encounters such as that of Menelaus with Proteus in Egypt; others encountered their demons upon entering their homes once more, as Agamemnon did. The poet uses this *nostos* material, when, for instance, Nestor and Menelaus are asked by Telemachus if they have any word of his father. Nor can we forget that the entire *Odyssey* is a giant *nostos*.

There are other instances of the poet's use of saga material. In the underworld scene Odysseus not only meets figures from the Trojan War such as Agamemnon and Achilles but also happens upon a bevy of ladies (whom the narrator lists) and other famous figures of Greek myth and saga such as Tantalus and Sisyphus. At the very end of the poem Achilles' funeral is described after the fashion of the great saga funerals. The typical battle narrative, the *androktasia* of the *Iliad*, is also to be found in the *Odyssey* story when Odysseus, Telemachus, and the suitors fight their climactic battle. The principal difficulty with this scene is that there are not adequate numbers of named warriors present to create a battle narrative with much substance. Few of the suitors have been distinguished with names, and Odysseus himself has only a few men helping him. The narrator confronts this problem masterfully: instead of the names in almost listlike fashion that characterize traditional battle narrative, the poet shows the suitors missing their very few human targets and hitting objects in the room; similarly, he calls Odysseus's helpers sometimes by their names, sometimes by their occupations: "the swineherd," or the "herdsman." In this way the narrator creates a sufficient number of subjects and objects for the action described in the typical battle narrative.

As noted in an earlier chapter, the poet immediately establishes an ethical and theological basis for his story different from that of the *Iliad*, one giving humans responsibility for the act of will. Since this idea is introduced in a speech of Zeus's only twenty-eight lines into the poem and in relatively abstract language, one is tempted to infer that the poet is answering Achilles' speech about the random and irrational distribution of good and evil from the jars of Zeus, a speech that comes at the end of the *Iliad* as a kind of summation of the action. In essence Achilles says that the universe in which mortals find themselves is indifferent, arbitrary, and wanton, a place in which they are senselessly subject to good and evil fortune. Zeus maintains quite the reverse in the *Odyssey*: "I must say, it's really something the way men blame the gods. For they claim that evil comes from us, whereas in fact they themselves, through their own stupidity and wrongdoing, suffer miseries beyond measure" (1.32ff.).

Zeus offers the example of Aegisthus, who was warned by the gods neither to seduce Clytemnestra nor to kill Agamemnon; Aegisthus disregarded their instructions and was himself killed by Orestes. The example becomes a leitmotif in the poem, in which each constituent of this conjugal and family catastrophe grows into a paradigm of behavior very relevant to the story of woman beset by suitors who wish her absent husband dead. The leitmotif charges every scene with those wonderful suspenseful questions from soap opera: will Penelope succumb to the blandishments of the men in her house who so desperately want her? how long can she endure the loneliness, the empty hope that her errant husband will return? The story outline was known, presumably, to all, so the questions are idle. But there are tensions in the plot which will make even the practiced listener of this story speculate and fantasize.

The emphasis on human responsibility, established so early, changes the main conception of the narrative. Events seem less fated than they are in the *Iliad* ("I know in my heart . . . the day will come when Troy will perish.") The gods do not enter the human scene; they neither look on as humankind is moved to some fate in an inexorable train nor affect the action. True enough, Athena gives Telemachus advice, but he acts upon it and gets the story moving. People seem more masters of their own affairs; they suffer more, therefore, in proportion to the mishandling of them. It is in part for this reason that the ancients considered the *Iliad* more tragic than the *Odyssey*.

Longinus called the *Odyssey* a comedy of manners. Literary critics cite these Homeric poems, which are the earliest literary pieces of the Western world along with the Bible (excluding the Gilgamesh story, which is only now slowly being absorbed into the Western literary canon), as the earliest representation of the tragic and the comic sensibilities. By a comic narrative they mean one that says yes to life, that exalts the life process, that takes its cues from sexual intercourse, love, birthing, eating, identifications of persons related but unknown to each other (that is to say, the reunions of lost persons, or we might call it the reintegration of family members)—all the things that sustain human life on this earth. Needless to say, a comic view will insist upon the success of action, upon the survival of persons, upon fulfillment in time. The reader will see that quite the opposite course of action dominates the narrative of the *Iliad* but that the *Odyssey* story does indeed show a family reunited, a man wandering the world and sleeping with great women but wanting to get home to the bed of his wife, a series of scenes in which persons are dining as a demonstration of the social compact (or of wanton appetites and selfish greed quite out of control). Furthermore, literary historians note that the *Odyssey* contains many motifs that will come to define the early romance, a genre the Greeks seem to have invented in the Hellenistic period but one that may have been gestating in tales, stories, and legends as early as the fifth century. Certainly, the principal narrative theme of romance is central to the *Odyssey* as well: star-crossed lovers separated by the cruel accident of fate struggle to reunite, she beset by forces that strive to rob her of her chastity, he boldly and bravely striving to reach her side before it is too late.

Critics must wrestle with the question whether such different life views as the *Iliad* and *Odyssey* portray can conceivably be the products of the same group of poets, the same tradition, the same poet—whatever is conceived as the instrument of creation. If these are public poems to the extent that their preservation results from their having served important public interests, then what was the social value of the *Odyssey*? What society decided that these two poems would survive as the fullest expression of their life view? It is not enough to say that for preliterate or semiliterate people the Homeric epics were the history of the culture, or that Homer along with Hesiod created the Greek gods. Both statements are true, but neither poem is a history or a religious or theological tract. Both profile human behavior as it will inevitably appear in certain stock circumstances; this aspect has far more didactic value. It is from this perspective that the critic needs to assess the social value of these poems. It is more to the point how the *Odyssey* is like *I Love Lucy* than how it compares with *The City of God*.

It has been argued that the Gilgamesh story, the Genesis story, and the *Odyssey* have in common a reference to the human life cycle. Just as Enkidu, the child of nature, and the biblical Eden describe human childhood, and other parts of these stories describe the later stages of human growth, so the *Odyssey* describes childhood in the Telemachia, a man's years of adventure and sexual questing in the travel stories, the time of nesting and acquiring wife and children in the return to Ithaca, and old age in the visit to the senile father, and Achilles' funeral as the seal of mankind's death at the very end. It then could be argued that just as the *Iliad* demonstrates the archaic age's concern with the tragedy of life—that is to say, the necessity of dying—so the *Odyssey* is a projection of the archaic age's interest in defining a life well lived. In both cases, of course, the preoccupation is with males, not with the whole of the human race.

The reader must consider whether the poets of the *Odyssey* tradition knew the *Iliad*. It is remarkable that there is no reference in the *Odyssey* to events of the *Iliad*. Many of the same people appear, and the Trojan war is the obvious backdrop to the story, yet nothing of what the *Iliad* describes is mentioned. It may be argued that anyone who ignores something that central to his audience is by his silence making constant reference. Or one can argue that the origins of these two poems are sufficiently disparate that in fact the *Odyssey* poets just did not know the *Iliad*. Or one can search the smallest details of the *Odyssey* narrative for subtle allusions to the *Iliad*. This last maneuver posits two fully established texts and the kind of interaction that one assumes for poets raised up in the Alexandrian aesthetic (see Chapter 7). Some contemporary critics insist that the *Odyssey* narrator plays off the *Iliad* constantly. It is worth remembering that in the constant digressive stories in the *Iliad* the narrator never introduces details of events that come from other moments in the war, such as, for instance, the Judgment of Paris, or the wounding of Philoctetes, or any of the many, many other stories that are part of his material. One could perhaps relate this practice to the reticence of the *Odyssey* poet and term it a convention of the narrator *not* to make reference to certain directly relevant material. Or one can imagine that the *Odyssey* poets were sufficiently competitive that they dismissed in silence the alternate *Iliad* tradition. The silence is and always will be an intriguing subject for speculation.

A previous chapter suggested that the distinction between the view of the universe in the *Iliad*, as revealed in the jars of Zeus speech, and that of the *Odyssey*, as Zeus tells it in the opening lines, could be said to reflect two views of a narrator's control. The *Odyssey* narrator takes a far greater interest in poets and performances. When Penelope complains about Phemius's song, Telemachus silences her, declaring that the poet is the authority and that people prefer to hear the latest song (1.351ff.), a critical judgment that betokens an interest in poetry and its creation not to be found in the *Iliad*. Then when Odysseus is invited to identify himself, Alcinous opines that it is better to speak out (8.549), bids the stranger "speak accurately; come now, don't lie" (8.574), and tells him halfway through that he is as good as a singer (11.363ff.), which identifies the king of the Phaeacians as a man of taste and critical standards. Odysseus himself is sufficiently conscious of the aesthetics of story-telling that when he arrives at the point where he commenced, he can say, "I hate telling a story over again, especially when it was well done the first time around" (12.450).

Such attention to the art of storytelling may well be an expression of what seems to be the heightened control that the poet exercises throughout the narrative. Almost every episode, for instance, is a variation on the typical scene of arrival and hosting. Athena arrives at Ithaca, Telemachus arrives at Pylos, Telemachus in the company of Nestor's son Pisistratus arrives at Sparta, Hermes arrives on Ogygia, Odysseus arrives at Scheria, Odysseus arrives at the palace of Alcinous, Odysseus arrives at Ithaca, Odysseus arrives at the hut of the swineherd Eumaeus, Telemachus arrives at Ithaca, Odysseus arrives at the palace, Odysseus arrives in Penelope's company, the suitors arrive in the underworld. These passages show the extraordinary ubiquity of the theme. The economy of using this typical scene to serve so many narrative goals is remarkable for its elegance; it suggests a mastery of the form far greater than the *Iliad* narrative demonstrates. The stereotypic women seem to be used for greater narrative value in the *Odyssey*. Calypso and Circe display both beneficent nurturance and destructive seduction, qualities that combine in Penelope as well. Nausicaa's and her mother's reception of Odysseus rehearse some of the interaction of Odysseus with his wife, eroticizing through association a scene that is otherwise relatively staid. These features make a tighter, more unified narrative than the *Iliad* seems to be. The *Iliad* may progress more smoothly with fewer shifts and interruptions of time, place, and point of view, but its narrative is more diffuse; it lacks the cross-referencing that marks the *Odyssey* narrative.

The Telemachia is the world's first *Bildungsroman*, and a number of themes that continue through the entire poem find their first expression in this part. The dilemma of Telemachus is one of them. Athena first comes upon him moping, dreaming of his father, powerless among the suitors. This impotent yearning is reflected in what Telemachus says as a kind of hesitant variation on the young hero's proud declaration of ancestry. To Athena, who has just identified him as Odysseus's son, the young man replies: "My mother says I am his son, but of course, I wouldn't know. For no one really knows his own parentage" (1.215–16).

One of the suspenseful issues in this story is whether Telemachus will mature, will finally be able to gain some mastery over the threatening affairs of his household. The references to Agamemnon's son Orestes and his unfortunate parents encourage the audience of this poem to wonder whether Telemachus has the same courage, or whether he will need it. Corollary to questions about his maturing is the question of whether he will ever come to know his father in any real sense. Will he identify with his father? Unless he grows more secure and aware of the heroic world his father represents, he will not. The question of Telemachus's identity, his self-identity, becomes equally important. We must not forget the normal male's anxiety over the identity of his father. It was probably acute in the period in which this poem took shape, a time, we may assume, when the occupation of warrior or merchant kept men away from home for long periods. Very young males could grow up without fathers. Girls can easily identify with their mothers, who obviously produced them; boys, who have a considerably more tenuous link with the reproductive process, are also not very well connected to traveling males who may or may not be their biological fathers.

As Telemachus becomes more aware of his heroic parentage, he does achieve heroic stature himself. Saga and epic poetry describe heroes with impotent fathers for the very good reason that either fathers must defer to their sons because of the strength of their youth, or sons must defer to their fathers by virtue of their seniority. Either posture cancels the heroic stance, which does not permit deference. Thus, Peleus is old and feeble, Laertes is senile, Tydeus is dead, Zeus is a god—and so it goes. In the *Iliad* only Nestor is on hand to nag his son, which he does by giving him elaborate advice on racing in the athletic contests in Book Twenty-three; the narrator is good to Antilochus, however, and makes him cheat to win rather than carry out his father's wholesome but tiresome instructions.

Homer is masterful at bringing Telemachus to manhood and to equality with his great father without diminishing either man. At home he can order his mother about. When she complains of Phemius's song, the boy says: "Go to your room. . . . Speech shall be the concern of men, of all of them, but mostly my concern. For I have authority in this house" (1.356ff.). But with the suitors in the subsequent assembly scene he is so unnerved that he bursts into tears and dashes the speaker's staff he is holding to the ground. On his voyage of discovery he is initially so shy that he cannot imagine passing time in Nestor's company. But at Sparta he fills the conversational void when Helen and Menelaus fall silent, exhausted by the repressed but animated hostility of the anecdotes they have just been telling. The next day Telemachus is even stronger, firm with Menelaus in politely rejecting his well-intended but useless gift of horses ("Ithaca is too rocky for horses, sir"). As he is about to sail back to Ithaca, he is sufficiently in command of himself to be able to refuse ever so politely to visit Nestor once again (15.200–201). Just on the verge of departure a certain refugee, Theoclymenus by name, comes up to ask if Telemachus will take him under his protection. Theoclymenus is a person who has no real importance in the narrative other than as a mechanical assistance for the narrator. Later, when a prophecy is needed, he will be there to make one. Here he has a similar function, to indicate relative strengths and powers. He is weak and vulnerable; Telemachus by contrast is protective and strong. When Telemachus agrees to take Theoclymenus along, the narrator has put the seal of adulthood upon the lad.

His meeting with his father, then, is fraught with the peril of imbalance: the narrator is in danger of having the one man overwhelm the other. His strategy has been to make Telemachus a man and his own person when Odysseus is not at hand but less sure of himself in the presence of the father. Thus, in the sixteenth book, when Odysseus and Telemachus begin to discuss strategy against the suitors, the son just cannot believe that he and his father have the strength to prevail against so many men. He still does not understand or know heroic temper or strength; the narrator makes his innocence a mark of his youth. Moments later, however, when the young man offers some sage and penetrating objections to Odysseus's plan of discovering the loyalties of the farmhands, he is for a moment his father's equal. Indications of Telemachus's newfound manhood are crucial to the story. Penelope (18.216–18; 269–71) says that Telemachus is now a man and recalls Odysseus's advice to remarry. Telemachus himself, just as he gave intimations of his new maturity when ordering his mother around at the beginning of the poem, is made by the narrator to speak harshly to the suitors, ordering them about (18.405–411; 20.262–67), and they are dumfounded. Just before the crucial stringing of the bow, the narrator combines the two themes as Telemachus again sharply orders his mother to leave the room and at the same time establishes in front of the suitors that the authority in this house is his (21.344–53). Any man who truly loves his wife will be delighted to see the way in which other men are excited by her as Odysseus is pleased when the suitors respond so heatedly to Penelope descending the stairs in book eighteen. Any man who truly loves his son will be equally delighted to see the young man demonstrate his capacity to exercise complete authority in the household he will someday inherit.

The story contained in the Epic Cycle poem *Telegonia* has been told in an earlier chapter. It is the tragic story of the young man Telegonus, who kills his father, Odysseus, whom he does not recognize. The *Odyssey* narrator devises quite another resolution to the meeting of father and son for his comic poem. When Telemachus returns from his travels to the mainland, he goes to Eumaeus's house, where in the absence of the swineherd his father reveals himself to his son. There is no killing here, no hostile act of aggression or territoriality. Instead, father and son fall into each other's arms, and the poet gives the reunion a simile: "And they cried shrilly, more insistently than birds cry, ospreys or vultures with their curving claws, whose young the farmers have taken off before the nestlings have learned to fly" (16.216–18). The simile is perfect for the scene, since it describes the loss of parents for the young and their children's youth for the parents, and this is exactly what Telemachus and Odysseus have to cry over: that loss of twenty years of each other's company which can never be recompensed or requited. Telemachus will never have a father while he is growing up; Odysseus has a man friend in Telemachus, not a baby son turned into a child turned into a man. Certainly this is one of the truly poignant moments in this story about men. Does it not perhaps reflect a universal truth of a seafaring society where male children are reared with the women while the grown men are abroad?

At Pylos the scene begins and ends with a sacrifice; at Sparta, with a party. The former demands knowledge of ritual detail; the latter, of social organization. The descriptions of Nestor's sacrifices are among the most detailed in either poem. The scenes also emphasize the importance of the knowledge of correct social behavior. The principal expression of social behavior in the *Odyssey* is in the show of hospitality, since the story turns again and again on the arrival of a stranger. It is very clear that in the time in which this poem took shape, as in many other times in many other lands, hospitality had divine sanction. Those who violated hospitality were doing something more than commiting a social blunder; they were offending against the gods. In a culture that had almost no absolute divine commandments (unlike the famous ten of the ancient Hebrews), the law of hospitality for strangers was universally observed. This no doubt stems from the fact that in a world without cities—hence without police, without hotels and restaurants—a traveling man was dependent upon those whom he chanced to meet. People who traveled frequently could build up a network of persons they could call on as they moved about, but the chance traveler was at the mercy of the human environment through which he passed. No doubt the law of hospitality, secured by divine sanction, came about so as to ensure elemental social stability. Or, more than that, the law of hospitality reverences the basic humanity that fellow humans are enjoined always to recognize, despite whatever other emotions are engendered at the sight of the stranger. In any case, it was incumbent upon a household to receive a stranger, bathe him, feed him, and bed him down before asking his name. Identification came at the very last so that if the parties turned out to be from families or peoples who were long-time enemies, the stranger could be quickly turned out, but well fed, clean, and rested. In this way the common humanity of the race was cherished and protected.

Immediately upon Telemachus's arrival in Pylos, the young man shows his confusion as to the proprieties of arrival. Not only young, Telemachus is a country rube. The poet consistently describes Ithaca as out of the way, a relatively poor and unimportant place. When, for instance, Menelaus tells Telemachus how he had hoped to settle Odysseus as king in one of his cities, he shows the insignificance of Odysseus's Ithacan principality. Telemachus, then, has much more to learn than simply the fate of his father. The boy's ignorance and his gradual education into the ways of men parallel the travels of his father, who much of the time is a human being among fantastics and marvels. Odysseus, too, is a student in these situations, although actively curious in a way that his son is not. Notice that when the disguised Odysseus asks himself whether he can endure being in the presence of the corrupt serving women of his household in Ithaca, he answers himself by saying that his horrible experience with the Cyclops had taught him to endure (20.18–21).

At Pylos, Athena (disguised as Mentor) answers Telemachus's nervous questions about proper behavior with words that contain the creed, the initial reason for self-respect, of an aristocrat: "Telemachus, part of the time you will think something up yourself, part of the time a god will help you. For I don't think you were born and reared without the gods being interested in you" (3.26ff.). This exchange is repeated between Odysseus and Athena: when he is doubtful that he will prevail over the suitors with so few to support him, she reminds him that he has a god on his side (20.37–51)—again a reminder of how the narrator uses the Telemachia as a rehearsal for the story of Odysseus which follows.

Odysseus's self-assured and courageous manner throughout most of the poem stems from the fact that he trusts in himself and in destiny or the gods because he has the security of someone who has been favored. One thinks of Jesus saying, "To them that have shall be given, from them that have not shall be taken away." In this sense Odysseus is the perfect comic hero. Slowly, Telemachus comes to acquire the same assurance. In the manner of theater the narrator makes the speeches dramatize the subtleties of social convention. No sooner has Telemachus arrived in Pylos than he meets Nestor's youngest boy, Pisistratus, who becomes, like Orestes, another model for the Ithacan. Pisistratus is the paragon of the young gentleman, his speech is a model of propriety as he passes the wine to Mentor. He bids Mentor pour a libation, then pass on the goblet to Telemachus, "since I believe that he, too, prays to the immortals. All men need gods. But he is younger, the same age as myself. Wherefore I shall offer the golden cup to you first" (3.47ff.).

Nestor is the first person of consequence whom Telemachus meets. The old man shows an old-fashioned piety, gentility, and serenity, grounded in the worship of gods and confidence in their ways. Nestor's attention to the detail of worship reveals a man who understands the ways of the world and the universe. He does things tidily, with precision and sureness. The poet has used far more concrete detail than is either customary or really necessary. The impression is one of routine, order, and knowledge. All this is lacking at Ithaca except in the swineherd's hut, where orderliness and mastery of technique are in evidence. Eumaeus, the counterpart to Nestor, is first shown cutting himself a pair of sandals (14.23f.), another example of man's control of his environment, so common a theme in this narrative. One thinks of the loving attention to detail in the narrator's description of Odysseus making the raft (5.243ff.). Control will perhaps seem insignificant when set beside the themes dramatized in the *Iliad*. Yet a threat of anarchy and imminent disaster lurks everywhere in the narrative of the *Odyssey* to which the themes of skill, control, endurance respond. Eumaeus's life story, fraught with chance disaster and sudden shifts, perhaps mirrors the chaotic times in which this poem took shape. The utter insecurity of life registered in this and in other biographies in the *Odyssey* draws attention to the haphazard quality of existence, to its irrationality and ruthless changeability. This has its metaphor in the boxing match of the two beggars, parodies of stouthearted men and true, set up by the suitors, whose own claim to physical strength and material prosperity is soon to be ruthlessly challenged (18.1–116). Those who are wise, the narrator seems to be saying, build a bulwark against life's insecurity by emphasizing order, precision, and technical skill. Those who are wiser still expect disaster to be a natural concomitant of the quotidian experience; hence, they husband their suspicion and cynicism, the sparks to the fire of Odyssean intensity.

Nestor has offered Telemachus a glimpse of normality, a way of life far removed from that of the lounging, partying, destructive suitors. Sparta offers another view. Menelaus and Helen live in a style still grander, more foreign to Telemachus's experience. He arrives just as an elaborate wedding party is ending; he sees a palace filled with a wealth he associates with gods, and the attention he receives is as elegant as the material possessions surrounding him. The narrator presents Menelaus as yet another role model in the education of Telemachus. Rich and magnificent as he is, Menelaus is not overwhelmed by the luxury of his life. He is, for instance, quick to reprimand a servant who delays admitting the young man, for he remembers what it is to be a wanderer, for whom the essentials of existence become sharply defined. Then, when Telemachus whispers to Pisistratus about the splendors of the palace, Menelaus overhears him and from his simple country-boy remarks extracts an important observation: "Dear child, no man at all could try to rival Zeus. For his house and possessions, you know, are immortal" (4.78–79). This is the only real distinction between humankind and the highly anthropomorphized Homeric gods. It allows for a philosophic view which Menelaus hints at here and which is more often and at greater length expressed by Odysseus. Mankind can only temporarily own possessions; they are at any time likely to disappear or be destroyed. The vicissitudes of his life have taught Menelaus to let go. Since this is a lesson that persons of advanced years tend to have learned and youngsters not, it supports Longinus's suspicion that the *Odyssey* is the work of a poet in his old age.

The conjugal scene at Sparta is only one of the loose ends of homecoming to be tied up in the aftermath of the Trojan War. Yet certainly any listener would be especially interested to discover how a narrator described that war's most famous couple in their adjustment to the postwar years. Audiences familiar with a tradition in which Helen castigates her lover Paris, who accepts her contempt with good humor and beds her just as easily (the story in the third book of the *Iliad*), would enjoy the way the *Odyssey* narrator sets up a contrast. Here, Helen is established as once again the wife of the local king, mistress of her palace, moving from room to room with her entourage of serving women. No outward show of estrangement mars the unruffled calm of the royal couple. This may be in part due to the low esteem in which women are held: if Helen is thought not to be capable of moral choice, no opprobrium attaches to her ill-starred departure in the night with Paris, and she can be reinstated with a minimum of fuss. On the other hand, it may be that the narrator is describing a scene in which social manners are on display. The scenario calls for the real dialogue to be created out of subtext. Consider the hilarious exchange between king and queen as they pretend to be reminiscing about Odysseus for the sake of his son (4.240ff.). When Helen describes how Odysseus came into Troy in a disguise which, although she penetrated it, she did not reveal to others, presumably she is teaching Telemachus of the laudable deceit of which his father is capable as well as his willingness to undergo degradation. More to the point, she is reminding everyone that she was loyal to the Achaean cause, despite having shared Paris's bed. Menelaus equally pleasantly offers another anecdote about Odysseus, that when Helen mimicked the voices of the wives of the Achaean men who were hidden in the wooden horse so as to get them to betray themselves it was Odysseus who smartly kept them quiet. We can read Menelaus as sarcastic when he delivers the commonplace Homeric thought "Some god must have made you do it"; certainly he seems a bit vicious when he then notes that "Godlike Deïphobos followed along with you" (the listener would know that Deïphobos—another son of Priam—succeeded Paris in Helen's bed after Paris was killed).

The *Odyssey* narrator is especially good at the kind of dialogue one finds in a comedy of manners, in which persons say one thing and mean another. Consider Nausicaa and the issue of washing clothes for the men in her family, when all the while she is thinking of her own future marriage (6.66). Exchanges of this delicate subtlety are not unusual. An Achilles who would find hateful as the gates of hell someone who says one thing and hides another in his heart would not be successful in such a comedy. This consideration may suggest something about the narrative tradition behind the *Odyssey* and its presumed audience. As is better understood today, males who, like Achilles, live lives at the center of the power structure are not good at decoding, since they, unlike the marginalized, despised, and oppressed, do not have to speak in doubletalk. Odysseus is, as everyone notes, different from Achilles, if only in his capacity for taking on roles that seem to derogate his status of power. Women in patriarchal societies such as this are, of course, definitely marginalized. Perhaps this poem speaks to women and to men who have lost power more than to other persons. Certainly the Cinderella motif that is central to Odysseus's homecoming and Athena's role in it is a story line fit for the disinherited who dream the impossible dream. Perhaps there is more about power or the loss of it waiting to be noticed in this poem. Observations about the subtlety of the dialogues, however, should not encourage the reader to imagine that Penelope carries on the lengthy conversation with the disguised beggar, and comports herself as she does with Telemachus and the suitors, all the while knowing that the beggar is Odysseus. If that were so, the narrator would neither describe her crying to herself in her bedchamber, yearning for her husband, nor fail to divulge at some point that she had indeed penetrated the beggar's disguise. Notice his clear indication that Nausicaa is thinking of her impending marriage while talking to her father of her brothers' dirty clothes. That kind of clarification, we must assume, is the narrator's obligation to his audience in the course of oral performance.

The exchange of reminiscences shows with perfect clarity the animosity of Helen and Menelaus and the social fabric of reconciliation that holds the household together. Nonetheless, the king and queen fall silent after this contrived communication, whereupon the narrator provides a slight revelation of Telemachus's growing familiarity with the ways of the world. At Sparta he has shyly allowed Pisistratus to speak for him—until the moment following this awkward exchange between Helen and Menelaus. As the king and queen remain silent, Telemachus enters the stalled conversation to change the subject. He has learned enough from his traveling companion to speak up and cover the impasse created by the royal couple. Not only does he speak; he motivates the action.

A second theme of great importance to this poem which has its beginning in the Telemachia is the overshadowing power of women. Marriage is its corollary. Athena, when she arrives at Ithaca and encounters the preparations for the suitors' usual banquet, asks whether a festival is in progress or a wedding, perhaps. Telemachus arrives at Sparta as a wedding party is taking place. Nausicaa has weddings in mind the entire time she is with Odysseus; her father asks the stranger if he will not stay and marry the girl. Calypso invites Odysseus to marry her. Mention of the marriage of Clytemnestra and Agamemnon runs throughout the poem. The suitors talk about nothing but marriage, and Penelope shivers with horror at the idea of her own remarriage. That the weddings are so often the idea of a woman, or at least proposed by a woman, attests to the importance of women in this narrative, a subject addressed in Chapter 2 of this book.

The patron saint or, better yet, the fairy godmother in this narrative is a woman, the goddess Athena. One is at first tempted to say that her gender is not decisive either in her role or in her relationship to Odysseus. As the divinity who represents or encourages intellectual action, ratiocination, strategies, devices, Athena is the natural choice. As the nurturant protector of cities—which is to say, of civilization and culture, human networks and bonding through talk and correct behavior—she is again the natural deity to assist this human. Also as a projection of Odysseus's thoughts, fantasies, hopes, and dreams, Athena is the suitable image. Yet Athena is protective and nurturant— she is guide to the son, comforter to the mother, inventive aide to the father—and we read these as the attributes, whether acculturated or not, of a woman.

The other women, however, are described as markedly feminine, either as the sexual partner of a male or in traditional activities, such as singing, working the loom, setting out the food. These are almost always threatening in one way or another, from a male's point of view, of course. The strong misogynistic strain in early Greek culture is evidenced in Hesiod's poetry, particularly in those maxims that mention women and even more particularly in the myth of Pandora in the *Works and Days*. This appears to be a story of the all-giving woman which a masculine culture has reread as the source of all the evils rampant in the world. The early Hebrews made a similar and considerably more vehement transformation of Eve, who seems to have begun life as the beneficent figure who provides food to man, situated in a garden, near the tree of life, with the snake emblem of immortality as her sign. But the crude misogynist bath to which these two great beneficent figures have been subjected is far from the subtle, balanced, appreciative, and yet fearful portrait of a stereotypic woman that appears in scene after scene of the *Odyssey*.

Even Penelope from the first bears a striking resemblance to Circe, the acknowledged witch of the *Odyssey*. The suitors, eating, drinking, and shouting in riotous debauch, resemble nothing so much as Circe's pigs, transformed from the men she has charmed. And there is something sinister about the shroud she weaves and unweaves. It seems a symbol of the way in which ultimately Penelope deliberately leads the suitors to their doom, since as the version of the shroud story in the twenty-fourth book is told, she finishes it just as Odysseus returns to wreak vengeance. Then there is her strange dream of the pet geese being killed—her suitors, as she herself admits, over whom in the dream she cries. Coupled with this is Penelope's defense of Helen (23.218–24), in itself a remarkable demonstration of the strength of women in this poem. Aristarchus, the great Hellenistic critic, and countless scholars thereafter condemned these lines; although they are unobjectionable as a specimen of Homeric Greek verse, the sentiment is startling and unsettling from the possessive male's point of view. Helen, says Penelope, would never have gone off with Paris if she had known that the Achaeans would go and bring her back again. Certainly, the narrator is at pains to describe Penelope as so emotionally dependent upon Odysseus that she whiles away most of the twenty years of his absence, it seems, in crying for him. The narrator perceives her as a woman and wife who lives through her husband. She is made to insist twice (18.251–56; 19.124–29) that her physical beauty and shape, her mark (as she claims) of excellence and identity, were destroyed when Odysseus left, but should he return and organize her life, she would enjoy twice the fame and better fame too. Nonetheless, as is plain to see, she has a mind and a libido of her own. What is more, the narrator chooses to employ the paradigm of Clytemnestra, Agamemnon, and Orestes almost as a leitmotif in the poem. Clytemnestra's great betrayal is every traveling husband's fear, which invests the homecoming of this poem with a certain anxiety.

Helen, the woman who sweeps into the room grandly and recognizes Telemachus instantly, is replicated in the narrator's conception of Arete. On the island of Scheria, Odysseus is directed by Nausicaa to present himself to her mother, Queen Arete; if she feels friendly toward you, says her daughter, then you may expect to see your friends and get to your homeland again (6.313–15). Needless to say, ancient and modern critics alike have been inclined to omit the lines or, in some cases, invent anthroplogical explanations for this strong female figure. Her daughter's view is supported, however, by Arete's first words to the suppliant Odysseus: "Let me ask you this one thing first. Where do you come from and who are you? Who gave you this clothing? Didn't you say you came from across the sea?" (7.237–39). Smart woman that she is, she immediately recognizes some of the clothes Nausicaa has given Odysseus, realizes immediately that they do not jibe with his story of coming from elsewhere. Arete has a quick mind—in contrast to that of her husband, Alcinous, who after Odysseus has entered and sunk to his knees, leaves the fellow there in the ashes until one of his courtiers has the presence of mind to suggest that he get the suppliant to a chair and to some food (7.159–66).

As Nausicaa had said, Arete is the important one. Well into the report of his travels Odysseus gets to the moment when he encounters the famous heroines of myth and legend (11.225–329), from which he asks to break off because it is getting late. Arete cuts into the ensuing silence: "Now what do you think of this man's brain and looks? He's my guest, but you may all share in the honor. Let's give him many gifts before we send him on his way" (11.336–41). A member of the royal gathering speaks up to say that Arete's idea is splendid, adding, "Let us do as she says. But the deed and the word derive from Alcinous." And then the king chimes in: "Yes, this will be my word, as long as I rule over the Phaeacians." The narrator leaves no doubt that Nausicaa was absolutely right about her mother. Female power is kept in the foreground here, even to setting up the Catalogue of Noble Heroines to inspire Arete to further heights of hospitality. In fact, throughout his travels Odysseus has been helped by women— Athene, Calypso, Circe, Nausicaa, Arete—whereas he has been almost destroyed by men: eaten alive by the one important male with whom he has to deal, deliberately set up for disaster in a storm by a male god, and faced with the prospect of a house full of hostile males once he returns to Ithaca. If one wishes to say that Odysseus relates better to women, and that this is perhaps part of the comic perspective when coming from the male point of view, then one might have the reverse to say about the tragic perspective. After all, it is Hades, the god of Death, a male, who snatches away the life principle, the blooming season: that is, the young girl Persephone at play in the flowering meadow with her girlfriends.

Circe is usually cast as the malign witch of this poem. True enough, when Odysseus and his crew land on her island, they spy smoke coming from a chimney in the forest. Enthusiasts of fairytale will think of the witch in Hansel and Gretel, who lives in a similar woods in a cottage. Circe's magic potion turns Odysseus's men into swine, but he is protected from her potions by an herb that Hermes gives him. When she proceeds to tap him with her wand, he, as instructed by the god, pulls his sword from its sheath. Twentieth-century children of Freud cannot resist seeing this as the archetypical duel of the sexes, the female with an enchantment that will turn men to swine, the male equipped with a death-dealing phallus. As if to make it more obvious, Hermes has told Odysseus that the drawn sword and his angry rush at her will prompt Circe to invite him to bed. Again on Hermes' instruction (since in this way he can save his transformed crew members) he accepts the invitation after getting her pledge to do him no harm. The conversation between the two prospective lovers is a masterpiece of mistrust, suspicion, and the calculated profiteering that they both take for granted. The phallic implications of the drawn sword in this sexual duel will return in the contest of the bow and arrows. Just as Odysseus is able to survive by being able to sleep with Calypso for seven years, just as he is able to save his crew and himself by being able to draw a sword, perhaps get an erection, with Circe, so he will be able to send phallic arrows through vaginal axe holes to save himself, his wife, his son, and their household. This poem is not only about a man who lives by his wits.

Malign witch Circe may be, but she is more than that. Hers is the advice that gets Odysseus to the underworld and back; she is the one who thoughtfully provisions the boat with a ram and a sheep. What is most telling is that Odysseus enjoys his stay at Circe's house so much that it is only the urgent pleading of his crew that finally tears him away. When he determines to go, he enters her bed and asks to leave, and she immediately agrees: "No point staying if you all want to go" (10.489). No doubt about it, Circe is the good-natured party girl of every man's dreams: no tiresome dependency here! Still, Circe can be mysterious and frightening, and she is a woman; as in so many other instances in the narrative, the sexual battle betokens male fears of women. The stereotypic woman of this poem has some mysterious power as well as clear intelligence; there is always some foreboding attached to her, a hint of danger. Circe fits this stereotype: she turns men to swine who eat her food; she enchants them and they have no power. The role of woman as feeder, from a mother's breasts to the wife's homecooked meal, lies behind the Circe character, it seems. All are suspect, since they cater to a necessity that can turn man to animal, surrendering to a need that cancels self-consciousness and free will. The Circe figure, however, is not only nurturer but also sexual provider. The contrasting roles of mother and wife as nurturers and wife as sexual consort are thoroughly mixed in the person of Circe, the woman of the travels we might say, as opposed to Calypso, Nausicaa, and Penelope. Calypso and Nausicaa are in the halfway realm of passage between outright fairytale and heroic narrative. With her magical powers and transformed men, Circe is a creature of the former just as the realistic Penelope resides in the latter.

In one way or another, however, men react to all the women of the poem as they do to Circe. She is frightening because she makes men weak. Perhaps it is only that males, who have such a pronounced need of control, are threatened by its loss in the physical paroxysms of orgasm brought on by their encounters with women. When Penelope descends the stairs and shows herself to the suitors in the eighteenth book, the narrator remarks that she drives them to a frenzy: "They went weak at the knees and passion overcame them, each one desperate to get to sleep with her" (18.212–13). Minutes later she has them sending servants home to bring back gifts for her, and the narrator mentions all kinds of precious material items. No doubt about it, Penelope casts a spell upon the suitors not unlike Circe's enchantment. In the second book the suitors defend their behavior to Telemachus in a way that elicits sympathy for them. Essentially, they seem to be within their rights, wooing the queen. Many of them are of the aristocratic class that might expect to be feasted by their overlord; that he is out of the country does not eliminate the obligation. The matter of Penelope's weaving the shroud is kept vague; her passing messages to the suitors is certainly a provocation. The narrator in an evenhanded way gives the suitors their due. The result is to cast them to some degree as victims.

In their stupidity, however, the suitors are also gluttonous and sensual, prefiguring Odysseus's crew, who are destroyed because they have no self-control and ravenously eat the forbidden cattle of the sun god (12.320ff.). Throughout the previous adventure stories Odysseus himself has caused their misery, partly by satisfying his curiosity in visiting a dangerous place. Later, when he returns to Ithaca, the suitors in turn become his victims. Penelope dazzles them into irresistible yearning, but it is Odysseus who provokes them into betraying themselves by the way they treat him when he is disguised as a beggar. Athena suggests that Odysseus go begging among the suitors in order to "learn which of them were just and which were lawless" (17.363). She forces one suitor to resist redemption so that he will be destroyed (18.153–55), and she stirs up the suitors' insolence to whet Odysseus's appetite for revenge (18.346–48; 20.284–86). Just as in the commonplace action of Greek tragic drama, Ate—Delusion or Temptation, we might call it, or perhaps better still, delusive Temptation or tempting Delusion—provokes men to evil action (it is what Agamemnon claims provoked him to quarrel with Achilles), so Odysseus moves through this scene. Antinous, the chief suitor, recklessly tries to cast him out, to deny him the hospitality of the palace, moving close to offending against unwritten law. Toward the last, Odysseus or the narrator has begun to think of the suitors as what would be the pagan equivalent of "sinners" (20.121). As they move inexorably toward disastrous denouement, they themselves sense it. The narrator gives their plight a kind of tragic inevitability as he makes their doom more and more obvious. At their last banquet he has Athena cause them to laugh. It is a hysterical outburst of "uncontrollable laughter, their wits were scrambled, they laughed again, with no control over the muscles of their faces, the food they ate turned to blood, their eyes bulged, tears coursed, and the laughter sounded more like crying" (20.346–49).

As in tragic drama the narrator lays on the ironies in the latter part of this story. When Odysseus appears before the suitors as a beggar and is forced into a boxing match with Iris, the resident beggar, there is one irony after another: when he has beaten Iris, the suitors compliment him and wish him success in whatever he desires (18.112–13); he warns the suitor named Amphinomus that the disregard for Odysseus's possessions and the disrespect shown the wife will not sit well with Odysseus, who may very well be just about to return (18.143–50); he expresses the wish that he could hold a contest with Eurymachus, another suitor, in scything or plowing a field or that Eurymachus could see him fight in battle (18.375–80). There are further tantalizing ironies in the exchanges between the beggar and Penelope, not the least of which is the dream she recounts in which a man just like Odysseus lay next to her in bed all the night long (21.88–89).

The situation of the disguised Odysseus, which permits the narrator so many ironies, simply intensifies that of the traveling Odysseus, who consistently lies or fictionalizes or gives no identity to those he meets. Appearance and reality play a great role in this story, as is clear from the start when Telemachus sets out to discover who his father is. What he will learn is his father's repute among the other heroes who were with him at Troy or from such reporters as Helen. His father emerges for him from the veil of obscurity as a figure of stories, a person in narrative rather than the flesh-and-blood man. Later on, Odysseus tells the Phaeacians stories of his travels in which he makes himself the central figure of adventure. Still later, in response to the commonplace invitation to identify himself, Odysseus as the stranger invents himself in a series of autobiographies that are or are not fictive. Again he is telling stories about himself. By setting out to learn who his father is, Telemachus learns who he himself is, which is to say, grows up and assumes his role in the society of Ithaca. By traveling, Odysseus learns much of the world and, perhaps in a more transcendent way, who he is; thus upon his return he is able to assume a role, again transcendent, in finding his place in life: that is, in the acceptance of the end of his life, as it must be in the aftermath of homecoming, which is itself the aftermath of the adventure of the war.

But appearance and reality are in tension elsewhere. Athena's lying to Telemachus about herself when first she meets him and when she subsequently accompanies him in the guise of the family friend, Mentor, is a counterpart to Odysseus's walking through the latter episodes of the poem in disguise. Penelope lies to the suitors about the shroud that she weaves in the day and unweaves at night. Telemachus lies to his mother about the trip he is planning to the mainland. Menelaus describes the old man Proteus, who continually changes shape until someone holds him down; he is an exact counterpart to Odysseus, who is given the epithet "man of many turns" at the very beginning of the poem and whose action throughout plays to this description. The poet of the *Odyssey*, when he describes someone as beginning to speak, very often comments upon the wisdom or the awareness or the deceitfulness or the cynicism of the speaker. Much of the *Odyssey* turns upon Odysseus's coming to know or be known.

Recognition is therefore reciprocal. For Odysseus the two-way recognition occurs when finally he is once more on the island of Ithaca, his homeland. Characteristically, the poet has his hero in the midst of his wanderings tell Polyphemus that his name is Nobody. This initiates a moment of great fun: when his fellow giants coming running to his anguished calls and ask who is the perpetrator of his woe, Polyphemus can only answer "Nobody." Nonetheless, it is Odysseus who has styled himself "Nobody." From this point in the story he moves forward to the discovery of self in the context of his homeland, where he is simultaneously acknowledged. Upon his arrival, he awakes to an island transformed into the unrecognizable; he meets Athena who is disguised. He is never more frustratingly alienated, especially in the cruelly surrealistic moment when the disguised goddess declares that the completely unfamiliar landscape is in fact Ithaca. In this crisis he maintains his integrity by keeping secret and hidden his true identity. That is, he lies to Athena, embroidering for her a fictive self. This act is the magic charm that swiftly opens the door to complete understanding. Three momentous revelations are contained in this instant of time. First, the goddess reveals herself to him not by sign or omen, not as a bird, but in the true and recognizable lineaments of an anthropomorphized divine being. Odysseus achieves an intimate and direct union with the supernatural force that in hidden ways has followed his life until now. One has only to think of the narrator's description in Telemachus's words of the numinous presence of Athena in something other than corporeal form (19.36–40). Suddenly this presence that has been with Odysseus so long and so often stands fully revealed to him. Second, Athena proceeds to list those characteristics that have made him her favorite. From the divine lips comes, one assumes, the substance of the man: "It would take someone quite cunning and deceitful who could surpass you in trickery. . . . Stubborn, clever, never tired of falsehood, . . . you are of all mortals best at planning and speaking. . . . I cannot ever desert you when you suffer, because you are so smooth, so intelligent, so sensible" (13.291ff.). In this encounter Odysseus has been initiated into the nature of things, including his own identity. As the goddess finishes speaking, she dispels the mists of unreality and Ithaca, his homeland, stands as the third revelation. Odysseus's personal homecoming is realized.

What is still to come is his reintegration into his house and home. Throughout the suspenseful events of mounting an attack upon the suitors, involving cunning, bold, and skillful actions, Odysseus gradually recovers the emotional and personal landscape of Ithaca through a sequence of recognition scenes. The theme of arrival is played out in miniature as the traveling man encounters a series of figures who need to know or discover who he is. First, he is reunited with his son; next his ancient dying dog recognizes him, and then the old household retainer Eurycleia, the suitors, Penelope, and finally his father. These revelations are all different: Telemachus, of course, must be prompted into identifying a man he has never seen; the dog Swifty, like all true, faithful beasts whose psychic depth compensates them for being dumb, instantly recognizes his master, absent these twenty years; Eurycleia, like any nursemaid who has bathed a youngster time and time again, knows when she sees the scar on Odysseus's thigh; the suitors must acknowledge his superior strength; and Penelope tricks him into revealing the secrets of their bedchamber.

When first he is alone with Telemachus at Eumaeus's hut, an act of Athena transforms Odysseus from his beggarly disguise into a man of commanding stature and beauty (just what any young man dreams that the father he does not know will look like!), and then he reveals himself to his son. After crying for their lost years, they immediately bond in plotting the destruction of the suitors. Man finds son in the defender of his property.

Swifty—Argus (swift or keen), as he is known in the Greek—rises, wags his tail feebly in recognition, and shortly thereafter falls dead (17.290ff.). It is a sentimental scene portraying something that cannot be registered in the language of a character's speech, the usual means of indicating emotional response. In Swifty's greeting it is as though the landscape and all the intangibles of place connected to it have received Odysseus back.

Eurycleia's discovery prompts the poet into a digression on the origin of the scar on Odysseus's leg. As preamble to that incident the narrator contrives to tell how Odysseus got his name. His grandfather Autolycus, the poet says, excelled all men in thievery and in bearing false witness, skills given him by the god Hermes, whose devoted acolyte Autolycus was. Asked to name the child, the old man replied: "I come here as a man who has been angry with many, both men and women, over the fruitful earth. Let his name then be anger" (19.407ff.). This etymology is very likely the poet's fancy, though "Odysseus" does resemble the not too common epic verb *odussomai*, which seems always to mean "angered at." Some critics would prefer to render it "object of anger," in view of the hostility that Odysseus excites in the course of the story, but the linguistic evidence does not really support that meaning. Then again, "Odysseus" may mean simply Anger, both the object and the source. He who is angry invites anger, and he who is the object of anger has usually bestowed it; the name works either way. The narrator has linked the name to the scar as though it were an external mark of the psychic blemish that is the state of anger or that the object of anger may acquire. The lines are enigmatic, hinting at the stranger side, the unheroic side of Odysseus's nature. His covert, dishonest, always distanced, and slightly hostile behavior is perhaps the natural manifestation of deep-seated anger. How ironic it is that the narrator of the *Iliad* has for his subject the anger of Achilles, which is finally the deep-seated anger at having to die, and here the narrator uncovers anger far deeper in the human psyche, the existential anger at having been born. Autolycus was, of course, only one grandfather; Zeus was the other. Still, it is Autolycus whom the narrator identifies. Notice that this passage, a digression of some length, sits in the narrative more or less in symmetry with the fourth book's description of Proteus (4.351–570), a creature who is constantly transforming himself until pinned down and forced to hold one shape. Through the medium of Eurycleia, who gazes upon the scar on the leg, the narrator holds Odysseus fast and reveals the innermost secret of his identity. The story of the scar can be a paradigm for Western man's peculiar dissatisfaction and disenchantment, the very psychological state that made Eve eat the apple.

Like Proteus, who contrives a kaleidoscopic succession of identities, Odysseus, once back at Ithaca, on four occasions gives a fictitious account of himself—yet perhaps not entirely fictitious, for they provide insights into how Odysseus sees himself, how he functions as a narrator of self, or the self he would be. Many have noted, for instance, that the events of these fictitious autobiographies parallel one another; furthermore, they are lodged firmly in the historical reality of the Achaean saga world, whereas many of the travel stories record events or creatures beyond the realm of human experience. The travel tales have from the very first been introduced so as to excite suspicion of their verisimilitude.

"Now then do not be devious in your answers to what I am about to ask you; it is far better to speak out," says Alcinous (8.548f.), when finally after some thousand suspenseful lines Odysseus's uncontrollable grief at Demodocus's song has given the king an opening for the question his guest has been so studiously avoiding. The court's long-felt suspense is echoed in the longest introduction ever to such a question from host to guest. Everything is poised for a great recital. Odysseus's initial reply emphasizes the majesty and artistry of what he will say. He talks of bards and the pleasure they bring people. This is the greatest joy at banquets. Slowly, rhetorically, by question, by advertisement, he builds to the revelation of his name. The prelude is so artfully contrived, so obviously and consciously so, that Odysseus seems actually to be supplanting Demodocus. The banquet is finished; we are in Alcinous's throne room. Demodocus finishes, and another entertainer begins. In earlier scenes the narrator has already demonstrated Odysseus's skills at verbal manipulation; Odysseus has even lied outright in describing how he found Alcinous's palace. It is not clear that his propensities in this direction would raise suspicions, were it not that Alcinous has seemed somewhat suspicious from the outset, certainly much more so later on when he compliments his visitor's skill ("You have told it all out in sequence, with skill, just like a bard" [11.368]) and remarks how unlike the world's many liars and cheats Odysseus is. In this way the light of speculation is made to fall upon Odysseus's veracity. The Phaeacians gathered at Alcinous's banquet must be augmented by the audience that the narrator of this story has assembled for his performance. Throughout this passage the narrator becomes an actor as he impersonates Odysseus telling his story. The audience enjoys what Odysseus has to say as though he were a storyteller, clearly enough. When he begs off, saying he is tired, Alcinous will have none of it, so on the man goes: "Alcinous, . . . there's a time for these long speeches, and then there's a time for sleep. But, if you insist . . ." (11.379–80). Arete even proposes to offer gifts as a mark of respect for his brilliant storytelling, just like those offered a successful bard.

It may be, however, that what is important here is the skill with which the speaker makes his identification, not the identification that he makes. In modern-day Crete there are country settlements whose residents applaud a brilliant narrative description offered by a stranger as identification, despite what may be perceived as inadequate or false facts. Perhaps in the many isolated centers of the ancient world where the chances for amusement or excitement were very few, the group who received any stranger demanded to be amused by his narrative as much as or more than to be given honest information about him. This is not an idle consideration; it may strike at a far more profound truth in the *Odyssey* narrative. The many scenes in which newly arrived persons must identify themselves are a simulacrum of the experience of everyday life, in which everyone is called upon to adjust his or her personality in some fashion in order to interact successfully with the persons encountered. Insofar as this is true, all persons contrive slightly fictitious autobiographies to suit the scene. Or more to the point, each person contrives a personality for the particular circumstance. There is no core person. Each of us is Nobody.

One might also claim that none of the autobiographical narratives that Odysseus delivers at Ithaca is really false because each one is made from ingredients of his own life and personality. In each of the fictions he offers to Athena, Eumaeus, Antinous (and the suitors in general), Penelope, and Laertes, he uses the same context: namely, that he is of a princely family on the island of Crete. He insists on an aristocratic background, either because it is true to the real Odysseus or because the narrator imagines that there is an aristocratic cast to his features which even beggary cannot hide; he has Menelaus say to Telemachus and Pisistratus: "The race of your fathers is not lost in you. You are of the race of god-nourished kings, the sceptered ones, since the lower orders could not have produced ones such as you" (4.62ff.). It is a not implausible notion, considering that in the ancient world the vast difference between the prenatal care and later food supply and work load of the two classes of people would make for sharp physical distinctions. Or perhaps Odysseus uses the aristocratic origin, as beggars the world over have done, to elicit sympathy. In other words, it may be part of the routine that Odysseus as beggar knows his auditor would be disappointed not to hear. He is always a family man as well in these stories, true to the peculiarly strong homing instinct in this hero. And he is often a victim; in one story someone of greater importance tries to force Odysseus to serve under him, and elsewhere his half-brothers try to do him out of an inheritance. He presents himself as an outcast when he claims to be the bastard but best-loved child of a ruler surrounded by jealous legitimate brothers (a male Cinderella, no less). He describes a misfit when he says he cannot serve another because he is too talented, or recounts how he, penniless, acquires a rich wife on his own merits. He is the runt as the younger brother of Idomeneus, and aware that he is not as competent or heroic. He is unheroic when he kills one man by night in a sneak attack, and again when he sees that a battle is being lost, throws away his shield, and turns suppliant before the conquering general.

The psychological facts of these stories coincide so well with the character traits given Odysseus by both the *Iliad* and the *Odyssey* that this man disguised as a beggar seems finally and paradoxically to be creating truth out of fiction. The narrator emphasizes that Odysseus is conscious of himself in almost every one of the stories. Certain elements of them are veiled allusions to events of the travels. For instance, going to Dodona to consult the oracle of Zeus (14.327; 19.296) is the equivalent of the underworld journey to Tiresias; the attack on his reconnoitering and plundering crew in Egypt (14.259ff.) resembles the real crew's experience of the Lastrygonians and others; and the mutiny of that crew is analogous to Odysseus's men's attempts to thwart his plans. It is easy enough to understand that the oral poet uses bits and pieces of stories available in his memory as he fashions these autobiographical tidbits, but it is also worth remarking that the *Odyssey* narrative does seem to be fashioned somehow more attentively or self-consciously than that of the *Iliad*. One sometimes has the impression, though perhaps it is overly sophisticated to consider this, that in using the themes of reality and unreality the poet is trying to bring out the paradox that fiction is often more truthful than reality, or that unreality can be a means to truth. Hesiod's Muses tell him (*Theogony* 27–28) that they know how to tell false things as though they were true, although they can also tell true things. That is a distinction the *Iliad* poet would not, one feels, understand, since the tradition with which he deals, which he transmits, which lies at the ready in his brain, is the truth, the final truth about the past. Perhaps the *Odyssey* poet, by contrast, or the poets of the tradition in its evolution, were beginning to deal with the momentous fact of what fiction is and how it can construe a reality stronger and more likely than can empirical evidence. It is notable that the first of those Hesiodic lines is used (with suitable grammatical changes) by the *Odyssey* narrator to describe Odysseus's speech to Penelope: "He knew how to say many false things as though they were true" (19.203).

The travel adventures that Odysseus tells the Phaeacians seem to be largely fairy-tale material, although it is also possible to locate several elements of the Gilgamesh story there. Cyclops is much like the giant Humbaba; Circe is partly a malign erotic force not unlike Ishtar; Tiresias in the journey to the underworld is the Greek equivalent of Utnapishtim; the crew who offend the god and die for it are like Enkidu, who threw the thigh bone at the god. Only Siduri is not in the travel tales, although she verges on a combination of Nausicaa and Calypso. But it has been suggested that the Gilgamesh elements in the travel tales are traditional and that the *Odyssey* audience would recognize them as such and thus consider each tale a fiction on Odysseus's part rather than a true story of his adventures. He would be giving them a routine. In that sense he might be doing what, as we mentioned, the modern-day Cretan audience expects of visitors: telling a very good tale and wrapping himself into it in order to give it context.

The Calypso story is a prelude. Calypso means "concealer"; mechanically, she performs as such for the narrator, keeping Odysseus away from Ithaca long enough to allow Telemachus to grow up and assume the place he must take in this story. Calypso seems to be no more than a pallid imitation of Circe, simply a plot device ready to hand. Yet the description of the natural setting surrounding her is unusual for Greek poets, who tend to prefer to describe the man-made rather than the natural world except in simile. It is a fantastic garden setting, a kind of natural-world equivalent of Alcinous's fantastic fairytale palace. Calypso's complaint that male gods get to keep their women, whereas female gods suffer when they want their men, turns into a very abbreviated list of women whose men have died on them; it is reminiscent of the list of men who have been damaged as a result of sleeping with the female deity Ishtar, the list used by Gilgamesh to decline her invitation to bed.

The Calypso episode is the introduction to Odysseus, who is first seen weeping on the shore of Calypso's island, longing for Ithaca. Calypso, while talking with Hermes, shows herself to be a warm, agreeable creature who loves Odysseus; she is generous when she tells him that she will not only let him go but help him, too. Yet Odysseus's immediate reaction to the woman with whom he has been sleeping and sharing a life for seven years is mistrust. He next realizes aloud that going by raft, as Calypso has directed, will not be easy. His mental agility sets him in contrast to the stereotypic Homeric epic characters, who have a habit of accepting without question the direction or management imposed upon them by divine or semidivine beings. His suspicious nature is such that he forces her to swear that she intends him no harm. A man who is alert, suspicious, aggressive, and quick to understand all the ramifications of the moment—this is the image of Odysseus which emerges from his first speech in reply to the goddess Calypso. Her reaction is the same as that of Menelaus when Telemachus speaks up aggressively and assertively in rejecting the gift of horses, or of Athena when she catches Odysseus in his lie to her: she smiles and strokes his hand. In some way she surrenders.

Directly after swearing in the solemn and awful fashion prescribed for deities, she cozily talks of her compassion, they wander home, and she herself proceeds to serve him his dinner, although there are maids who perform the same task for her.

She is ready to make one last pitch: forecasts of great suffering, an offer of immortality if he stays, the prospect of a bed partner sexually superior to what he may expect at Ithaca. His response begins as a diplomat's would. True enough, he concedes, Penelope cannot compare, yet I must go home. In this momentous scene, the first meeting with the central figure of this poem, he is shown rejecting immortality. It is the key to understanding him and the values of the entire narrative. Odysseus accepts human life over anything else. True to the comic spirit that animates the narrative everywhere, the superiority of humanness to everything else is insisted upon. That is what is meant when the comic spirit is defined by the vague expression "saying yes to life."

Having affirmed human life over everything else, Odysseus is fully prepared for the suffering that Calypso has forecast. It is part of living. The contrast with his crew could not be more profound. Eurylochus, a distant relative of Odysseus and his second in command, is set up by the narrator to represent the craven human attitude toward life. The Greek words for good and bad, *kalos* and *kakos*, also meant beautiful and ugly or, more basically, beautiful and cowardly. The distinction is fundamental in a society of action-oriented physically strong men who defend or attack. Either they are physically beautiful, strong, stalwart, eager, joyous, tough, aggressive, sure of themselves, and arrogant, or they are craven, physically inept, socially unacceptable, retiring, unimportant, whining—wimps, nerds, or nebbishes, take your pick. Again to repeat the words of Jesus, "To them that have shall be given, from them that have not shall be taken away," or "Many are called, but few are chosen."

Eurylochus begins to get on Odysseus's nerves when they are on Circe's island. After he and Circe have had their night together and she has returned his swinish crew to their human shapes, he goes back to the ships to get the rest of the crew to come up for the banquet promised to all. Eurylochus begins to complain that they will only let themselves in for trouble (10.431–37). He reminds them of the disaster in the cave of the Cyclops. Odysseus thinks to kill him then and there to shut him up, he tells his Phaeacian audience, but the rest of the crew calm him and promise that they will come, leaving Eurylochus behind—though once they set out, of course, Eurylochus insists upon coming, too. He is a type common throughout history, psychiatrists must have a name for it. Later, when they are on the island of the Sun God and strictly enjoined from eating his cattle, it is Eurylochus who convinces the crew to do so as they slowly begin to starve (12.340–51). Death by starvation, he points out, is most hideously painful. Better to eat the cattle and suffer instant death from the god's retribution than endure this slow torture. In other words, he counsels a kind of suicide. Odysseus represents a love of life so extreme that every experience of it, including suffering and finally death, is valuable and desirable. Eurylochus demonstrates another extreme, what one might call lust for existence, and when that is threatened or no longer seen as whole, then better to be snuffed out. Eurylochus, the craven, would opt for any system that promised him immortality, one imagines, even though as Achilles describes it in the underworld scene it is entirely horrible.

Odysseus rejects immortality after he has visited the underworld, where Tiresias has told him that death from old age will come gently to him. It is, of course, an interesting critical question in the comprehending of orally generated narrative whether that which is chronologically prior but narrated later is truly earlier or later for the auditor. It seems most likely that it is later, since unless the narrator makes a point of it, that kind of temporal perspective is lost in the ongoing flow of episodes, each of which stands so briefly in an evanescent present. In that case, the priority of Tiresias's prophecy is of little consequence. One could say, instead, that a man can be promised a happy old age *only* after having rejected immortality.

The narrator sets up Achilles, Agamemnon, and Ajax as a contrast to Odysseus. The first cries out: "Don't speak to me of death. . . . I'd rather be a day laborer, migratory worker on earth . . . than lord of all the dead in the underworld" (11.488–91). The gray nothingness of this underworld is not for the vigorous Achilles. Agamemnon can only complain of his murder, as though the ugly manner in which he died has canceled out all his life, true to the commonplace Greek saying "Never count a man happy until he is dead," since up to the last moment some ugly event might negate the previous good. Ajax refuses to speak because, as we know from other sources for the saga tradition, the army assembly voted to give Achilles' armor to Odysseus instead of to him. Depressed, bitter, and enraged: these are the outcomes of the stereotypic emotional stances of *Iliad* warriors. Odysseus talks with them and moves on. The narrator who has placed him in a very different kind of poem has also endowed him with a very different philosophy of life. After he has fought with the beggar Iris in a boxing match that is a parody of the test of physical skill and endurance of strong young men, a kind of perversion that the constraints and accidents of life bring to decrepit beggars, he tries to talk some sense into Amphinomus, one among the suitors who had just been laughing and egging the old beggars on:

> Of all the things that breathe and crawl on this earth, nothing does earth produce of less consequence than man. For as long as the gods give him manliness and his knees work, he thinks that he won't suffer evil in the future. But when, as will happen, the blessed gods make things wretched, these too he must bear with an enduring spirit though he be suffering. For man's mind and disposition are no more or less than the father of men and gods causes them to be each day. . . . Wherefore let no man ignore the unwritten laws of the universe, but keep in dignity and silence whatever gifts the gods may happen to give. [18.131–37]

When Odysseus sets forth on his raft from Calypso's island, Poseidon blows up a frightening storm that nearly kills him. His struggle to maintain himself and keep his wits about him throughout this nightmare scene is an episode that ranks as Odysseus's *aristeia* in a poem that has no place for a formal one. The narrator introduces a significant number of similes, as though to give it the quality of battle narratives, which in the *Iliad* are heavily laced with similes. Odysseus is often praised for his endurance; indeed, he praises himself for his endurance. Throughout the travels, he must endure one misfortune or mental torture after another. Once back at Ithaca, the proud aristocrat dressed in beggar's clothing must endure the insults of young untried men and people of the serving class. He must endure sitting by his erstwhile wife, talking with her, hearing her cry. Odysseus's endurance in the storm scene of the fifth book is a marvel. He remains throughout a man aware and in control. When the nymph Ino offers him a lifesaving veil, he is instantly suspicious and does not accept it immediately in a frenzy of self-preservation. At the point of being driven to his death on surf-battered rocks, he continues to think logically and completely. His prayer to the river he finds flowing into the sea asks the customary sanctuary and protection offered to the wanderer and stranger. The human being as an alien in the natural world, having confronted the enemy in the storm, knows the rhythm of the universe. It is an extension of the skill and technique Odysseus previously showed on Calypso's island when he built the raft, a passage in which the narrator brought out all the vocabulary available for a truly detailed account. As Archilochus, a Greek poet of a slightly later date, said: "Rejoice not in your blessings nor grieve at your misfortunes, overmuch. Learn the rhythm that holds man." Even when he has been finally thrown up on shore, after suffering untold battering, privation, and total desolation, Odysseus still can reason with himself about where to hide for the night. The moment caps the entire episode that began with Odysseus on another shore, weeping, looking out to the sea. Nowhere else in epic does one get so quickly, so incisively established a character.

In the subsequent visit with the Phaeacians recounted in the next several books the narrator plays out the implications of this character. Nowhere else in the poem does he manage to create quite so perfect a comedy of manners; the subtlety of every line is breathtaking— perhaps the evidence most difficult to accommodate to the notion of a tradition as "author" of this poem. In the establishment of the story the two principal scenes will be Odysseus's account of his travels and the killing of the suitors. One way to handle these would be to have him kill the suitors and be reunited with Penelope, to whom he would then tell the travel tales. In the version we possess he does just this, of course. But the narrator paraphrases his account for the wife (in which by the way there is no mention by Odysseus to his wife of the Circe episode, where after a year he had to be torn from her bed by his complaining crew, who wanted to get home), having created instead a rehearsal version of these events in this marvelous Phaeacian episode, where Odysseus encounters a woman, vanquishes her suitors at games, and then proceeds to reveal himself and tell his story. The woman, of course, is Nausicaa; around their meeting the narrator has cast such an erotic nimbus that it perhaps resides as a subtext to the meeting of Odysseus and Penelope. The vanquished suitors are no more than the arrogant young lads of Scheria who laugh when the old seaworn stranger asks to join their games and are dismayed when he wins. The revelation and the story are Odysseus's legitimate star turn in this poem.

The Phaeacians, as remarked earlier, live in something like the biblical paradise, a never-never land like so many places Odysseus has visited during the travels he is soon to recount. The constant theme of these travels, as he tells them, is the temptation of curiosity: the disasters that result from surrendering to it, and the escape from them. The Telemachia, preceding this scene on Scheria, has described the process of growing up and learning. Odysseus comes to the Phaeacians as a stranger who learns how to handle himself among these alien people and at the same time to hold himself aloof from the temptation that is Nausicaa. The narrator describes the rich and embellished palace of Alcinous in all its fantastic detail as Odysseus approaches and goes in. It is somehow a replay of Telemachus, the country rube from Ithaca, mouth agape at the splendour of Menelaus's palace. Odysseus in never-never-land is a hero's adventure in its way, a tale that has had its own history, down to the ever so serious and complicated adventures of Alice in her wonderland and through her looking glass.

Having managed to extricate himself from the marital expectations of Calypso, Odysseus now requires all his tact to avoid the marital ambitions of Nausicaa and her family; an equal test of his endurance is, on the one hand, keeping himself from any erotic entanglement with the young girl and, on the other, not succumbing to the temptation to stay. The temptation of Scheria is very real. For a traveling man in middle years the prospect of a teenaged virgin as a bride and the throne of her father in the future, all of which represents the commonplace male ecstatic fantasy of starting all over again, is probably harder to resist than the lure of immortality. If Odysseus has rejected sexual bondage in saying goodbye to Calypso, now he denies himself the sexual renewal that a partner such as Nausicaa promises.

In his dealings with Nausicaa, Odysseus displays supreme sensitivity, grace, and intelligence; the episode is as subtle and complicated as his reunion with Penelope. The Nausicaa episode has a frame that begins with the narrator's comparison of the young Phaeacian princess to Artemis, the virginal, chaste, and robust goddess, which Odysseus repeats in his initial speech to the girl: "If you are a goddess . . . I myself would compare you to Artemis" (6.150ff.) Not only does this emphasize the Artemis quality of Nausicaa, but also, in reiterating the narrator's comparison, Odysseus is made to demonstrate that he is altogether the narrator's equal in creating the story, thus foreshadowing the travel tales soon to follow. The frame closes with Demodocus's story of Aphrodite and Ares caught in bed together, (8. 266–366) in which quite the opposite qualities were presented: indulgent sensuality, foolish adultery, and public scandal. Shortly after

Demodocus has delivered this song, Nausicaa says farewell to Odysseus. In the entire episode she is almost a protagonist. She tries to seduce Odysseus, politely enough, to be sure, and she rejects him at the end. That she is alert first to the possibility of marriage and later to its impossibility marks her as one of the cleverest, most sensitive young girls in literature. Nausicaa is yet another instance of the narrator's insistent valorization of intelligence, sensitivity, and verbal skill.

The initial meeting between Odysseus and Nausicaa is both charming and intensely erotic. Athena brings to the sleeping girl a dream command to wash clothes for her impending wedding: "You won't remain a maiden very long. You are already being courted by the best men among the Phaeacians" (6.33–34). Nausicaa, awake, alludes to her bachelor brothers' need for fresh clothes, for, as the narrator remarks, she is too shy to speak of her own possible marriage. It is a stage direction the narrator needs as well in order to motivate the carrying of items of male clothing to the beach; they must be there, of course, to clothe the naked Odysseus. Once the tensions between desire, propriety, and maidenly shyness have been established, this superb scene of human beings reacting to each other unfolds like a stage performance.

Nausicaa at play on the beach with her girlfriends has cast aside the veil with which young women protect their modesty. As the naked Odysseus emerges from his place of concealment, the narrator notes that he hides his genitals, thereby drawing attention to them. Odysseus's naked masculine predicament is further defined by his refusal to embrace Nausicaa's knees, the commonplace gesture of supplication. Again the narrator forces proximity, flesh upon flesh, into the imagination of the reader or auditor. Odysseus furthermore spurns the customary hospitable gesture, which Nausicaa offers, of being bathed by young women. This overt contradiction of the normal social rule now makes not only the narrator's audience but, one may imagine, the young women on the beach acutely aware of the stranger's situation. He is naked, alive, and—the male audience will instantly assume—desiring among desirable young girls. They are virginal and naive; his defenses are down; he seeks to prevent anything from rising.

The narrator has set this initial encounter (6.127ff.) into the context of an *androktasia* by comparing Odysseus as he emerges from hiding to a hungry lion as it comes to a pen of sheep—a simile of the type

and subject matter so often found in battle scenes. The girls are described as fleeing at the sight of him, except for Nausicaa "who stands
her ground" (139) as "Athena puts courage into her heart" (140)—
language taken from battle formulas. For the student of the history
of literature, this is the moment when the persistent image of love as
a battle, with the male lover as the attacking warrior and the female
recipient of his love as the beleaguered party, finds its first expression.
What marks this passage, however, is that the hungry lion of the
simile is almost instantly dependent on the sheep. He is given clothes,
directed toward the city, told what to do when arriving there. The
sheep tells her companions that he would make a wonderful husband;
she indicates as much to him by describing why she will not let him
enter the city with her. One almost imagines a sheep standing trium-
phantly with leg atop the recumbent body of the lion. The scene is
one of the great moments of double-talk in the brilliant comedy of
manners that unfolds among the Phaeacians and principally in the
royal household of King Alcinous.

Odysseus's visit to Polyphemus, the Cyclops (9.216ff.), is also a
tale of social behavior. Here, however, none of the rules that Odysseus knows applies. He brings wine as a conventional response to
the hospitality that he imagines to find. The gesture rewards him,
however, since it is the wine that makes the Cyclops drunk and
thereby ensures his escape. The entire nightmare visit is a surrealistic
revision of men in groups, banqueting, the reception of strangers,
and the rules of hospitality. As in his initial experience with Circe,
Odysseus is made to confront a perversion of everything he knows.
Just as Telemachus emerges from the perversion of human behavior
that the suitors are enacting in his childhood home to encounter
proper behavior at Pylos and Sparta, so his father leaves behind a
lifetime of conventional social behavior to meet with the perversion
of it in the fairytale world of his travel adventures. Odysseus is constantly tempted by his curiosity. It brings him to Polyphemus's cave
(and indeed to the disaster there, for once the place is reconnoitered
and found empty, the crew wish only to steal some food and go,
while Odysseus demands that they stay); it is curiosity that sends
him among the Lastrygonians; it is curiosity that drives him to stand
tied to the mast listening to the enchanting Sirens while his crew rows
on.

The visit with Aeolus contrasts Odysseus with his crew. His curiosity is satisfied by talking with the god of the winds, whereas the

crew cannot wait for departure and Odysseus's nap so that they can open the sack of winds in the mistaken, greedy, and imprudent notion of finding gold therein. Imprudent as the crew may be, they are frequently the victims of Odysseus. Members of the crew are sent ahead unwillingly to the Lastrygonians only to satisfy their master's curiosity, and the crew is later destroyed and eaten except for those who escape with the ship. He cheers on his men in the only language they understand: "Come now, while there's food and drink on the swift ship, let us think of food" (10.176f.). Later, he forces some to investigate the smoke he spies on Circe's island, obdurate before their tears ("But nothing came of their crying," he can coldly, or perhaps even cheerfully, tell the Phaecians [10.202]), and once more those who are sent ahead are ruined, again through eating.

The narrator outlines in these travel stories what was no doubt the truth of social distinctions of the time as seen by those who were or who served aristocrats. The people were only so many bodies to be used, thought to be motivated by nothing more than the basic needs of hunger and other elemental wants, not worthy of devotion or respect or even simple good will. Persons such as Eumaeus and Eurycleia, on the other hand, by virtue of their slavish devotion to their masters, are accorded some affection. Consider how the narrator in the fourteenth book gives to Eumaeus a speech in praise of Odysseus. Of course, this establishes that Eumaeus is to be trusted in the coming battle, but more to the point it functions as any Uncle Tom–like speech from the mouth of a house slave in the American antebellum South: it shows that the "good" enslaved people are happy with their masters. To speak of the crew as victims is to set them up as in some way parallel to the suitors. In reality, however, though the original audiences for this narrative no doubt could see the suitors as to some extent the victims of Penelope and Odysseus, it is doubtful that the victimization of the crew would occur to them on a conscious level. As a matter of broad comedy the image of a group of stupid, crude, silly men, many certainly inferiors, shivering with fear, getting into trouble, and even dying must have provoked many a good laugh.

But Odysseus himself at last gets his comeuppance when he meets Penelope as husband to wife. The narrator has used the simile of a goldsmith gilding a silver object to describe how Athena improved on Odysseus's good looks when he emerged from his bath, clothed in pieces of Nausicaa's brothers' laundry. Now he repeats the simile to describe Odysseus—once he has washed off the blood and gore of the slaughtered suitors—as he proceeds to woo his wife of many years. Penelope is utterly suspicious of the stranger and resists, repeating Nausicaa's initial stance on the beach. But like Nausicaa she takes command. The woman who is finally the combination of the superior assurance and intelligence of Helen and Arete, the mysterious power and danger of Circe and Calypso, the appealing sexuality of all these women (best rendered in Nausicaa's virginity, the always thrilling challenge to a male that such innocence represents)—this woman, the wife, Penelope, for twenty years dependent on the hope of her husband's return, forces him to reveal himself in a way that will be satisfactory to her (23.177ff.). For once he will not win the day with an autobiography or a travel story. Penelope bids Eurycleia to make up their bed outside the bedchamber; she is lying and stage-acting as only her husband has previously succeeded in doing. And he, a master craftsman who knows the secrets of bed building and had himself constructed this bed as an immovable object inside the chamber, this man who has always been in control, identifies himself by the spontaneous, unguarded, shocked response to her command to have the bed moved outside. Suddenly many things come together: the knowledge and craft with which he constructed the marriage bed; its permanence, like the determination of the two of them to be together again; their knowledge of it, which like the conjugal knowledge of two long-time wed persons is unique and not replicable; her utter control of the situation, which is the culmination of womanly determination and domination throughout the narrative. Penelope and Odysseus, like the star-crossed lovers of romance narrative, are together again.

No one can ever know Penelope in any depth, because the narrator is finally not much interested in women as persons. But Odysseus, despite the fact that he responds exactly the same way to each situation, earning from narratologists the definition of monolithic, is a character on the way to being fully realized. What is presented by the narrator who promises at the beginning to concentrate on the man, the "man of many turns," is probably the best representation of pagan man in all of Greco-Roman literature.

Masking inward joy with outward cool, humble in his understanding of the powers that hold humankind, arrogant in his assumption of his own worth, sociable and personable toward every kind of person though never sympathetic, always private, sensual, and fastidious, cruel and cunning, serious and dignified, Odysseus is the superlative role model for the males of the ancient world. The fifth-century Athenian tragic dramatists grew to be ambivalent in portraying him; they hinted at a cynical and corrupt person. Their hints found considerably stronger expression in the conceptions of Renaissance Christian poets and playwrights, grounded as they were in ideas of good and evil, heroism and villainy; from them was realized an Odysseus or, better, a Ulysses essentially alien to archaic and classical Greek culture.

· 6 ·

The *Argonautica*

She would have taken out her soul from her breast,
and given it to him, so thrilled was she at his desiring her.
Desire cast its sweet flame out from Jason's blond head;
It captured her gleaming eyes. Her wits relaxed in the warmth,
melting, fading, as the dew fades, warmed in dawn's early rays.

—Argonautica 3.1016–21

Relentless Love, great bane of the human race, abomination,
from you comes destructive strife, come groans and lamentations,
from you come countless woes to trouble and cause confusion.

—Argonautica 4.445–47

Tradition had it that the sixth-century Athenian tyrant Pisistratus established the custom of reciting the *Iliad* and the *Odyssey* at the Panathenaic Festival. Whatever the truth of that tradition, it is probably fair to say that as the sixth century B.C.E. came to its end, the Homeric poems had become an institution. And one might also assume that the original social needs and aesthetic impulses that had led to creating epic poetry were by this time beginning to dissipate. But the Homeric poems, which seem to have been universally acknowledged as superior to all other epic poetry, were valuable as cultural icons. Their preservation became almost a religion. On the island of Chios, for instance, there appeared a guild known as the Homeridai, "the men of Homer" (if not "the fans of Homer"), who took it upon themselves to maintain an authoritative tradition of the recitation of the poems. It is said that they preserved the original pronunciation of the *Iliad* and the *Odyssey* down to Alexandrian times.

As noted earlier, we have little knowledge and only minimal fragments of the works of the epic poets who created a series of poems that more or less systematized the saga and myth tradition of the early Hellenes. The poems of the Epic Cycle for the most part filled in the gaps in the story line from the origin of the world to the death of Odysseus, which might be called the end of the heroic age. They were widely read and influential; seven or eight centuries later the Roman poet Virgil seems to have composed the second book of his *Aeneid* from material contained in the so-called *Ilioupersis* (The fall of Troy). Four centuries after Virgil a Greek poet, Quintus of Smyrna, took some of the material of the Epic Cycle to create a poem called *Posthomerica* (What came after Homer), in which he scrupulously reproduced the narrative style of the Homeric poems. It is probable that the Epic Cycle poems were valued more as repositories of the ancient stories than anything else. The Hellenistic poet and critic Callimachus did not like them as poetry, complaining that the poems of the Epic Cycle depended for their coherence and fluency on the very mechanical narrative device of "and then."

The literary history of Greece in the fifth century B.C.E. is marked by the emergence of tragic drama and history writing. Both literary forms are a logical extension of the process of epic poetry. As collections of ancient stories in an age still barely literate and with minimal access to the written word, the poems of the Epic Cycle along with the Homeric poems constituted the archival record of the Hellenes. The historians took this material, particularized it, endowed it with motives, space, and time. As highly stylized, conventional narratives depicting stereotypic people in stereotypic scenes, the epic poems constituted a manual of behavior for archaic Greece. Tragedy mythologizes this conventional epic action by severely restricting details and rigidly schematizing action, thereby taking it one step further into abstraction.

Throughout the fifth century, epic poetry continued to be sung, and some new epic poems were even written. Apart from the Homeridai, professional singers known as *rhapsodes*, recited parts of epic poems at festivals and at other public gatherings. We have a portrait of such a man in Plato's dialogue *Ion*. The reader who gets past the ridiculous line of argument with which Socrates harasses poor Ion discovers a *rhapsode* who is a thoroughgoing professional, dedicated to his art and to the poetry of Homer.

A poetic form as routine, automatic, and unoriginal as epic had become either dies or is revised and reconstrued. In the late fifth century a certain Antimachus of Colophon composed *Thebais*, an epic poem, narrating the first expedition against Thebes. Antimachus borrowed from the style of the early epic poets but reordered his material to give it new meaning. He varied the language and development; he introduced new forms, stylistic elements from other genres, and every other kind of obscurity. It must have been an awful poem, even if an interesting commentary on literary practice and genre. Unfortunately, the surviving fragments of *Thebais* have been preserved because they illustrate its oddities; these tend to reinforce its idiosyncrasy. But Callimachus himself pronounced the poem slow and pedantic. One might argue that Antimachus shared Euripides' preoccupation with what Ezra Pound was forever enjoining his contemporaries to do: "Only make it New." This last of the great fifth-century tragic playwrights is remarkable for reconstituting the stories of tragic drama. Euripides' *Alcestis* and *Electra* and *Orestes* are dramas in which the characters act out behavior that is implicit in the legends but scarcely explicit or conventional. Compare Euripides' portrait of Alcestis, a wife who is willing to die for her husband only after making some rather harsh demands upon him, with Phaedrus's far more conventional description in Plato's *Symposium* of her thoroughly self-sacrificing wifely act of altruism.

From the vantage point of the twentieth century c.e., Antimachus seems to presage the third-century b.c.e. literary and cultural movement that literary historians call Alexandrianism. The term derives from the city of Alexandria, founded in 332 b.c.e. by the Macedonian king and conqueror Alexander himself on the Egyptian shores of the Mediterranean. After his death in 323 his general, Ptolemy, consolidated the position of the Greek-speaking conquerors in Egypt and made himself the ruler. He adopted the style of the Pharaohs and ruled absolutely, something new for Greeks, who were used either to illegal tyrants of dubious authority or to democratic city-states. But Ptolemy's philosophers were able to legitimate his position by language and logic from which descends the theory of the divine right of kings, which accounts for the words *Dieu et mon Droit* on the arms of the English royal family as well as for the pope's claim to be the Vicar of Christ on Earth.

Ptolemy chose to legitimate not only his royal person but also the colonial city of Alexandria, a Greek-speaking entity surrounded by Egyptians. He strove to make it a kind of new Athens, looking not to the declining city of the fourth century but back to what the self-advertising fifth-century Athenians characterized as their glorious experiment in democracy, art, and literature. He invited Demetrius of Phalerum, who had been involved in the Athenian school of Aristotle, to come to Alexandria and create a library. The Library and the so-called *Museion* (our word is "Museum"; at Alexandria it was a kind of think tank for scholars) attached to it deeply influenced all the literature produced in Alexandria during this most productive third century. In Western literary history the Alexandrian period is most important not only for what was produced but for the highly influential literary critical theories that arose then.

Ptolemy and Demetrius set out to collect copies of everything written in the Greek language. Eventually the Library contained 700,000 papyrus rolls, the largest collection in the world for a very long time to come. As noted earlier, the word for roll in Greek is *biblion*, generally translated as book, which is why so many ancient works are divided up into what are called "books" rather than "chapters." The division of the *Iliad* and the *Odyssey*, which are of such unequal length, into the same number of books seems artificial. Further artificiality appears in their each being divided into as many books as there were letters in the conventional Athenian alphabet. The divisions seem more obedient to the arbitrary logicalities of a library system than to the aesthetic principles of a poet, poets, or a poetic tradition. The problem of book division, like the aesthetic question of framing a painting, must have engaged the writers of the Alexandrian Age. In fact, the book divisions of the *Argonautica* seem to be speaking to this problem

The librarians who gathered the papyrus rolls and disposed them in the collection were at pains to authenticate and classify the texts. Remarks in the margins of Homeric manuscripts reveal that scholars of the time were concerned to remove from the poems lines that they believed offensive either to the Homeric manner, to the nature of epic poetry, or at times, obviously, to the scholars themselves. They wanted to delete Achilles at his most selfish when he is demanding that Patroclus not take too much glory for himself, Thetis telling Achilles to get over Patroclus's death by sleeping with a woman, Zeus being excessively violent, Dionysus described as afraid, and an entirely too tedious (to an Alexandrian whose medium was reading) ten-line verbatim repetition. Concerns such as these betoken an overriding emphasis on genre and concern for poetic decorum.

We are fortunate in having fragments of poetry by Callimachus, whose critical theories set the standard of poetry for the age and greatly influenced the Romans when they discovered the Alexandrian Age two centuries later. His major work was a poem of seven thousand lines called *Aetia* (Causes), about the origins or causes of things. Like Hesoid's *Works and Days* and *Theogony*, the poem reveals the antiquarian mind of its author, a collector of lore and curiosities, far more interested in fact than in fiction. So far as we can tell from the fragments, the poem was episodic, a grand catalogue more than anything else. His celebrated poem *Hecale* is in dactylic hexameters, a meter that immediately suggests heroic narrative, but it is heroic in miniature, since there are no more than a thousand lines. Here again Callimachus plays with conventional narrative values by skewing the focus. The story concerns Theseus coming to fight the bull of Marathon. Whereas a traditional narrative describing heroic action would have concentrated on the labor of Theseus—and there were many poems on such themes—this narrator spends the greater amount of time recounting Theseus's visit to an old woman, Hecale, and describing the dinner she serves him. The contest with the bull is casually sandwiched between that episode and Theseus's return to Hecale's house, where he finds her dead. The conclusion of the poem is a description of Theseus's grief and the rites instituted in the old woman's honor.

Callimachus calls for poetry that is brief, peeled down to the essence; he wants a sound that is clear and pure. He uses the images of a clean path, of priestesses bringing their water from the clear spring and not the muddied river, of the path untrod by the many, a narrow path where carts cannot go. Elegance, economy, refinement, and novelty, especially novelty, are the operative terms of the Callimachean aesthetic. As his parodies of the archaic Homeric hymns suggest, he also urged wit, that eighteenth-century term for the elegant juxtaposition of the incongruous. An amused tone, altogether foreign to the high seriousness of archaic and fifth-century Greek literature, permeates almost everything written in the Alexandrian Age.

Little remains of the enormous literary production of that age. There are fragments, but few complete works. Theocritus's pastoral poems, the notable invention of the period, survive intact. Alongside them, the most significant other work is the *Argonautica* of Apollonius Rhodius. We know very little about the life and times of Apollonius. He was born sometime in the early third century B.C.E., perhaps at Alexandria. He studied with Callimachus. His career got off to a shaky start with a hostile reception of his *Argonautica*, but he was much esteemed later on. He may have spent time on the island of Rhodes (hence Rhodius in his name to distinguish him from every other Apollonius). He may have been tutor to the prince and heir to the throne as well as director of the Library. He may have quarreled with Callimachus. The paucity of information, most of it dubious, requires us therefore to dispense with the poet for our understanding of the poem.

It is probably best to lay to rest, however, the ancient tradition of a quarrel between Apollonius and Callimachus, since it accounts for a critical bias against the *Argonautica*. Modern scholarly critics have argued that Callimachus, Theocritus, all Callimachus's disciples must have considered the poem an entire contradiction of Callimachus's aesthetic principles: it was too long, too imitative of Homeric epic, too dependent on a conventional story line for its coherence—in sum, not original, new, different. But the many Callimachean and Theocritan quotations in the *Argonautica* might suggest quite the opposite, that Apollonius was insisting on his adherence to the Callimachean ideal. Then, too, a 5,835-line poem is scarcely long when compared with the *Iliad* or the *Odyssey*, which are more than twelve and fifteen thousand lines respectively. In the *Poetics* Aristotle had said that the successful new-style epic poem must be far shorter than the typical old epics; it should approximate "the size of tragedies performed for one hearing." If he meant the time allotted to the three tragedies and one satyr play that were performed at one continuous sitting at the Festival of Dionysos at Athens, then the four books of the *Argonautica*, each of them approximately the length of a typical tragedy, would satisfy his prescription.

Apollonius is far from imitating Homer, as anyone who reads the poem sympathetically can quickly see. But perhaps this is something only twentieth-century critics will recognize. For the author is recreating, rereading, reconstituting the Homeric poems after the fashion of the experimental twentieth-century painters and poets of the Modernist movement who have reconstituted the entire Western European tradition. It is true that the *Argonautica* demonstrates an immense knowledge of the Homeric poems and an intuitive understanding of the Homeric manner. The narrator's habit of playing off the Homeric originals requires that the reader know the *Iliad* and the *Odyssey* equally well. In addition, the work is studded with allusions to all aspects of the Greek world. Since the narrator demands a reader who is thoroughly familiar with Greek culture, the poem probably reflects, on the one hand, the insularity of the Greek-speaking population of Alexandria and, on the other, the obsessive exclusivity common to colonial elites.

This development marks an important turning point in literary history. In earlier epochs epic poetry and tragic drama were important forms of social communication, the characters and action in every instance emblematic of the culture at large; these art forms were completely accessible to the people. The Alexandrian poet did not strive to communicate with his audience so much as require the audience to understand the poet. The poet spoke exclusively to the Greek-speaking population; eventually, Hellenistic poets and their Roman followers spoke only to the *cognoscenti*—whence the Latin poet Horace's haughty declaration *Odi profanum volgus et arceo* ("I hate the people who must stand outside the temple door [i.e. the uninitiated] and distance myself from them"). One might say that this is the true stance of serious twentieth-century art, music, poetry, and criticism as well. Modernism, as this elite culture is known, has had a very different history from Greco-Roman Alexandrian elitism, however. Apollonius's uninitiated were first of all the non-Greek-speaking population surrounding Alexandria and in its foreign ghettos. Horace's uninitiated were the uneducated proletariat of the city of Rome. The masses of the twentieth century, however, are members of a consumer society that demands and can afford a vibrant alternative artistic, cultural experience in film, television, rock concerts, and the like. American Modernism has long since capitulated to it. As the consumer society goes global, so goes vulgar culture as well; it has a power and vitality that elite cultures around the world cannot withstand. Nothing like it has occurred in the Western world since the destruction of aristocratic pagan culture by the emergent ideology of Christianity.

The *Argonautica* is the story of Jason's voyage on the ship *Argo* to get the golden fleece at the command of his malevolent uncle Pelias. The first book describes the gathering of the crew (the Argonauts), in the form of a catalogue similar to that in the second book of the *Iliad*, and their setting sail; then come three quite unrelated episodes that establish Jason's role in this story. The second book is an account of the voyage to Colchis. It begins, however, with a boxing match in which the shining young hero Polydeuces defeats and kills the giant bogeyman Amycus. One might say that the narrator has positioned

Amycus at the beginning of Book Two as an obstacle. He stands as a kind of gatekeeper defying anyone who would enter the second book and the adventure of travel to be encountered there, as well as the world of love and danger thereafter. The boxing match ends in the triumph of shining youth, beauty, and goodness over ugly, old, brutish strength; this is the outcome one would expect in a story of Jason, the beautiful youth who triumphs through his charm and graceful manners over the demands of the harsh old King Aeetes, father of Medea. But the second book also presents the aged prophet Phineus, who tells the crew what direction their trip will take. As they proceed from place to place, what he has told them comes true, although sometimes with minor variations. The multiple versions of supposedly the same reality seem to betray an Alexandrian interest in narrative point of view. The voyage of the Argonauts takes them past many interesting peoples and places, most of them truly extraordinary and exotic, which the narrator describes after the fashion of an anthropologist or geographer from the temporal position of the reader. The narrator is thus ironically depicting men who are indeed out of a fable, or from heroic myth, as they pass through the so-called "real world," which is studded with descriptions relating to the reader's contemporary experience yet is a world so bizarre that it could be labeled fabulous even more reasonably than can the mythic men traveling through it. The third book is the story of how Medea's father, Aeetes, challenges Jason to an impossible contest of strength as the price of the fleece, of how Medea falls in love with Jason and decides to give him charms to help him in his contest with the bulls that guard the fleece, and of Jason's decisive success in the contest. The fourth recounts Medea's leaving home to join Jason, their getting the fleece, their flight from her father's army, her brother's murder, and then a series of episodes set in a landscape that evokes their mood until finally they return to Greece.

Callimachus could never accuse Apollonius of leaning on the stale narrative device of "and then," like the poets of the Epic Cycle. There is little attempt at making a story in this poem, other than in the breathtaking adventure of Jason and Medea in Colchis and later in flight. Essentially, the work is a reading of the Homeric poems in particular and epic poetry in general. As such it is quintessentially Alexandrian, mirroring the scholarly preoccupation with literary forms and stylistic authenticity. The age ushered in an entirely new way of looking at literature. Previous writers may have considered

their predecessors when they composed; certainly any society so traditional, in which the opinions of the old were privileged, would
encourage an originality based upon what had gone before. But just
as Ptolemy tried to recreate Athens in Alexandria, so the writers in
his capital city tried to recreate their literary past in their own writings.
Rather than through slavish imitation, however, these entirely original poets imitated through distancing, looked to the past by rereading
the past, and in their reading—that is, their willful misreading, their
deliberate perversion and parody of what had come before—they
recreated the past by demanding that their readers notice the difference between their models and what they made in seeming imitation.

The book divisions of the *Argonautica*, for example, require the
reader to reconsider the nature of continuous narrative and the aesthetics of arbitrary interruptions of it. Some features would startle or
at the least unsettle a constant reader of traditional epic poetry. The
Homeric poems, for instance, have been made to divide where episodes end in sunset and sleep, whereas Apollonius's first and second
books close with the sunrise and the commencement of new action,
which seems to be a kind of perversion of the notion of an ending.
The first, third, and fourth books begin with an invocation, calling
upon a deity for aid in narrating the story, but the symmetry of this
very conventional manner of introduction is flawed by the simple and
unadorned first line of the second book: "Here were the stables and
farms of Amycus." It is unlikely that a modern reader would even
notice this anomalous opening line; to someone who knows the constant symmetries of ancient literature, however, the raw, unadorned
beginning to the second book comes as a surprise.

In the first line of the first book the narrator calls upon Apollo to
help him with the story of the entire poem. A few lines later he calls
upon the Muses to act as interpreters in his telling of the first two
books of his poem. The third book commences with an appeal to the
Muse Erato to help the narrator tell the tale of the last two books.
This appeal stands in symmetry with the call to the Muses in the first
book. What is more, Erato is a love nymph and thus entirely appropriate for these books that focus on the love of Jason and Medea. The
beginning of the fourth book, however, is so peculiar that it threatens
the rationale of the entire scheme. The narrator calls upon both the
goddess of the *Iliad* and the Muse of the *Odyssey*, adding other words
that remind the reader of those texts. Then, having summoned up
this out-of-scale and intrusive aid to recitation which recalls the com-

mencement of two entire monumental narratives, he proceeds to ask a simple question that deals only with the immediate psychology of Medea: did she flee her home out of fear of her father or love for Jason? Then the narrator makes a very grammatical connection between this and the preceding book which is interesting for its subtle penetration of the narrative. The third book ends with a description of the angry Aeetes and a notice that night has fallen, an entirely conventional and thus satisfying conclusion. But the fourth book, after the overelaborate invocation, picks up Aeetes in a pronoun ("now he . . ."), as though the narrative of the fourth book were a seamless continuation of the third, just as the second book's first word "here" implies that there has been no break in the narration between Books One and Two. These several features cause the reader to stop, to notice, to ponder the form. And since the book divisions do not seem to clarify or reflect the narrative, the reader must think about the nature of the Apollonian books still further.

Consider, for instance, that the third book is often treated as though it were an independent whole. It alone is the truly popular book of the poem, sometimes printed separately as an individual story. As such it is unusual among the surviving pieces of ancient Greek literature because it builds to a climax at its conclusion. Yet of course the third book is not independent; the story continues, the traditional description of the action's outcome, the capture of the fleece, fills the first part of the fourth. Apollonius again demonstrates his amazing complexity in balancing the various elements of his story. The third book *seems* complete until we enter the fourth. Not only is the grammatical carry-over decisive in bonding the two narratives, but our hero has yet to get what he came for. Again, Jason *seems* to be the hero, the only hero, the true traditional centerpiece of the action, until in the middle of the third book Medea starts to debate her great moral choice. Suddenly all that is crucial is hers; she begins to emerge as Jason's equal. The reader is forced to make some adjustments. Thus, though the conventional *aristeia* with which the third book concludes *seems* to be also a conventional climax, it recedes in our interest, becomes the traditional postclimax or outcome; it is replaced by the love scene between the two principals, an *agon* moment of far more tension and movement, from which Jason's *aristeia* proceeds as a foregone conclusion. What is truly remarkable throughout the third and fourth books is that the poet manages to contrive a narrative in the third which has a theatrical beginning, middle, and end, is complete in itself, and yet when extended into the fourth book easily dissolves into a larger unity that culminates in the murder of Medea's brother Apsyrtus. Then in turn the narrator brings the reader into a still larger narrative structure that reaches back into the second book; the travels of the fourth parallel the travels of the second until, when finally we arrive again on shore ("you go ashore," the very last word of the poem), we are once more at the poem's beginning ("setting out," one of the two meanings of the first word of the poem). Suddenly a still greater overarching unity has been realized. Noticing this process of narrative was, we may assume, the way in which the Alexandrians intended their poetry to be addressed. For one thing, it requires *reading*, which makes for a response entirely different from that fostered by the traditional oral poems; for another, it requires the reader to take on the text as a problem in categorization and authenticity—just what one would expect of someone trained in a library.

The question the narrator asks his divine helpers at the beginning of the fourth book betrays his own ignorance of the events in his narration. We may recall that the *Iliad* narrator, after calling upon the Muse for his story, enters the narrative twice again to emphasize how difficult his task is; otherwise, the story proceeds on its own with an absolute authority. By contrast, the Apollonian narrator enters the poem often: he talks to the reader ("you would imagine . . . "); he lectures the reader about strange customs or unusual natural phenomena; he talks to his characters, bidding them farewell at the poem's end; he twice shows his human heroes calling upon a god, only to enter the narrative to address the deity himself as though he were presiding over the events on some Olympian plane similar to theirs.

Moreover, he omits information that the constant reader of Homer would expect to be given. For instance, in the opening lines of the poem the narrator mentions Pelias's fear of a man wearing one sandal, and then Jason arrives at Pelias's banquet shod in only one sandal. This brief notice is entirely, if not shockingly, un-Homeric. The details are omitted, particularly Jason's progress from the moment he lost a sandal in the river (which the narrator does mention) to the scene of his arrival at the banquet. Why didn't he stop to get another? we want to know. Later, when two members of the crew arrive at the beach after all the others are assembled, the narrator not only does not tell why they are late; he does not put one word in their mouths to account for their actions, and what is more, he says "Jason forebore to ask them." What is going on here? Why were they late? Why didn't Jason speak to them? Homer tells all; this narrator perhaps does not know, certainly will not tell. The reader is distanced from the narrative, which suddenly becomes the private property of the characters. Throughout this poem the characters preserve their privacy; whereas early epic presented only public figures who acted out their lives and spoke their thoughts completely to their audience, the Apollonian characters live at one remove. It is a feature of the early romance and the later novel that the characters are private individuals in this manner, and one may say that the Apollonian narrative looks forward to that genre of narration. If the *Odyssey*, as remarked earlier, has features associated with prose romance—most important, the star-crossed and separated lovers who struggle under a variety of fortunes and misfortunes to reunite—it is in the Alexandrian period that romance begins to take shape as an overtly fictional prose narrative, although our few surviving examples come from several centuries later.

The beach scene in which Argus and Acastus arrive late (1.317ff.) is also important as the moment in which the narrator begins to betray his hero. The Homeric narrator is almost perfectly consistent in his approval of Achilles or Odysseus; it is evident that they are superior to their fellows, that their actions reveal strength, authority, and intelligence. Even the gods with whom these heroes have such rapport are almost always approving. Consider, however, the beach scene in the *Argonautica:* "Jason stood there at the point of entering," says the narrator, "and all the heroes were gathered together opposite" (which is perhaps to say, in anticipation, or as a group facing someone singled out). In conventional epic narrative this language signals the designation of Jason as the centerpiece of the scene if not the story. But then Argus and Acastus arrive late; their clothing is described, and the narrator remarks that all the others marveled that they had come in defiance of Pelias. In several ways the narrator has taken the attention from Jason, has, as it were, upstaged him. What is more, when Jason thereafter calls upon the assembly to choose a leader, the reader naturally expects Jason to be named: first, because the myth tradition has Jason as the leader of the expedition to get the fleece, then because in the opening lines he has been mentioned as the central figure in this narrative, and finally because the arrangement of this scene conventionally requires it. But instead, the crew in one voice calls out for Hercules. The contradiction of expectation is exhilarating and witty, possibly witty enough to provoke a laugh, although one is never sure what made the ancient Greeks laugh. The perversion of the convention also reminds the reader of the extreme selfishness and narcissism of an Achilles or an Odysseus and in this fashion reconstructs yet more clearly the underlying truths of the earlier epics.

Hercules, of course, demurs; the narrator, riding the crest of the irony, has him magisterially insist, while remaining seated, that the crew choose Jason as the leader. Throughout the poem Jason's capacities as a conventional leader remain dubious. He cries, for instance, as they set sail, moments after the narrator has described Hercules entering the ship with such weight that it sinks significantly in the water. And Jason is never really sure of himself thereafter. The other episodes in the first book function as establishing scenes rather than standing as parts of an ongoing story. They show Jason inadequate in battle, splendid in bed; by the end of Book 1 his rival Hercules, the old-style military strongman, has left the narrative, thus ceding to Jason the authority that the reader and the narrator know would never otherwise be his.

Shortly after their departure the heroes arrive at the island of Lemnos (1.608ff.). Here is Jason's first triumph but as usual the narrator undercuts it by describing a situation of which Jason is not altogether the master. The narrator tells us that the women of Lemnos some years earlier killed off all their men in retaliation for their infidelities. Now, faced with a childless future, these women suddenly need men, just as the *Argo* sails opportunely into port. Jason and some others go ashore and up to the town to reconnoiter, recalling Odysseus's exploration of Circe's island. The difference is vast, however. Jason is equipped with a magnificent cloak upon which various scenes from myth are embroidered. He is beautiful; the women of Lemnos are excited by him and his men. A reminiscence of Circe's capacity for baleful enchantment perhaps resides in Princess Hypsipyle's lies to Jason about the absence of Lemnian men; she tells him something quite different from what the narrator had told the reader. But Jason stays with Hypsipyle until the much disapproving Hercules, who has remained on the beach with some of the crew, exercises sufficient moral force to cause the lovemaking men to leave their Lemnian beds and return to the *Argo*. Hypsipyle in tears bids Jason goodbye, asking to hear from him and expressing the hope that she is bearing his child. The conventional tears of goodbye, the wish for communication, and the hope of a tender remembrance of the departed lover in the shape of a baby have a somewhat unconventional effect when the reader remembers that these women are in desperate need of babies. For once, the tables are turned. The ancient Greek males traditionally married to have offspring; they viewed their wives as so many brood mares. Here it is the Lemnian women who have thoroughly exploited a band of visiting males for their semen.

Jason's success as lover is immediately set in balance with his misadventure as a warrior in the ensuing disastrous visit to the homeland of the young Prince Cyzikus, who greets and entertains Jason, his equally young guest. After the *Argo* sets sail again, a nighttime storm sends the ship back to the same shore. But with the land and people unrecognizable, Jason and his men are on the alert, while Cyzikus and his men fear an invading enemy. The two sides engage in battle, and Jason kills his erstwhile host. In describing this nightmare encounter, the narrator returns exactly to the language of Homer and reproduces a stock battle scene of the *Iliad* (1.1039ff.). The outcome is a perversion of a Homeric *androktasia*—by mistake a good man kills his friend. Once again the old-style epic poetry has failed this Alexandrian hero.

The final scene of the first book sets the stage for Jason's triumph as something other than the traditional warrior-hero. With the Argonauts' earlier instinctive call for Hercules as their leader, the narrator introduced into this very Alexandrian poem a reminder of the conventional hero of the tradition. Somewhat later, as the crew enjoys a picnic, a dejected and worried Jason sits by until a drunken crew member, Idas, jeers at him, deriding his fear. At the same time Idas brandishes his spear, claiming that his strength and his weapon are all that are needed. But as the reader knows and Jason will discover, spears and strength are not what is required to win the love of a woman who will provide the only means to yoke the magic bulls of Aeetes; it is sweet talk, diplomacy, politesse, and physical beauty. Gruff, tough Idas is an anachronism. So is Hercules, and he leaves the narrative in a significant way. The final scene of the first book describes the rape of Hylas, Hercules' young companion, by a nymph. (The ancients, we must remember, for reasons probably self-serving to the males, called any sudden, physically energetic act of possession—not always for sexual purposes—a rape, even if the "victim," either at the time or eventually, acquiesced in or actually enjoyed the attentions of the raper.) The episode poses a special historical problem for the reader because the story of the rape of Hylas is treated by Theocritus in the thirteenth of his Idylls, just as the opening scene of the second book is also to be found in a Theocritean version in the twenty-second. Since we have no way of knowing which version was prior, we cannot detect how the one plays off the other.

In any case, although Apollonius does not say so (Theocritus does), Hylas is Hercules' young male lover, taken away by him (indeed, raped) after Hercules, in one of his commonplace acts of violent aggression, has killed the boy's father. True to the almost universal custom in fifth-century Greece, Hercules not only nurtures Hylas and teaches him but also makes love to him. (It is not too much to say that behind the niceties of the story lies the brutal truth that in a world of minimal civic protection strong men could easily kill fathers in order to take their teenaged sons as docile servants and compliant sexual partners.) In the Apollonian scene Hercules goes into the forest and yanks a tree trunk out of the ground to replace the oar he has broken while trying to paddle too vigorously, while Hylas goes to the spring to get water for the evening meal. Their respective activities exactly mirror their relationship in all its sexual and psychological complexity. As the boy Hylas bends down to dip his pitcher into the spring, his skin glistening in the light of the moon, a nymph, captivated by his beauty, reaches up and draws him down under the water to make him her own (1.1228ff.). Hercules' companion, Polyphemus, hears the boy cry out and rushes in search of him, shouting to Hercules. The two in desperation go off to seek the boy, and eventually Jason determines that the *Argo* must sail on, leaving these archaic pederastic heroes behind.

Brilliant writing marks this episode; its sensuality leaves a lasting impression in the poem. For the boy, it is the transition from boyhood to heterosexually aware manhood. The cry that Polyphemus heard was perhaps Hylas's first orgasmic shout as he transferred his sexuality from the adolescent boy's penetrated anus to the adult male's ejaculating penis. Just as Jason seems to have lost his virginity with Hypsipyle, to have become authoritative and active through adult masculine sexuality, so Hylas, on the other side of the coin, has left the shelter and comfort of a strong male protector to be seduced into the vast unknown pool of water, and possibly to some kind of death, by a woman. Jason will replicate this frightening immersion in the unknown (3.1194ff.) when on the night before he meets the contest of the bulls, following Medea's instructions, he goes naked into a pool and then, wrapped in a robe given him by Hypsipyle, makes sacrifice to the dread goddess Hecate, whose frightening apparition Apollonius describes in detail.

Making love, not war, seems to carry the day in this poem, but it requires a special kind of courage for the male who must encounter a woman on her own terms. Ancient Greek males consistently repressed and exploited their womenfolk. The surviving literature is uniformly misogynistic, more often than not describing women as killers, betrayers, or at the least sexual predators who ensnare and weaken their males. These characterizations are more likely the projection of the men's fear of their quasi-enslaved women than any realistic assessment of female power. In the third-century world of Alexandria, however, there is evidence to suggest that women were considerably freer in their actions than in previous centuries. Theocritus's fifteenth Idyll, portraying two women in dialogue on an outing to the Ptolemies' palace to see a show and on the way sparring in a tough way with a bystanding man, probably illustrates the way in which women were beginning to participate more in the culture. These women seem also to have commanded greater respect from men. Perhaps for this reason the age-old custom of males fulfilling their deepest needs for affection, love, and respect with adolescent male lovers seemed to disappear. Theocritus wrote poems of love between a man and a woman—a boy and a girl, really—which describe the playful side of passion; Apollonius writes of the other side to love, its problematic, frightening, all-consuming, dangerous passion in which a man encounters that which he can never really know or understand: to wit, a woman. Apollonius could draw on a long tradition of portraying women as a fundamentally negative force in a man's life to tinge all the encounters of male and female in his poem with a hint of the female's destructive force.

His reader would also know Euripides' fifth-century play *Medea*, which takes up the tragic events in the last days of Jason and Medea's life together. In Corinth, to which they flee after Medea has been instrumental in the death of Pelias, King Creon proposes that Jason jettison Medea and marry his daughter Creusa. The action of the play begins shortly after Medea learns that Jason has agreed to this scheme. Essentially, it is a collision between a traveling prince, whose only form of support is to marry the local princess, and his foreign wife, whose claims to her husband in Greece are perhaps shaky but who wants him for something other than the formal fact of marriage. He cannot see why, if she is well provided for, she has cause to complain if he decamps. She cannot believe that he does not want her anymore. Furthermore, Medea is possessed with love or at least overwhelming desire for Jason, a passion that the ancients assumed to be a bodily sickness like typhus or malaria. To remind Jason of her claim upon him—that she is the brood mare who has provided him with a dynasty—her only recourse is to kill her children. The tragic fact is that she is killing the only justification for a woman's existence in ancient Greek society. It is a bitter play, and the two of them fight it out, hurling bitter, cruel insults at one another. For the reader, the memory of it can only cast a pall over the developing romance in the *Argonautica*. He or she will read that memory into the words of the narrator after Jason has proposed marriage to Medea: "And thus he spoke. Her soul melted at his words, and yet, the deeds of destruction, she shuddered to think of them" (3.1131f.).

Apollonius's Medea is a remarkable literary construction. The Homeric epic figures are monoliths, utterly consistent and predictable in their behavior. Achilles is essentially a self-pitying, narcissistic male whose self-preoccupation never falters. Odysseus is a man whose need to reinvent himself motivates his stoic determination to get home and resume the mantle of husband, father, squire as much as it does his notable artistry in creating new identities whenever he is asked who he is. But Medea is not so simple. The narrator amply describes the naiveté of her virginal passion as Eros wounds her with his arrow, but then he shows her wielding her gruesome charms and reminds the reader that she knows the landscape from her expeditions to scout for corpses. Medea is both witch and maiden. But she is still more than that. In his creation of her Apollonius plays upon his reader's expectations, which are built up from familiarity with other myths and other narratives. Among the major epic and tragic associations are these: (1) Ariadne, the girl who helps Theseus and is abandoned by him on Naxos; (2) Penelope, the wife who waits and helps by keeping the household intact and then is in effect abandoned by her husband and the narrator of the *Odyssey* once she and Odysseus have gone to bed after his return; (3) Euripides' Medea, a tragic female figure who on the one hand must destroy her living issue, which is almost herself, yet who on the other hand is the daughter of the Sun and a malevolent figure because she survives her evil deed, unlike the purely tragic Deianeira of Sophocles' *Trachinian Women*, who dies; (4) Homer's Circe, who enchants men to their doom, a malign witch/

goddess figure who is sexually dangerous to males on the model of Aphrodite (Adonis perishes in his relationship with her) and Artemis (Actaeon perishes when he has seen her nude, a quasi-sexual relationship) and many others; (5) Aeschylus's Clytemnestra, who seduces Agamemnon into entering the warm bath where he is stabbed to death, the paradigmatic threatening mortal woman whose power to kill is directly related to the intimacy of the matrimonial chamber. Medea's behavior in this poem, therefore, often comes as a surprise. For instance, there is a great difference between the frightened and vulnerable young girl who calls out to her nephew for protection after she has run away from her father's house, the coldly resolute woman of action who plans with the ineffectual Jason her own brother's death, and the charming and insincere girl in love who beguiles Arete (far more credulous than her Homeric counterpart) into believing that she and Jason have committed the merest peccadillo. These turns in character surprise the reader, and this is a new development in the history of ancient Greek literature.

Apollonius is often congratulated for his psychological realism. The story of Medea and Jason falling in love is superb precisely for this quality. Perhaps nowhere else does he achieve such subtle psychological truth as in the three monologues that Medea delivers in her bedroom. These are interesting as well for the changes they reveal in audience perception between the time of the oral Homeric poems and that of the written *Argonautica* meant for readers. A Homeric monologue is nothing more than a conventional speech delivered by a character to himself or herself by virtue of that curious dichotomous sense of self that Homeric heroes display. The monologues have absolute validity for the audience; there is no sense of the unconscious, of another level to the psyche hidden by the speakers from themselves. Thus a character may not lie to himself or herself. But Medea's monologues reveal a woman who, if not self-deceived exactly, is at least (to use a vague term) exceedingly muddleheaded. One might say that in oral performance the immediate and complete symbiosis between speaker and auditor—visceral, sensual, intellectual, totally compelling—gives absolute authority to the words spoken. Apollonius, however, is dealing with an audience who will read his poem, not hear it. In a literate culture where readers must decipher for themselves and by themselves the words of an absent and thus far less compelling writer, the problematic quality of what is said becomes in its written form something the narrator can play with.

Medea's moral travail is expressed in these three monologues in the third book. Like Achilles' three great refusals in the ninth book of the *Iliad*, which grow increasingly equivocal in their denunciation of the request made to him, Medea says no while she means yes, gradually weakening until she finishes by agreeing to aid the stranger. That there are *three* monologues gives the passage the fairytale sense of her having made the enchanting, transforming decision. Medea begins by telling herself that she does not want to get involved but that she does not want to see the stranger hurt (464–70). Then she sees in a dream (619–31) what is indeed the underlying truth of the poem, that the golden fleece is somehow symbolic of her virginity, and that Aeetes' anger at losing the fleece is a father's anger at losing his daughter to another man. The dream provokes the second monologue (636–44), in which Medea determines to remain a virgin, hoping that the stranger will woo some Greek girl—entirely ignoring the fact that Jason has not yet cast a glance in her direction. In the third monologue (772–801) she wishes he would die and asks for her own death. Once having divorced action from its consequences by allowing herself the fantasized luxury of suicide, she proceeds to contemplate helping the stranger, betraying her parents, and losing her reputation in a series of rhetorical questions that have no answer.

In the course of these three speeches, Medea wrestles with and overcomes her guilt at betraying her father for a lover. The monologues portray a Medea more active and decisive than Jason is anywhere. The result is to constitute her as a major figure, at least equivalent to Jason, in the narrative. Jason does not have a shadow companion like Achilles' Patroclus, nor do the members of his crew interact with him as Odysseus's do. He is quite alone. Into this void emerges Medea, who develops in the fourth book into Jason's absolute equal, if not superior, in power, energy, and daring. Apollonius has again contradicted the expectations of his reader. The traditional bonded males in heroic action stories establish a superior figure (an Achilles, an Odysseus, a Gilgamesh) set beside his inferior (Patroclus, the crew, Enkidu). But here is a *woman* as the second figure in the traveling duo. That is not all. The reader, acculturated to the values of the ancient Greek world, would naturally assume that the woman would take the inferior place, but the narrator increasingly reveals her strengths as Jason remains weak, with the result that she becomes the dominant figure. In his creation of Medea, Apollonius is again absolutely original.

The *Argonautica* may explore the manner and values of heroic narrative, but it is also a great love story, the earliest in a long tradition of love stories in the Western world. Apollonius is also original in describing aftermath, something with which the ancients seldom dealt. One may compare his version of the story of the golden fleece with that of Pindar, the fifth-century B.C.E. choral lyricist. *Pythian IV* is Pindar's longest surviving poem; one may assume that he gave himself ample scope to include whatever details he chose. Yet it is significant that once Jason has the fleece, the poem is nearly over, just as the *Odyssey* narrator takes Penelope out of the narrative as soon as the couple has been reunited and spent a night together in bed. Apollonius, by contrast, fully describes the onset of Medea's love, the passion of the couple's first meeting alone, their interaction while getting the fleece, their tension with each other as they seem to be cornered by their pursuers, their desperate act of murder, and the heavy depression that engulfs them until they finally marry—by which time it seems to the reader that love has gone away. This poem mirrors the common experience of Western romantic love, which flares up so prominently in the raptures of first meetings and fades so quickly in the deadening quotidian conjugal routine. As such, the poem is hard to place. Epic stories like the *Iliad* are tragic because they are founded on the realization that the hero must die, revealed through the mechanism of the death of the friend, the alter ego, the surrogate. The prose romance is comic because at the end the two lovers who have struggled through so much adversity and have preserved their love are reunited and "live happily ever after." The *Argonautica* tells a cynical and sad story of two lovers who stick together through adversity, even going to the extreme of murder, but who, when they are at last united in marriage, are not happy. Nor do they live happily ever after, since the reader knows what Euripides has already prepared for them. In a sense the bonded traveling couple *has* been split, even if it is not death that carries one off, as it does Patroclus. This is not exactly tragic (although if one accepts the notion that Apollonius is describing the universal human conjugal condition, it approaches something like a tragic event); still, when Hera tells Thetis near the very end of the poem that someday Medea will pass all eternity in the Elysian Fields with Achilles, the narrator has introduced a somewhat lopsided happy ending (though it is not clear that female readers of this poem who also know the *Iliad* would congratulate Medea on the prospect of spending eternity with Achilles).

Because centuries of critics faulted Apollonius for what he was not or seemingly ever intended to be, his particular virtues as a narrator are generally in danger of being scanted. The *Argonautica* in fact constantly attests to his skill. One thinks, for instance, of the moment in which Medea is struck by Eros's arrow. Love is described as overcoming her as a fire bursts up from dry twigs. The poet embellishes the simile by describing the woman who builds up this fire, a woman who must struggle at the hard work of spinning wool, getting up at the crack of dawn to start her fire (3.291–95). The image returns in the fourth book (4.1062–65) as Medea cries, awake and restless during the night, just like a woman who must turn her spindle through the night, as her orphaned children hang about her and she thinks how awful her life has become. In the first simile the woman of toil parallels a woman in love and dependent, in bondage forever to a man, as this culture saw it. The second simile finds the poor working woman now bereft and deserted, just like Medea, who has had to fight not to be rejected by Jason and turned over to her family.

Another superb image is contained in a description of night:

> Then night brought the dark over the earth. Sailors
> on the sea looked out from their ships to Orion
> and the Bear. Both the traveler out there on the road
> and the gatekeeper by this time were longing for sleep.
> And a heavy slumber enclosed all around that woman
> whose children had died, nor was there any dog barking
> through the town, nor the echoing voices of men.
> Silence held the black darkness.
>
> [3.744–50]

Apollonius recalls Homeric ring composition in returning to the darkness with which he begins. Like Homer, he presents conventional night figures, except for the startling image of the bereft mother in slumber. The description moves in time from early evening, when the traveler is hurrying along and the doorkeeper waits, to the dead of the night, when the men have all gone home and the dogs sleep. Apollonius goes from the porter who waits up for someone to the mother in deep sleep because her children are dead and no one any longer will make demands on her. Her cares are over and she can sleep, as the porter cannot. But her sleep is perverse; it is the heavy sleep of the depressed and recently bereaved mother, the sleep of escape. It is the sleep of the dead of the night. The image is completely woeful, befitting the moment in which Medea debates with herself her future course, which, as we know, will end in her killing her brother, her husband's uncle, and finally her children. It is a simile so grim and perverse, so unlike "the classical," that we must marvel at its originality.

The sailing of the *Argo* (1.536–68) is an example of Apollonius's ability to stage a scene. He begins with a simile that describes the mood of the scene and the men: the crew cleaving the sea with their oars, to the rhythm of Orpheus's lyre, are compared to youths dancing to the sound of the lyre in honor of Apollo. Next, Apollonius moves his reader farther away from the scene by describing the armor glistening from the ship as it speeds along, then still farther with the comparison of the *Argo*'s wake to a path stretching over a green plain. This takes the focus to the horizon line, where the poet pauses to recapitulate the now greatly enlarged view by describing the scene from the Olympian vantage point: all the gods, he says, looked down from heaven. Thereafter, the poet begins to redirect the focus, moving down and closing the view when he says that the nymphs gazed down from the top of Mount Pelion upon the heroes. He continues the downward movement now to the lowest point and adds a scale figure to the foreground, exactly in the tradition of heroic landscape painters of the eighteenth and nineteenth centuries. "Down from the mountaintop came Chiron . . . and at the surf he waved, calling out *bon voyage*" (1.553–56). The final sentence of the description ("And his wife, carrying Peleus's son Achilles, displayed the child for his father") ties the foreground and the frame into the picture, adding domestic human interest to heroics. What narrator ever before thought of the woman who changed Achilles' diapers?

In the third book Apollonius creates his bittersweet love story with splendid writing. The book begins with a portrait of Aphrodite and her son Eros, upon whom Athena and Hera call to ask for aid in getting Medea to help Jason. A modern will note that the gods' intervention marks Medea as the victim of love. An ancient would not have considered otherwise, since, as has been remarked, love was thought to be a disease of the body over which its owner had no control. Desire (*eros* in Greek) is the better word, a condition manifested by sweat, trembling, secretions, erections, taut nipples, and all the other disagreeable yet agreeable, wayward yet thrilling sensations of extreme sexual passion. Apollonius's portrait of the goddess and her son reveals much about love. She is narcissistically brushing her long hair, taking it up in her hands. The boy has just beaten Ganymede at dice; his mother wonders if the lad cheated. She offers him a grand toy, a golden ball; he greedily yearns for it. Before setting off on his mother's mission, he hands her his dice, first counting them. Love, the narrator shows us, is narcissism, greed, bribery, mistrust, and cheating. What has appeared in this scene will be re-enacted shortly by Jason and Medea. No wonder the lovers finally arrive at their nuptials so dispirited. One could also argue that the poem bears a message of doom to those who would marry for love.

The tone of the third book's opening scene is cynical, clever, and humorous, thereby saving the reader from taking the ensuing story too seriously. It may sometimes be thrilling, sometimes sad, but it is always amusing. When, for instance, Medea goes with her maiden attendants to her assignation, a simile compares her to Artemis, the very same simile used to describe Nausicaa in the *Odyssey* (quoted in Chapter 5). Readers will recall the innocent Nausicaa, dreaming of marriage, sturdily standing her ground as the naked stranger comes forth from the bushes, and the sang-froid with which she handles the business of getting him bathed, clothed, and directed to her parents' palace. Medea, by contrast, has just mastered thoughts of suicide; she arranges her hair, just as Aphrodite did eight hundred lines earlier; she arrays herself in shining clothing and goes forth with her handmaidens. There is no cart filled with clothes for washing here. Instead, Medea selects a magic ointment to take with her for Jason's use in his contest with the bulls. The narrator gives every detail of its gruesome origin, then offers one of those marvelously unsettling juxtapositions which generations of critics so disliked in Apollonius but which today's critics so applaud: "She took up the charm and set it in the perfumed band of cloth that encircled her as support for her ambrosial bosom" (3.867ff.).

As she and the girls approach the shrine, Medea demonstrates as much courage as Nausicaa showed. She tells her attendants to wait while she goes to the meeting alone. She has already proved courageous, if not downright foolhardy, noting that no women are at the precinct today because so many strangers are out on the town. With this the narrator reminds us that in this ancient village there are fifty sailors off a ship. Such were the conditions of life in those times that the reader would immediately imagine the extraordinary threat of rape which such a situation implies for a woman, the extraordinary daring—whether courage or sheer recklessness—which possesses

Medea. She must bribe her girls: "We'll sing and pick flowers, and you will go home with many a gift from me, if you will humor me." So they are to risk themselves in this dangerous journey through town, and they are to stand discreetly aside and let her speak to the stranger alone (imagine what Aeetes would do to them, if he learned). No sweet Nausicaa here, although someone just as tough, we may say.

Jason's trip to the shrine is equally amusing. He sets out with Argus, Medea's nephew, and Mopsus the prophet to beseech Medea for her aid—and the reader will be reminded of the Embassy to Achilles in the ninth book of the *Iliad*, when a similar triad went to seek the army's salvation from the great hero. Of course, Jason is more beautiful, sexy, charming than any of the heroes in days of yore, the narrator says, thus placing this gorgeous youth incongruously in the ranks of those brawny men of heroic narrative. And, of course, it is not Achilles these three will supplicate but a sweet young maiden. As they proceed, a crow in the tree cries out to Mopsus: "Are you so simpleminded that you don't know what even children know, that a girl won't say anything to a young man in front of others? . . . Stay away, you idiot!" (3.933ff.). The crow effectively bursts the balloon of pretension in this imitation heroic embassy.

The passion of their meeting is described (956ff.) in one of the strongest evocations of erotic desire surviving from antiquity. The narrator lavishes detail on Medea's physical collapse before this beautiful man and couples it with a simile taken from Sappho describing trees standing side by side in silence in the mountain, then suddenly stirring and whispering to one another when the wind comes up. When Medea takes the charm from her bosom and hands it to Jason, the narrator again describes her extreme weakness and excitement, adds that she would have given him her whole soul, so thrilled was she at his desiring her. They grow shy, they stare at each other, they smile. Conventional epic poetry, indeed all the poetry of high seriousness from antiquity, minimized descriptions of physical desire. Male desire especially, because it must inevitably center upon the erection, is inherently ridiculous, just as any sculpture of the nude male must contend with the penis, which offends against the aesthetic perfection of the torso. (A modern may argue that the penis punctuates the sublimity of the torso, but the ancient Greeks, who emphatically preferred small penises on men real or sculpted, would probably disagree.) Apollonius has powerfully imagined Medea's passion and given to Jason as much physical emotion as possible. The epic form does not allow for any precise acknowledgment of sexual intercourse; furthermore, epic describes a class of people whom the ancient Greek reader would know to have been governed by archaic or even contemporary strictures on female virginity. Jason and Medea could not, therefore, be imagined to have performed the physical act of sexual intercourse before their marriage in the fourth book. But the eroticism of this passage describes the same passion as that of the young boys and girls who make love in pastoral poetry or in the many love poems of the period which survive in a contemporary collection titled *The Anthology* (which we might translate as "The Bouquet of Flowers"). Jason's request to Medea and gift of the charm, set in this swirling sea of passion, plus the profound change in their relationship that gradually occurs in the dialogue that follows, seem like the irreversible transaction of physical love between a virgin and her young boyfriend. It is not unreasonable to read it that way through the convention.

After it is all over Medea goes home, so lovestruck that she cannot even speak to her sister, and sits alone in her room. Jason, as in the cliché of males through all time, goes back to his comrades and tells them the whole story. However vulnerable this leaves women in general, Medea, it seems, has won for herself exactly what she wanted in return for the charm: before they have parted company in this passionate moment Jason has asked her to marry him and go back to Greece. The scene immediately following the moment of extreme passion, in which it looked as though Medea were losing all self-control, is a striking reversal.

Aphrodite needed Eros to enchant Medea, and bribed him to do it with a golden ball. Jason needs Medea to enchant the bulls. His glowing sexuality suggests one thing, but, when he speaks to her (3.990–95), he offers her fame—his version of the golden ball. Medea, with her eyes fastened on Jason, has other ideas. Her negotiation with Jason (3.1060ff.) is thoroughly amusing and, though touching, gently cynical.

"Take the fleece and go away. Go nevertheless where you will." That telltale "nevertheless" marks her opposition to his departure. She acts it out with tears, thinking of him gone; then she speaks to him face to face and—dropping all her sense of shame, as the narrator remarks—takes his hand. Passive Jason must be trembling, the reader imagines. This is Medea's great moment.

"Remember me," she continues (3.1069) just like Nausicaa, no doubt enkindling some guilt in Jason's breast. For when he replies, he is fervent: "One thing I know all too well, I shall never forget you night or day" (3.1079–80). She has asked about his country, too, and also more about Ariadne, taking up homecoming and an accompanying maiden as a means to maneuver the conversation in the direction of her goal. Ariadne, whose help to Theseus parallels what Medea has been asked to do for Jason, can enter the text only with irony, however, because although Jason has mentioned Ariadne's going on board ship with Theseus and leaving her homeland, he omits to mention that Theseus left her on Naxos, where he was able to give her the slip while she was sleeping.

Pressing her point still further, Medea points out to Jason that Aeetes is not the same as Minos, being untrustworthy, and adds ambiguously, "I can't compare myself to Ariadne" (3.1107–8)— which, of course, she has indeed done, if only in negation. The persuasive rhetoric of these speeches is formidable. Then she hints more forcibly: "May a little bird come with a message to you when you forget me [still more guilt for Jason!], or, better still, would that a swift wind would carry me across the sea to Iolcus so that I can reproach you for having forgotten that it was my aid that saved you [guilt, guilt!]. Oh, if only I could be sitting in your great hall, a surprise guest!"

She bursts into tears, and Jason is lost. "Forget winds and messenger birds! If you were to come to Hellas . . ." So far he is in the subjunctive mood and the thought is hypothetical, but he is clearly testing the water. He falls back on the subject of fame. Then suddenly in the indicative mood he takes the big plunge: "In our bridal chamber you will prepare the marriage couch. Nothing shall take our love away till death envelops us" (3.1128–30).

Like Odysseus, who approached Nausicaa speaking soothing words to gain his ends (*Odyssey* 6.146,148), Jason has taken his glamor to the temple of Hecate and spoken as a practiced courtier—as Apollonius remarks, "fawning" (3.974). He has gotten what he wanted, but he has paid a price. And that is what love is all about.

The fourth book begins with Medea's surreptitious flight from home to Jason's encampment. Medea is like a serving girl fleeing a cruel mistress, the narrator says. He has just mentioned Aeetes' night-long angry meeting with his lieutenants and put Medea's reaction in another telling simile: "like a fawn whom the baying of hounds frightens as she lies hidden in the underbrush deep in the woods," which calls up an image of the terrified girl as inevitable victim, property of the possessive men whose angry shouts and cries float up and into her window from the meeting downstairs in the palace. Now the narrator compares Medea to a serving girl, one who, having recently been taken away from her native land and still quite ignorant of life's struggles and all its misery, sneaks away from a rich house, terrified of her harsh mistress. This simile, too, projects in all its detail what lies ahead for the sheltered princess daughter of Aeetes. Both similes underscore her vulnerability.

Upon reaching Jason's camp, Medea calls out to the younger of her two nephews who are there; by stressing the *younger* nephew and mentioning the crew's absolute amazement at hearing her voice, the narrator aptly reflects the mores of the time. Medea would not dare to call out to Jason, a man not of her family, for protection; and she will not call out to the older nephew, Argus, who has been the authoritative representative of her family throughout, no doubt for fear he will oppose her extraordinary breach of decorum. Her subsequent speech of supplication presents an interesting mixture of motives, arranged by the narrator for the delight of the cynics, since its persuasive strength depends finally on what is buried in its center: the goods Medea can deliver. "Save me, and save yourselves from Aeetes' anger," she says to her nephews. And "Honor your proposal of marriage to me, o stranger," she says to Jason. "I shall put the guardian serpent to sleep and get the fleece for you; now that I have fled, do not leave me vulnerable to blame and infamy because I have no kinsmen" (4.83ff.).

Jason responds to her by vowing marriage. Shortly thereafter, through her ministrations, the fleece is his. The narrator describes (4.167ff.) Jason's ecstacy at holding and possessing the fleece in language again suggesting that the subtext goal throughout has been the possession of Medea's body (when the two of them are finally married, they use the fleece as their wedding-night bed). Just after getting it, and while he is so deep in the emotional experience of its possession, Jason will let no one touch the fleece. Similarly, once back on the *Argo*, he seats Medea in the stern and delivers a speech in which he speaks of his marriage vow and asks the crew to "preserve" her. This injunction is guaranteed to protect her virtue while she travels unchaperoned and unprotected by female attendants on a ship with ifty males.

Ariadne got left on Naxos while Theseus, mission accomplished, sailed on to Athens. Medea is in danger of being left as well, when, shortly after Jason's vow, an army of Colchians, led by her brother Apsyrtus in hot pursuit, blocks their passage. Jason and the crew agree to a truce that gives them the fleece and puts under arbitration the question of whether Medea will be returned to her father or continue with Jason. This is the very extreme of dependency in which this hitherto powerful woman has been placed simply because of her sex. In ancient Greece a woman was legally a minor for her entire life, always under the jurisdiction of a male relative or spouse—a fact of social life which generates enormous tension in the fourth book. It was certainly true then and in much of the world is still true that a woman exercises what little control males allow her only in the bidding for her body. Once Medea agrees to help Jason, she has made a commitment to him utterly, since she has so betrayed her father that she is no longer safe in his jurisdiction. She has thus for all practical purposes surrendered her body to Jason; at the same time, however, she has managed to extract a promise of marriage from him. These negotiations emanate from the remarkable intelligence of a girl who must struggle to rise above the violent physical pangs and delirium of sexual passion to assure herself some safe passage in the unsparing, cruel world of men. Apollonius is being neither sentimental about women nor particularly sympathetic to them, any more than Euripides is in his *Medea*. Rather he is coolly viewing the conditions in which women live as a factor in their (from the male viewpoint) sometimes suspicious behavior.

Thus, when the Argonauts consider a truce with Apsyrtus, the possibility that Jason will abandon Medea is a cynical commentary on male moral weakness, a humorous recognition of the fate of human contracts made on both sides from simple self-interest in a poem that is meant to be an amusing yet tragic commentary on women's alienated position in the larger world. Medea's subsequent anguished speech about dependency and betrayal speaks to that female position (4.355ff.); Jason's reply, which is ambiguous to the point of vacillation, is simply another revelation of this very young lad's inexperience of the moral world. Her reply to him is the climax of the emotional journey of this union, and yet another revelation of her strength and Jason's weakness. As she had the daring to defy her father, to come to assignation with Jason alone, to flee her house and board the ship, she now sums it all up with the courage to kill her brother.

The murder of Apsyrtus, the ultimate gesture of betrayal of her own family, represents the cutting of all ties with them which every new bride in ancient Greece had to do as she both accepted and was assumed into her husband's family and household. Apollonius, of course, makes it something more in this story. For his traveling duo, murder is the extremity to which they go in finding their own special bond. As a metaphor for the emotions that have animated the relationship from its start, the murder and the subsequent guilt and depression are apt expressions of the aftermath of romantic ecstacy when the inevitable ugly truths of the relationship become clearer. If one were to psychoanalyze Jason and Medea, one would say that although weak Jason wanted a sweet submissive wife such as he imagined the very young virginal Medea would be, his subconscious recognized and wanted the strong bully she turned out to be; strong Medea confused the simple facts of Jason's maleness and physical beauty with strength and resolution, while all along her subconscious saw in him the very person she could effectively dominate. Their relationship had no other way to evolve than to turn sour. Thus, while Apollonius was no doubt describing what males in his misogynistic culture imagined to happen always in male-female relationships of real duration, he had the instinct to create two characters whose psychologies could only lead to misery when coupled.

The murder scene is again an example of bravura Apollonian writing; it reads like a scene from tragic drama, so well does the narrator indicate the setting and detail the action. "In the entryway to the temple he [Apsyrtus] fell to his knees; there as he breathed out his life, in his one last act he took the dark blood at the wound with both his hands, and he made red his sister's silver veil and her gown as she tried to dodge away" (4.471–74). All the horror and guilt of murder are in this scene. Resonating through several scenes thereafter, the horror and guilt are played out through a fantastical geography: the Po, Rhone, and Danube rivers in Apollonius's imagination form an inland waterway that allows the Argonauts to make their way from the Black Sea across a great land mass to what is now the Italian Riviera. Just as the poet uses the various reactions to the fleece to illustrate all the various emotions and attitudes that love inspires—desire, possessiveness, seduction, joy, and glitter—so he uses the landscape in the fourth book to express the couple's state of mind, brilliantly describing guilt in the group's progress up the Po River. At the lake where the sun god's offspring fell to his death—"No bird is able to cross the water, spreading out its fragile wings. Mid-course it falls into the flaming water, fluttering"—daughters of Helios, the sun god, enclosed in poplar trees stand at the lake lamenting; from their eyes fall tears of amber. "No desire for food or drink came to the heroes, nor did their minds turn to joyful thoughts. All day they were strung out, exceedingly weak, weighed down by the dreadful smell, intolerable, which the streams of the Eridanus [Po] sent forth from the burning son of Helios. All night they had to listen to the shrill cry of the daughters of Helios wailing in a sharp voice. As they cried, their tears were borne upon the waters like drops of oil" (4.619ff.).

Depression is the emotion suggested by the landscape of North Africa. The impotence and cyclic nature of the depressed state are caught in verbal repetitions: "Everywhere shoals, everywhere thick seaweed from the bottom, the foam of the wave lightly flows over them. Sand stretches out until the eye mistakes it for air. Nothing creeps here, nothing flies . . . pain overcame them as they gazed at the air and the broad expanse of earth looking like air, stretching far away without end. No watering hole, no path, no shepherd's enclosure could they see anywhere. Everything was held in dead calm (4.1237ff.)." Their prior meeting with Medea's aunt, the sorceress Circe, has done nothing to change the mood, since she is so scornful, so disapproving of them. Even their marriage, a hasty, frightened affair, rushed through to protect Medea from yet another band of pursuing Colchians, is desperate and sad (4.1161ff.).

Still Apollonius is not done with them. True enough, he gives little more to Jason than a kind of superficial blessing from the god Apollo, to whom Jason, yet again in tears, cries out as he finds himself lost in the Pall of Darkness, a night so dark that not one star shines forth. For Medea, however, the narrator has reserved one final triumph as she conquerors the monster Talos. And a triumph it is indeed: the narrator expands his description of it, using the language of old heroism to describe the monster's fall to earth. As the fourth book began with Medea's lulling the fleece-guarding serpent to sleep, so it ends with her sending Talos to his destruction.

The fourth book is more complex than the other three, since it contains a gripping story of suspense in the pursuit and flight of Medea and the Argonauts, the pace of which is suddenly much slowed by the episodes of journeying that have landscapes as their central purpose. The murder of Apsyrtus turns the narrative somber, a mood from which the reader is rescued by the highly humorous account of the desperate couple's visit to Circe, who is, on the one hand, very bourgeois, proper, and nervous, and, on the other, surrounded by grotesques that suggest a Circe even more crazily outrée than the witch figure of the *Odyssey*. The narrator makes her violate the propriety of epic poetry by speaking to her niece in Colchian, while Jason, the presumed hero of this poem, is to be imagined by the reader as sitting about impotently twiddling his thumbs.

Curiously enough, one thoroughly lighthearted passage (4.930–64) pierces the persistent gloom of the fourth book. It is a parody of the description of the *Argo's* passage through the Symplegades, which occurs in the second book. Here, when Thetis marshals the Nereids to lift the boat on high, they are first compared to dolphins at play around the ship and then, as they hike up their dresses to keep them out of the water, to frolicking girls at play with a ball, which they pass from one to another. When they succeed in their task, Apollonius describes Hera's joy as she throws her arms around Athena. We could be at a soccer match. Once the ship is past the Wandering Rocks, Apollonius devises a charming pastoral landscape to go with the euphoric mood. The daughters of Helios here are not amber-crying poplars, but two shepherdesses, one with a silver crook, one with a crook of *orichalcum*, an even more exotic metal, to be found only in fable. The cows are as white as milk and have horns of gold. We are reminded of Dresden porcelain shepherdesses, or Marie Antoinette at her milking. The narrator uses the figures to remind his readers of the absurdity, the artificiality, and the essential, delightful charm of a grim tale that they might otherwise take all too seriously. The wandering twosome has just been shown the door by Medea's aunt, and there is little cause for joy. But the unexpected passage is an imagistic outpouring of the comic resolution to Medea's plight, which Hera has just announced (4.810–15): someday all her troubles will be over, and she will be in the Elysian Fields married to Achilles, a man as bold and overbearing as she herself and hence finally her own true mate.

The prophecy is followed by the narration of the marital career of Achilles' mother, Thetis (4.866–79). A strong woman, a goddess, she was married to the mortal Peleus, who was incapable of understanding her attempts to render their son immortal. In wrath she left him. In this narrative, at Hera's command, she communicates with Peleus but as briefly as possible: she touches the tip of his hand, and leaves the minute the message has been delivered. As Apollonius's readers know from Euripides' play, someday Aegeus will offer Medea sanctuary, and she will leave Jason and Corinth in a skyborne vehicle. She, like Thetis, like the Nereids, will be in control. True to the comic vision, Apollonius is reminding us that perils, problems, and tears are here only for a moment; finally, even through the Pall of Darkness, Apollo sends light.

The *Aeneid*

But, Rome, 'tis thine alone, with awful sway,
To rule mankind, and make the world obey,
Disposing peace and war by thy own majestic way;
To tame the proud, the fetter'd slave to free;
These are imperial arts, and worthy thee.

—*Aeneid* 6.851–53 (Dryden translation)

The city of Rome was originally no more than a small settlement on the banks of the Tiber River, a few kilometers upstream from where its waters emptied into the Mediterranean. As any schoolchild once knew, the Romans calculated that the founding of their city had taken place in the year now identified as 753 B.C.E. The Latin that the settlers there spoke was only one small dialect branch of the Italic language that evolved from the dialect of Indo-European that migrating people brought into the Italian peninsula sometime in the second millennium B.C.E. These were, as they say, humble beginnings. Yet some 870 years later, by the time of the death of the Emperor Trajan in 117 C.E., the Romans controlled a land mass that stretched from present-day Scotland to the Sudan, from the Atlantic Ocean to the Caspian Sea. Latin was the official language for all the people living under Roman rule. Latin survived into the nineteenth century as the language of scholarship; to this day it remains the official language of the Vatican. It otherwise became the source for numerous dialectal variations which in time evolved into what are known as the Romance languages.

The legend of ancient Rome has been just as powerful. Roman civilization has been the inspiration behind one successive revival of art and learning after another. The story of the rise of Rome to its imperial greatness, its descent into obscurity around 500 C.E. as a consequence of the invasion of German tribes from the north, and its revival in the thirteenth century and thereafter remains the enduring legend of the Western world, as potent a mythology as the stories of the Greek or Christian gods. A reader of the *Aeneid* used to come to the poem knowing this tradition. It could be daunting; some critics in the nineteenth century and, indeed, even well into the twentieth reacted as though they were dealing with a sacred text. It is a blessing that present-day ignorance of history frees the *Aeneid* from the burden of sanctity, although, sadly enough, ignorance of the history of Greek and Roman antiquity often causes the reader to draw a blank at what Virgil would quite legitimately have expected his reader to know.

The *Aeneid* is a Latin poem written by a Roman, but it presumes a knowledge of the ancient Greek world. From the seventh century B.C.E., Greek-speaking peoples migrating from various cities on the Greek mainland in search of more room and better land settled all along the coast of southern Italy and Sicily. They built cities, some of which rivaled their hometowns in the quality and size of public building. As the Romans slowly began to expand the territory in which they lived, they eventually came into contact with these Greeks. Even before that they had encountered Greek culture in the towns of their neighbors to the north, the Etruscans, who had taken over from the Greeks all sorts of features of their civilization, among them many of the names and stories of their gods and goddesses.

The Romans had no system of mythology; they did not anthropomorphize any deities except a kind of father god, Jupiter, his wife, Juno (her name means "joining," so one might think of this colorless figure as the male definition of the female as conjugation, not unlike Adam's rib), and a nurturant female city protector named Minerva. The Romans took over from the Etruscans the stories and the idea of identifiable, anthropomorphic gods, as well as a myriad of names that were often subject to a radical change in spelling. Through the medium of the Etruscan system of writing and spelling, for instance, the name of the Greek hero Polydeukes, the brother of Helen, went through a phase in which the consonants shifted as vowels disappeared; in the Roman mouth the *d* sound coalesced with the *l* sound, and they wrote *x* for the *ks* sound. The result, when vowels are added, is Pollux.

The effects of this quirk of history are still with us. Knowledge of antiquity has come down in the Western world through the Romans, and hence through Latin. Even when talking about the Greeks, their literature, their gods, their culture, it has not been uncommon to speak of Pollux instead of Polydeukes; of Jupiter, not Zeus; of Ulysses, not Odysseus—all reminders of the centuries of Roman hegemony and the subsequent power and ubiquity of the Latin language (just as the British of the nineteenth century said Leghorn for the Italian seaside resort of Livorno, or Florence for the city of Firenze, to underscore their sense of world domination). In the twentieth century, however, there has been a reaction to this practice. Some people think it more honest to transliterate from the Greek: Aias, not Ajax; Korinthos, not Corinth. The reader, therefore, will encounter a melange of spellings of the same word. In fact, the spelling of Virgil's name, which is really Vergilius but by tradition spelled with an *i* (Christians, who thought Virgil had intimations of their faith before its god had even been born, saw the Latin word for the Virgin, *virgo*, in his name), is one of these irrationalities. (There are those who would argue that there is nothing irrational at all about maintaining these absurd variants in spelling, that they represent yet another elitist strategy, probably unconscious, of devising a complicated code that only the cognoscenti can penetrate, one that will at the same elude and defeat the uneducated.)

The reader who is thinking of the Greek epics while reading about the *Aeneid* would do well to bear in mind the names of the principal Greek deities and the Latin equivalents: Zeus/Jupiter [or Jove], Hera/Juno, Aphrodite/Venus, Athena/Minerva, Artemis/Diana, Apollo/Apollo, Poseidon/Neptune, Hades/Pluto, Hephaestus/Vulcan, Hermes/Mercury, Demeter/Ceres, Dionysus/Bacchus.

Roman literary history really begins with a Greek. Around 250 B.C.E. there came to Rome one Livius Andronicus, a citizen of the Greek community of Tarentum (modern Taranto), located on the southern coast of Italy. Tarentum had recently been besieged and captured by the Romans, who were engaged in bringing under their command all Greek-speaking southern Italy. Andronicus, like many others, had been sold into slavery and brought to Rome, where he was installed as a teacher of boys. In the mid-third century any cultured Greek, and certainly Andronicus was that, carried as his principal baggage the literary experience of Greece from Homer to the tragedies, comedies, and histories of the classical period to the new refinements, introspections, and revenants of Egyptian Alexandria, which was at that time riding the very crest of its citizens' creative powers. Formal education in ancient Greece, which was mostly character development and aesthetic awareness, achieved its ends through the presentation of examples from literature, which the students memorized. All educated Greek boys could recite the Homeric poems from memory. Andronicus cast about but found no Latin equivalent to the epic poems or, for that matter, to any other Greek literary masterpieces. He found nothing that he could call literature. He set to, therefore, and translated the *Odyssey* into Latin in a meter native to the Romans called Saturnian, about which we know very little except that it had stress accent. He wanted to provide his charges with an *exemplum*. Whether he knew it or not, he had also begun the giant task of creating a literary language.

Virgil's self-consciousness in language, his obvious expectation that his audience will bring a comparable awareness to a reading of the poem, the strong impression that the poem makes of a verbal construct delighting in its music and in the cunning of its word arrangements are in the long tradition of the sharpened sensitivity to language that Livius Andronicus brought to his translation of the *Odyssey*. The surviving fragments show him using Latin archaisms not only to capture the sense of antiquity which persons in the third century recognized in the Homeric language but to offer a Latin equivalent of the compelling Greek poetic diction. For instance, he found a pure Latin name, Camena, that he then elevated to the equivalent of the Greek word *Mousa*, "Muse."

Greek poetry begins with the formulaic language of the oral poets, from which all their later poetry derives. Serious, formal prose came about later, created from quite different verbal experience and expectations. The Greeks did not confuse poetry with prose, even apart from the meter. To read Greek poetry is to enter another realm, to speak another language. The language of archaic Greek epic became over time sometimes quaint, sometimes incomprehensible, but all Greek poetry is constructed out of a poetic diction altogether unlike vernacular speech. Livius Andronicus strove to capture that sense of otherness which is the hallmark of Greek poetry; he inspired all his successors.

The remains of early Latin reveal a constant preoccupation with the shaping of a poetic language. When Aristotle established standards of vocabulary for the different genres of Greek literature, he singled out the rare or strange word as particularly appropriate for the epic genre. Obviously, he was influenced by the history and reception of epic language in his own time. The Roman poets searched through archaic law texts, religious formulas, and early folksongs for the special words that would take their poetry out of the commonplace. From the start, therefore, there was a self-consciously "poetic" sensibility alive in the writing. Perhaps the early poet Ennius seems ridiculously exuberant when he composes an aggressively alliterative line such as *O Tite tute Tati tibi tanta, tyranne, tulisti* (which, being a mere fragment, doesn't mean much by itself—something like "O Titus Tatius, tyrant, what a great thing you have brought for [or on] yourself"), but he was surely struggling to make a language that no one would confuse with prose.

The most influential Greek convention that the Roman poets adopted for epic was the dactylic hexameter meter. The numerous uncontracted short vowels in Greek make natural dactyls plentiful, but Latin, like English, is poor in dactyls. Perhaps there is no greater measure of the profound artificiality of poetic Latin than the rich invention of dactylic phraseology. For instance, the verb "to command" in its common form *imperare* cannot, in many of its personal and tense endings, stand in a hexameter line because it contains a metrical shape known as the cretic: that is, a short syllable sandwiched between two long syllables ($-\smile-$), a metrical shape that can never be part of a dactyl. So the Roman poets found another verb form from this root, the so-called frequentative (because it implies action performed again and again) *imperitare* and used it. Abitrarily they denied its original special meaning. Likewise, words that end in a consonant create problems in the formation of dactyls, so the Roman poets discarded a word like *gaudium*, "joy", and used instead the plural form *gaudia*, "joys", but denied its plural meaning. These perversions in meaning became conventions that people who read poetry understood and did not confuse with the prose usage of the same word. It was a practice that made the Latin hexameter in its own way as peculiar and artificial as the Homeric dialect seemed to have been.

Once Livius Andronicus set the example for the production of literature, Romans began creating. Unfortunately, only the merest fragments of this material survive, often only words or phrases culled by ancient grammarians to illustrate linguistic usage, so it is difficult to gauge the quality of these pieces or even their character. The fragmentary nature of early Latin literature works a special disadvantage for readers of the *Aeneid*, because it is obvious that Virgil plays off his Latin predecessors as well as his Greek. While it seems likely that the literary circle in which he moved and for whom he wrote would know the Greek masters far better than they knew the early Latin poets, who were considered by comparison crude and harsh, we cannot take that as certain. Virgil, who was self-consciously Roman, was writing a Roman epic; as such, the local Latin tradition from which it sprang would be significant. There are numerous indications in the late fourth century C.E. scholarly commentary of Servius that Virgil's debt to his Latin predecessors was, indeed, large.

Two early epic poets were Gnaeus Naevius, who lived in the second half of the third century B.C.E., and Quintus Ennius, who was born in 239 and died in 169. Using the native Roman meter, the Saturnian, Naevius wrote a poem about the first Punic War in which much of his verse was devoted to the background history of the Romans. This included among other things their flight from Troy, their wanderings, and Aeneas's meeting with Dido. Ennius, who was born in what is now Calabria, grew up knowing the Greek of the townspeople, the Oscan of the local Italic peoples, and the Latin of government and the military. His poem, the *Annales*, is an eighteen-book-long account of the history of Rome, based on the chronological scheme of the yearly tenure of the chief priest (*annales pontificum*)—not, one would think, a very exciting topic or narrative structure, though the historian Tacitus, who used the same scheme, made a fascinating prose narrative of it. Ennius is important in the history of literature, however, because he chose to write in dactylic hexameter. He began the process of making Latin over into a medium for this alien metrical scheme— not only began it but accomplished so much that successors such as Lucretius and Virgil were able to experiment with and refine from a completely realized poetic diction and verse pattern. He and Naevius are also important for their decision to make poems based on historical fact. This had, of course, been done by the Alexandrians; one thinks of Apollonius's contemporary, the poet-scholar Rhianus, whose four epic poems, though not preserved, were often cited by scholars of antiquity, especially for their geographical lore. Ennius, especially, set the standard for Roman epic, and he made history an important theme. One can see instantly why historical fact should appeal to the Romans; they had no native mythology or any developed body of saga material. They were heavily dependent upon the Greeks for the direction in which their nascent culture was evolving. Creative artists in this predicament must struggle not only for their personal originality but also for their cultural identity. History, obviously, was of supreme importance to them. This consideration will not escape the reader of the *Aeneid*.

The Romans had created a great deal of turbulent history by the time Publius Vergilius Maro arrived on the scene in 70 B.C.E. More was to come before he began writing the *Aeneid* in 29. As the Romans continued to enlarge their territorial interests and their trading routes, they naturally encountered, whether hostilely or not, more and more peoples of the Mediterranean. Their principal enemy became the Carthaginians, with whom they waged a series of wars, once enduring a devastating invasion of Italy. Victorious at last, the Romans became master of considerable land as a consequence; the territories of Spain, North Africa, Sardinia, and Sicily all became Roman provinces. Invading Gauls sent them northward, and their victories in this area secured for them all of what is now Italy above the Po River and to the Alps, the Italian and French Rivieras to Marseilles, and the land along the eastern coast of the Adriatic Sea. When they were drawn into Greek affairs, the intervention resulted in their conquering the many city-states of the Greek-speaking people. In the face of the inevitability of Roman power, Attalus, the king of Pergamon, bequeathed his kingdom (on the northwestern coast of present-day Turkey) to Rome in 133; it was formed into the Roman province of Asia.

The Roman Senate persisted in believing that the rise of the Romans to imperial power was without conscious design on their part. Enemies had attacked, the Romans had responded; allies had asked for aid, the Romans had responded. What had once been an insignificant settlement on the banks of the Tiber had for no discernible reason become master of the Mediterranean. The matter, therefore, was beyond reason. It was there, even in the ironic fact that the Greek word *rhomē*, so like the Latin name of the capital city, Roma, means strength. It was the will of the gods; it was the Romans' manifest destiny. The narrator of the *Aeneid* plays to the Roman sense of destiny when he presents as future action for his characters or their progeny events that for the Roman readers would have long since become part of their history.

The Romans had a genius for political structures. By trial and error, through negotiation and pressures, they had by the late second century B.C.E. created various forms of government which Polybius, a Greek who spent considerable time in Rome and with Romans, called the realization in practice of what Aristotle and other philosophers of government had called the ideal in theory: a mixed constitution, with two consuls to represent the monarchical principle, the Senate to reflect the aristocracy, and the public assemblies for democracy. To the Roman mind it seemed that, just as some kind of divine hand, some providence, had led the Romans to world supremacy, so they had of their own accord, quite unwitting, created the perfect constitution, had realized in fact what the Greeks had imagined in theory. It was again confirmation of their being the ideal made real, as it were. A great number of Romans were devoted to the Hellenistic philosophy known as Stoicism, which became for them a kind of religion, as we moderns understand the term. A principal article of faith for Stoics was the existence of a benevolent Providence, God, Eternal Fire, call it what you will, which moves all things toward the best. Roman success, then, was a kind of working-out in the visible world of this great supreme force. This notion seems to inform all the action of the *Aeneid*.

The second-century political arrangements looked, from the vantage point of nostalgia in the mid-first century, to have been a Golden Age: a happy populace exercising its sovereignty with the benevolent assistance of a patriarchal aristocracy, all watched over by two authoritative consuls. Whether myth or reality, this stable and beneficent consensus of the various classes of the populace broke down in the last decades of the second century, when men began to jockey for extreme personal power under the guise of helping the people or restoring the dignity of the old constitution. The names from the next century of civil turmoil are familiar: Tiberius and Caius Gracchus, Marius, Sulla, Pompey—and then, of course, Julius Caesar, assassinated by jealous fellow aristocrats who could not stomach his notion (picked up on his travels to Egypt) that something so unwieldy as the Roman Empire would be better served by a king at its head, an absolute monarch after the fashion of the Ptolemies. In fact, Caesar had been sleeping with Cleopatra VII, of Egypt's brother-sister rulers, whose royal power, intelligence, and courage equaled if they did not eclipse those of her Roman lover.

Throughout the first century B.C.E. the warring parties crisscrossed the Roman lands, bringing death and devastation to the people. The waste in human life and resources was appalling; the absolute selfishness of all concerned was naked, palpable, and relentless. When Julius Caesar died, his nineteen-year-old great-nephew Octavian, grandson of his sister, joined with the elders of his great-uncle's party, who perhaps thought they could use him for his illustrious name. Immediately, however, he started his own rise to power, trading on the famous name, fueled by iron will and inflexible ambition.

After innumerable murders, intrigue, and brute thrusts of naked strength, Octavian eventually confronted his principal rival for all Roman power, his great-uncle's lieutenant and successor in the seductive bed of Cleopatra: Marcus Antonius, who was Cleopatra's means to become ruler of the eastern Roman world. At Actium in August of 31 B.C.E., however, Octavian defeated Antony and Cleopatra, who fled back to Egypt and suicide. It was all over but the mopping up. In 27 the Roman Senate gave Octavian the title of Augustus, "worthy of honor," "sacred." They even offered him the title of "Romulus," the name of the legendary founder of Rome, which he wisely refused. Instead, he gradually took upon himself the titles, honorifics, and powers of the various instruments of state that had existed in the previous period, the so-called Republican Period. He had learned his lesson from the fate of Julius: despotism in the closet, republicanism in the forum.

History's opinion of Augustus will always be divided: did he make the trains run on time, or was he a monster tyrant? By staying his hand from a crown and by working within the nominal framework of the previous political arrangements, one could argue, Augustus, managed to establish a kind of stage setting in which the Romans could act out the illusion of a city, republic, and state. There had scarcely been much in the way of workable government in the preceding decades, merely anarchy and ruin. Now there would be stability in which at least the forms of government would exist. Perhaps he realized that in the previous centuries the people and the aristocracy had never found any common rallying point that would engage their loyalties and sympathies as the city-state had done for the Greeks; hence, he set about to substitute the glamor of the imperial person for the impersonal and ill-focused state. He then spent his life turning himself into an icon so that an icon, an idea, and a cult would survive his personal death. He is reputed to have asked on his deathbed, "Have I not played my part well?"

There is great praise for Augustus Caesar to be found in the *Aeneid*, particularly in the eighth book's description of the shield on which the battle of Actium is depicted. Some critics choose to believe that Virgil had no choice but to praise the strong man; others argue that he was a bootlicking toady who knew where the stipends came from;

still others believe that he acknowledged but lamented the historical necessity for Augustus. Virgil, we know, had personally experienced the devastation of the civil wars. It is easy to find fault with a man who would choose order over liberty, but perhaps the chaos, anarchy, and bloodshed of the decades prior to the firm establishment of the Augustan regime in the twenties made people so thirsty for law and order that they welcomed it even from the dispensing hand of a single powerful figure. Indeed, one could argue that the glorious young men who go to their tragic deaths in the latter half of the poem while Aeneas survives are so many reminders of the power-mad strong men of the years of Rome's civil strife, whose glamor resided in their daring and delinquency. In sum, it seems perfectly reasonable—and makes the *Aeneid* an infinitely better poem—to believe that Virgil was quite sincere in his praise of Augustus. After all, the world had been waiting for a savior for the previous three centuries. And just as Aeneas gives up a personal life in order to accomplish his destiny in Italy, just as the Christian savior would forgo human relationships, saying "I must be about my Father's business," so Augustus seemed to be transforming himself into some transcendent icon.

Despite the public turmoil of the first century, the Romans grew ever more confident of their literary strengths. Nonetheless, the generation of poets preceding Virgil had committed themselves deeply to the Alexandrian manner. They were much influenced by a certain Parthenius from Nicaea, who was brought to Rome as a prisoner of war in 73 B.C.E. and there freed. He proceeded to set up shop as a teacher; Virgil was said to have studied with him in Naples. Parthenius was committed to the aesthetic principles of Callimachus, which he impressed upon the young poets of the time. Catullus's Poem 64, on the wedding of Peleus and Thetis, is a brilliant example of the powerful and beneficial influence of Alexandrianism on the generation of Latin poets preceding Virgil (Catullus is thought to have lived from the eighties until the mid-fifties of the first century B.C.E.). The poem begins by describing the wedding feast, but the focus soon changes as the poet turns to a detail of decoration in the house of Peleus that depicts Ariadne deserted on the island of Naxos by Theseus. True to the Alexandrian way of viewing things, this small detail in the design of the tapestry inspires a narrative account of Ariadne's predicament, which constitutes about half the lines of the poem.

Virgil himself began his career writing short poems after the fashion of Theocritus or more like those of two of Theocritus's successors, Bion and Moschus. These poems were called *Eclogues*. He then turned to another favorite of the Alexandrian world and a special favorite of Callimachus, the archaic Greek poet Hesiod. In his four poems entitled *Georgics* (which might be translated as something like "All about Working the Land"), Virgil very loosely used Hesiod's *Works and Days* as his model. Hesiod's piece, put together from agricultural maxims, rules, and epigrammatic remarks (not unlike *Poor Richard's Almanack*), might seem to be a kind of manual of agricultural lore, but it is in fact a disquisition on justice in which the agricultural world reveals the rhythm of the universe from which justice springs. Hesiod's poetry appealed to Callimachus in part because it dealt with fact rather than what the Alexandrian critic considered the thoroughly shopworn saga tradition. Virgil makes fact into something quite other than material for instruction. The *Georgics* with their gorgeous pictures of Roman landscape insist upon the absolute value of the natural world. In these poems that celebrate country life the poet makes animal husbandry, beekeeping, and the growing of crops into metaphors for human existence. Above all, the sheer sensual pleasure of Virgil's Latin verse keeps the reader enthralled.

Finally, he turned to a relatively long epic poem, long enough surely to offend against Callimachean objections to long epic poems. The fact seems, however, to be simply part of the evidence that proclaims the *Aeneid* a truly original poem, a Roman poem, a confident poet's amalgamation of his tradition and his culture, not an imitation of any other poet's work. Virgil apparently wrote the story in outline first, then proceeded to compose portions of it as they came to him, rather than in studied chronological fashion. We are told that it was his custom to dictate several lines to his secretary in the morning, then to return to the poem later in the day, polishing and repolishing, getting the perfect expression, or leaving part of a line blank if its perfection eluded him. In 19 B.C.E., ten years after he began it, Virgil lay dying in the Italian port city of Brundisium. The tradition is that he instructed his literary executors to destroy the manuscript, because it was unfinished and he was not yet satisfied with it, but that Augustus countermanded the order. Evidently he, even if no one else, could recognize genuine praise of himself.

The story of the *Aeneid* is that of the band of Trojans who survived the destruction of Troy and wandered the Mediterranean until they finally landed in Italy and there laid the foundations for that great city that eventually became the center of the Roman Empire. The narrator begins:

> Of arms and the man I sing, who first from the shores of Troy,
> sent into exile by fate, to Italy and the Lavinian shores came,
> much tossed about on land and on the deep sea,
> by the power of the heavenly gods, because of the ever mindful wrath
> of Juno,
> suffering much as well from war, to the purpose that he found a city,
> bring his gods to Latium, whence sprang the Latin race
> and the senatorial fathers of Alba and the lofty walls of Rome.

The reader will immediately notice similarities with the narrative manner of both the *Iliad* and the *Odyssey*. The greater similarity is with the opening lines of the *Odyssey*, as the *Aeneid* narrator focuses on the traveling man, but the way the narrator expands his ideas and recapitulates them is very much like that of the opening lines of the *Iliad*. Yet the narrator begins "I sing" rather than calling upon the Muse for his story. Whereas Homer's call to the Muse assigns the story to another agency, Virgil signals the narrator's control and responsibility for the poem; he is very much the Alexandrian poet. Only after seven lines in which he outlines his story, does the narrator make his bow to the tradition: "Tell me, o Muse . . . "

What are we to make of the constant reminders throughout the poem of the *Iliad*, the *Odyssey*, the *Argonautica*, and countless other works less markedly emphasized? There is a school of criticism as old as antiquity which will notice the similarities and term them "Virgilian borrowings," as though the Roman poet used his predecessors for inspiration when the construction of a scene or a simile stumped him. It seems far more likely, however, that Virgil, clearly enough devoted to the Alexandrian point of view, meant to allude to his predecessors in such a way that the reader would bring over into the *Aeneid* the context of a passage or characteristic taken from the earlier piece. Though it is true that neither Aristotle nor any other ancient literary theorist refers to the literary practice of allusion, the surviving literature from the great Alexandrian poets seems to demand that the reader take into account the tradition upon which their poetry is based. Theocritus's experiments with miniature epics gain significantly in sense when compared with conventional long epics; Callimachus's hymns depend upon the Homeric hymns for their absurdist and deconstructive effect. Apollonius's poem is in constant dialogue with the Homeric poems. Modern-day critics who consider Alexandrian poetry decidedly second rate, at best playful and witty but scarcely substantial, do not take kindly to what is really an Alexandrian notion that the *Aeneid* deliberately reads best in some limbo between its text and its predecessors. That is to say, somewhat ambiguously, Virgil works with so many allusions, echoes so many other works, that his reader must construct a narrative far richer and larger than what the *Aeneid* offers as a surface. The reader imagines a narrative fuller and deeper than either this poem or its literary predecessors or its historical context.

What is distinctly monumental in the *Aeneid*, what has given it authority over twenty centuries, is exactly this fact: that it contains the whole of human existence in its narrative. This has been achieved, on the one hand, by the poet's brilliant use of past and future, history and myth—which for once makes the word "transcendent" correct in describing the poem's action—and, on the other hand, by his use of the literature of all time which allows the reader to imagine a depth and breadth to almost every scene beyond what any narrator could possibly achieve in description. It is absolutely essential for the reader to know as much as possible of the Greek and Roman history and culture of the centuries preceding the *Aeneid*. Such is the poem's centrality to the Western literary experience that in fact twentieth-century readers can rightly bring the history of the last two millennia to it with equal profit. The reaction to the poem can never be complete, since we lack knowledge of so much of the literature to which Virgil seems or may be assumed to be referring. But then no one reader can know everything in any case. The old truism is, we may say, even truer of the *Aeneid*—that the poem is always a unique experience for each of its readers.

Therefore, the call to the Muse, to whom the narrator turns in the line following those quoted above, is not simply a mechanical bow to his great Homeric models. Like the good Alexandrian he is, Virgil makes the tradition speak to his time and to his poem. Here at the very beginning the poet calls upon his reader to invest his knowledge of the Homeric poems in the moment. The narrator asks the Muse to explain Juno's implacable hostility to Aeneas. What could seem nothing more than epic ornament in fact makes narrative structure; the question to the Muse takes the reader away from here and now, the terrestrial scene, to some abstract plane where the narrator can begin the flashback with which the story proper begins. What is more, in asking the rhetorical question (rather more an exclamation) "Can such anger reside in the hearts of gods?" the narrator establishes an important theological depth to Juno's behavior throughout the poem. For on the simplest level, she functions in the *Aeneid* as the retarding agent, just as her brother god Poseidon (Neptune) does in the *Odyssey*. The narrator positions Poseidon in the narrative when he wishes to keep Odysseus from getting home too quickly; every good storyteller, after all, has to be able to put on the brakes to prevent the too rapid denouement of his tale. Here the narrator turns to the Muse for clarification and then, while he is that far away from the immediate telling of the story, asks a question that poses still larger questions about the nature of evil in the universe, about the fundamental malignancy of gods. Virgil's readers will remember that the narrator of the *Odyssey* also raises the subject of theodicy at the start; in the very first lines Zeus is made to complain that mortals blame all their misfortunes upon the gods, when in fact it is their own folly that brings them trouble. The *Odyssey* is the story of one good, wise man's triumph over adversity and evil. The *Aeneid* narrator is speaking to that passage as well but from another perspective, because, while allowing his question wider scope by addressing it to the Muse, he is nevertheless a *human* who asks, not a god like Zeus of the *Odyssey*, who pontificates. The reader will also recall the last words of Achilles on the subject of good and evil at the close of the *Iliad*: Zeus rains down now evil, now good mixed with evil into mortal lives. Achilles describes an indifferent universe, indiscriminate and random. Virgil's Juno, however, as the reader grows to realize, is persistent, focused malignity, a far more threatening presence in this poem than her brother Poseidon was in the *Odyssey*. Aeneas, one might say, lives in a far grimmer world than his Homeric counterparts.

Because the poet begins by saying he will sing of a traveling man, he invites his reader to remember the *Odyssey*. By using language that recalls the *Iliad*, he brings that poem into perspective as well. The position of the question to the Muse about divine responsibility for human suffering recalls Zeus's remarks, but the idea of divine hostility recalls the more general view of Achilles. These are the immediate observations that might occur to the practiced reader. Familiarity with the Homeric poems allows for a much fuller interpretation of the *Aeneid*. What is more, Virgil's narrative style is sufficiently abstract and allusive to persuade readers to interpret as they read. Certainly this constitutes one of the great distinctions between oral poetry and written verse. Freed of the voice of the singer-poet, to whom rapt attention must be paid, the reader may engage the text as slowly and meditatively as he or she chooses. The writer has left space in the narrative, and there the reader may enter. Apollonius had departed from the Homeric manner of seeming to tell everything; much was deliberately unsaid by his narrator. Virgil also practices this manner of narration, but his constant allusions to previous epic poetry give the reader yet another source of inspiration for imagining the text. The narrative of the *Aeneid* has maintained its centuries-long capacity to attract and satisfy partly because the poem is open to so many and such varied interpretations.

The narrator's creation of Dido is an excellent example of Virgil's method. She is presented as the ruler of Carthage, a queen beleaguered by neighboring people, a widow bound by oath to her late husband's memory. Her psychology, her motives, however, come through the reader's investment in the story. A woman who is described in a simile comparing her to Diana (Artemis) meets the shipwrecked Aeneas after he has come ashore. Exotic royal figure that she is, she entertains him in her palace, nurturing him, protecting him, desperately wanting to keep him there, in a way seducing him with her beauty and fairytale richness and splendor, dressing him in the local native costume which he exchanges for his Trojan military gear. When he is determined to go, she rages at him in a series of harsh, cruel rhetorical questions and vows eternal enmity, then kills herself. Later, meeting him in the underworld, she is silent when he tries to address her.

The experienced reader will invest Dido with (1) the sweet, virginal innocence of the sturdy young Nausicaa, who is also compared to Artemis when she goes to the beach where she will meet the shipwreck; (2) the tenacity of Calypso, mistress also of the bed and breakfast; (3) the sinister seductiveness of Circe, who transforms men's appearance; (4) the memory of the war with Carthage, when Rome's future security was for once seriously challenged; (5) the disastrous seductiveness of the royal bed of Cleopatra, where two traveling Roman leaders stopped and one was destroyed; (6) the rage of the betrayed and deserted Medea; and (7) the same sense of being a failed anachronism that leads Ajax to his suicide, whose bitterness keeps him so angry at Odysseus even after death that he refuses to speak to him in the underworld. The combination of sensations that these reminiscences introduce into the story would be beyond the range of a more literal narration. Since the allusions suggest rather than insist, the reader is very much the master, able to fill in the tone and depth of each scene as he or she wishes. Every reading is a radically new experience of the poem.

"Of arms and the man I sing": so goes the opening line, and critics distinguish between the war story of the last six books, the so-called Iliadic *Aeneid*, and the story of a man and his travels in the first six, the Odyssean. Yet the poem can never be so simply categorized, for Virgil is a master of the complicated architecture of narrative. Some critics see a pattern of light and dark in which the odd numbered books tend to have a more sanguine view of things than the even numbered books. Sometimes the scheme seems only relatively true; for instance, Book Three can be called light only because it is set between the very somber Books Two and Four. Still, there is a pattern to be observed: Dido receives the anguished, shipwrecked Aeneas and gives him a banquet in the first book; he describes the woeful fall of Troy in the second, then his relatively happier and finally more optimistic travels in the third; the fourth recounts the couple's fatal love affair, the fifth a jolly day of athletic contests; the sixth details the grim and awesome descent into the underworld; the seventh inaugurates the Trojans' triumphant arrival at their destined homeland, and so forth until the last, the twelfth book, ends in the tragic death of Turnus.

Yet another pattern that one might establish in this poem is a triadic structure. The first four books are a third-person narrative much in the Alexandrian mode, in the center of which (Books Two and Three) the principal figure is made to create two first-person narratives: one a miniature battle epic (like the *Iliad*), the other a miniature travel narrative (like the *Odyssey*). The second four books contain action lodged one way or another in a temporal scheme that is either the present or the future for the characters in the story and is established fact for the reader of the poem. The final four books constitute a drama of battle in which good triumphs over evil, age over youth, destiny over free will, and comedy over tragedy. As these last books make clear, the entire poem is more the story of the *Odyssey* than anything else. Aeneas travels the world over, confronting and overcoming obstacles, until he arrives at the homeland destined for him by fate, where he fights a suitor to win for wife the princess of the land over which he and his sons will rule. Ancient literary theorists seem to have distinguished between the tragedy of the *Iliad* and the comedy of the *Odyssey;* in this context it is fair to say, although we have no evidence that the ancients had worked out the notion in theory, that Aeneas is a comic hero in the grand sense of the word. In the same way, the history of Rome is comic; a small city succeeds, by destiny's design, to the ownership and control of the whole world.

The reader, however, as well as Aeneas himself, must be prepared for this concept. The reader's anticipations based on epic convention must be shattered; this means that Aeneas must misconceive things, lose his way, proceed by trial and error. In various scenes of the early books the hero seems to stumble; he appears in an awkward light. In the first book, for instance, he encounters his mother, Venus, who is disguised as a young country girl (1.314ff.). When she asks him who he is, he replies in the high-heroic style appropriate to scenes before thrones and at courts. Only a few lines into his grand reply the narrator says that Venus, able to stand no more, interrupts him. The incident recalls the humiliations that the narrator of the *Argonautica* inflicts upon Jason, particularly the moment when Aeetes more or less shuts him up just after the young lad has launched into his own introductory speech to the king (3.401). Venus's dismissal contrasts particularly with the enthusiastic response of Athena to Odysseus when he gives her a false autobiography in circumstances that almost exactly parallel those of this scene.

In the second book, after he has been asked by Dido to tell his experiences, Aeneas describes the last days of the city of Troy. As his original reader would know, he has taken the material of his story from one of the poems of the Epic Cycle. Aeneas is thus acting as his very own poet, just like Odysseus, presenting a miniature epic story, a fighting story much like the material of the *Iliad,* a story in which he has a chance to star. He does in fact commence by mentioning his considerable role in this period of fighting. As the poem unfolds, however, the reader discovers that Aeneas has been more spectator than warrior. As a poem, the second book is a fine verbal construct, but it lacks a hero; Aeneas, whose reminiscence this is, does not succeed in filling that role. There is also the awkward incident he describes (2.567ff.) when in the last desperate moments of the fighting he chances upon Helen and goes to kill her, only to be stopped by his mother, Venus. The scene is altogether amusingly dubious, considering that Helen's and Aeneas's claims to Venus's protection and concern stem respectively from her disparate roles, that of goddess of love and reproduction, and that of national goddess, titular mother of the Julian clan, divine mother of the Roman people. It is the kind of incongruous juxtaposition beloved of the Alexandrians. Venus takes this moment to reveal to her son that Troy is lost; she shows him behind the scenes, as it were, the entire Olympian divine entourage fighting to destroy the city and its people. It is as though Aeneas, in striking out at Helen, is locked into the old heroic belief in the validity of human action, as though he is in some other poem, as though the war at Troy is being fought over Menelaus's and Paris's possessiveness—whereas, as his mother shows him, Helen is not relevant to what is really happening. Troy is doomed; the fighting is immaterial; it is rather a matter of historical process. Although the poetry that the narrator places in Aeneas's mouth is thrilling (the Laocoön scene and the Priam scene are two of the best moments in the entire work), on the whole, Aeneas's war poem seems somehow empty and off the mark; it lacks the very essence of epic narrative, a strong central character. Certainly Aeneas does not stand in his own narrative as Odysseus stands in his travel stories (*Od.* 9–12).

Aeneas's next try (the third book) is a travel narrative, very much a miniature *Odyssey*. Here again he fails to succeed as a poet, since he does not lead this poem to the happy conclusion that travel stories—the *Odyssey* in particular—demonstrate. Instead, the poem ends with the death of his father, Anchises, a sorry event for Aeneas if not for the entire band of Trojans. Book Three is weary in tone, even sometimes unhappy, beginning with the group's departure from Troy with Aeneas in tears. Jason's tearful departure from Iolcus comes to mind, as well as the grim journey of the second book of the *Argonautica*. Readers of this book of the *Aeneid* will not forget, either (since they are reminded of it), that while Aeneas and his band are traversing the seas, often dismally misguided as to their destination, Odysseus is living out the highhearted adventures that make the central books of the *Odyssey* eternally attractive. Despite their terrors and perils, Odysseus's adventures at least in the telling are exciting. Those of Aeneas, by contrast, are grim and plodding, the telling tight-lipped. The third book of the *Aeneid* is universally condemned as boring. Virgil, it seems, is onto something his readers do not understand.

The narrator, who began this story with a third-person account in the first book, takes over again in the fourth. Whereas Aeneas was the stand-in for a Demodocus figure, telling his story before a live audience, performing like the oral poet of the very early Greek epics, the narrator of the first and fourth books is writing a love story after the fashion of the third-century Alexandrian stories. But here again the narration fails; love does not succeed for Aeneas any more than does war, travel, or storytelling. The first four books of the *Aeneid* dismiss the cultural and literary past to which the Romans had clung ever since Livius Andronicus introduced them to the seductive authority of things Greek. Aeneas fails in his attempt to introduce himself in the heroic mode: he cannot recite a poem of his adventures in which he is the star, as his self-centered predecessor Odysseus can do; his battle narrative fails as heroic epic, since it is curiously empty of his own exploits; his travel narrative, in which he appears small because he leans on the presence of his father, is both depressing and misguided and ends in failure. Even Greek intellectual superiority has been degraded when in the second book the narrator introduces Sinon, a protegé of Ulysses who debases himself by lying shamelessly, acting out the part of a sniveling victim to touch Trojan hearts. Such is Trojan directness and honesty that they are helpless against Sinon, who proceeds to initiate the action that brings on Troy's final catastrophe. Sinon's ability to persuade through lying, one feels, is the legacy of Greek rhetoric and philosophy set against the Roman inclination—at least as seen through a Roman narrator's eyes—to make things whole and get things done. Anchises' death in the third book parallels Hercules' departure from the narrative in the *Argonautica*. The Trojan prince Anchises is a figure from the heroic past; as the third book begins, he directs the sailing out while his son languishes in tears, but thereafter he is confused and misled about the oracles that have revealed a promised land to these Trojans. He leaves this narrative as Hercules left the *Argonautica*, a symbol of values and beliefs that are alien to the narrative under way.

Now in the fourth book Aeneas has the chance of love that Jason also had, once Hercules was no longer center stage. The narrator presents Aeneas in yet one more situation in which he tries on an attitude of the past: he falls in love. Love, as remarked earlier, is the great Hellenistic form of self-realization; romantic love was the invention of the Greeks in the age after the collapse of the city-state, in a world controlled by god-kings, when the private self eclipsed the public self in importance, when love became the affirmation of the private self as the private life of the romance novel and Menandrian comedy replaced the public hero of epic and Aristophanic comedy. Yet when Jupiter commands, Aeneas leaves. He chooses something other than love. He has a son to provide a future for; he has followers to make secure. One might also argue that Aeneas has a destiny that promises him some kind of stardom. This last is implicit in his action, his aristocratic or regal class, and the narrative genre. A heroic male cannot stay at the side of a woman. Notice that Penelope disappears from the narrative after she and Odysseus have reunited; notice how Jason is diminished when he brings Medea aboard ship.

The poet reveals the elemental conflict of Dido and Aeneas through a marvelous collision of genres when he describes the couple's meeting in the underworld (6.450ff.). She, the suicide, is silent, recalling the tragic dramatic character Ajax; Aeneas, on the contrary, has called out to her, "Invitus, regina, tuo de litore cessi" (unwilling, o queen, did I leave your shore). This is a direct imitation of the line of the earlier, very Alexandrian poet Catullus: "Invita, o regina, tuo de vertice cessi" (unwilling, o queen, did I leave the top of your head). The Catullan poem is a translation of a Callimachean original, "The Lock of Berenice," in which a lock of hair shorn from the head of Egypt's Queen Berenice laments its separation from the queen. The Callimachean-Catullan piece is a typically charming, lighthearted, mocking poem describing something utterly trivial in momentous terms. That Aeneas speaks the line seems utterly shocking yet says better than anything else could how mistaken was Dido's deep emotional dependency. It is rejected by Aeneas, whom the divine command to leave has brought to his senses. In the flippant, witty, and charming manner of a Callimachus or Theocritus, he puts their passionate coupling in the cave and their days of romance thereafter into a broader perspective and has seen that it was no more than great fun that all began on a stormy afternoon. Dido and Aeneas are in different poems!

It is difficult for readers who believe in true love, long-term relationships, and commitment not to fault Aeneas for leaving Dido. It becomes even harder when the last scenes between the two remind one so much of Euripides' tortured Medea and the smug Jason. Yet the fourth book is a story of misplaced loyalties. Because Dido has sworn an oath that she will not remarry, her love for Aeneas is a violation of her conception of herself as wife and widow, a capitulation to personal feeling. She is head of state, yet she allows personal emotion so to captivate her that royal projects in the kingdom are stopped. A romp through the meadows of personal feeling would be entirely in keeping with Hellenistic love poetry, but Dido, makes the mistake of sinking into feminine dependency upon a male, becoming or at least resembling nothing so much as a heroine from the tragic stage. For female dependency, whether aculturated or not, is one of the true tragedies of the human condition (at least as male writers have construed it); it is a condition to which the ancient tragic dramatists turned again and again. Dido betrays herself by indulging in private emotions.

Aeneas does not see their relationship as marriage at all. Emotional involvement and social contracts are entirely separate. Consider the epithets that the narrator gives him; only occasionally is he allotted the kind that accompanies a Homeric hero at all times. Instead of something so physical as "swift-footed" or so psychological as "man of many turns," Aeneas is called *pius*—a word that does not translate easily into English but, whatever else, does not mean "pious." "Responsible" is better, or "aware of obligations to others," or "devoted." These do not have a glamorous ring to them, and Aeneas has always seemed a little dreary because of this characterizing epithet. If one were to consider him as an ancient version of a very contemporary cliché, however—that is, the man who gives up everything to pursue career and find success—Aeneas would attract more sympathy and more luster. For what he does, in fact, is just that. He is not successful in the traditional role of the self-obsessed Homeric hero; he hasn't the self-serving, self-congratulating way of Achilles or Odysseus. He is not allowed to succeed in the role of love hero as Jason has done; that experiment in private life and personal ecstacy is taken away from him when Jupiter sends Mercury to tell him to leave Dido and move on. When Zeus sent Hermes to Calypso to tell her to give up the fun, she did so with ill will, while Odysseus set out to leave enthusiastically. In the *Aeneid* Aeneas takes the part of Calypso, as it were: it is he who must stiffen resolve and find the will to do what he does not altogether wish to do. It is another exercise in his *pietas*.

Aeneas is a strong man, a responsible man, who leaves Carthage. The poet has arranged a sequence of events that articulates the journey of Aeneas' soul. He says goodbye to Dido and chooses instead the career that destiny rather than his personal will has assigned to him, thereby effectively killing in himself any further chance of authentic individual human experience. He journeys to Sicily, where the group puts on athletic contests to commemorate the death of Anchises. These funeral games, standing between his own self-abnegation in Carthage and his descent into the underworld, celebrate in a way Aeneas's own kind of death. The descent into the underworld and his return bring Aeneas through a change comprising spiritual death and resurrection, which is the logical movement for one who has symbolically died and will be born again as an icon for his age.

Roman history is what holds together the narrative of the central four books. It gives a peculiar authority to the entire story as myth and legend are suddenly revealed in historical fact. The wanderings of the Trojans, their hope and expectation of a promised land, bears a real resemblance to the Hebrew story of the biblical Exodus. Some would like to believe that young Virgil must have moved in circles in Rome where he was able to hear such Hebrew stories as this. There is also the Hebrew prophecy of a messiah, the god who would enter history. One would not, of course, have to know Hebrews to think of saviors; it was a common enough idea among all the Mediterranean peoples in this century. Virgil himself wrote a poem (*Eclogue IV*) in congratulation of the birth of a friend's child which so much resembles the verses of Isaiah prophesying a messiah that the Roman poet acquired an enormous reputation among the Christians. The poem's messianic glow, however, is no doubt a tongue-in-cheek exercise in hyperbolic irony to accompany a set of booties or a layette; the recipients would likely smile as they recognized the commonplace sentiments inflated in the poem. In any case, the *Aeneid* is filled with the Trojans' expectation of their future, with divine pronouncements on Roman future. The great prophecy of Jupiter, which he tells to Venus in the first book, more or less sets the comic tone of success for the entire poem. Jupiter prophesies Roman power without end. For Roman readers of the *Aeneid* the prophecy was a historical reality.

Two episodes in particular thrill the reader by the way events and persons realized in Roman history are anticipated in the temporal plane in which the story unfolds. In Book Six Aeneas descends to the underworld, where his father shows him the souls of Romans waiting to be born; in Book Eight Venus brings him a shield upon which Vulcan has set out scenes from future Roman history. An extraordinary parade crosses Aeneas's vision as he stands with his father Anchises who provides running commentary. The early kings of Rome are there, the great generals, the Scipios, Quintus Fabius Maximus, known as the "Delayer," who protected Rome from Hannibal's invasion—a selection of men whose actions are emblematic of their noble or evil character. On the shield the conflict of good and evil appears in still greater relief. The description passes from the noble heroes of Rome—Cocles, Cloelia, and Manlius, youngsters whose daring and courage provide the fables of Rome's founding—to Catiline, the criminal-minded enemy of the state, to Cato, ancient conservator of Rome's pristine mores; it ends in a large panoramic scene of the battle of Actium. In describing that scene, Virgil has repeated the values of the Herodotean portrayal of Xerxes confronting the Greeks: the Persian king savage, deranged, inflated in passion and opulence; the Greeks staid, sober, simple, sagacious. Here, Antony and Cleopatra and their exotic unbridled retinue accompanied by wild, strange gods are dispatched into disarray by Augustus, whose subsequent triumph is the final scene upon this shield. The scene of the battle of Actium does far more than recall Herodotus; it plays to the Greco-Roman conviction of their cultural superiority to Eastern peoples. It reenacts Aeneas's departure from Dido. It replays the agonizing war against Carthage, when for brief moments Rome and the West seemed about to succumb to this Semitic-African power. The fearful Roman temptation to turn eastward resonates in the shield scene as well. Actium had saved the Romans from many things. Now Aeneas will wear this shield and be protected from the emotions that the East exemplified and that will be repeated in the young men who confront his warriors and himself in battle.

From Romulus to Augustus, Virgil has allegorized Roman history. He has mythologized it as well. The Greeks organized their shared experience on several planes, one being the saga and myth world that provided them with a set of familiars whose deeds constituted a thorough repertory of responses to the human condition. Agamemnon, Clytemnestra, Antigone, Creon, Oedipus, Medea, Actaeon, Sisyphus—the list is endless. These names conjure up an entire other world in which events have been played out and will be repeated to the end of time as icons and models for our lives, as instruction for us all. Virgil's brilliant originality is to make Roman history over into something more than a chronology of past events or their interpretation. He turns the dead figures of Rome's past into eternally living symbols, emblems of attitudes, behaviors, and values. It is true, of course, that all history is in some sense mythology, since it involves juxtaposing events and persons so as to make sense or meaning. But Virgil went far beyond this: he made abstractions; he made Roman history into something more than enactments confined by the straits of past time; he opened up Roman history to a universal stage. For the Western European world Virgil made a new mythology. The history of Rome stands to this day beside the Judeo-Christian religion and Greco-Roman mythology as one of the fictive staples of inspiration for Western culture.

Aeneas, who denies Dido and leaves Carthage, by this choice gives up the individual that he might be to enter into this greater world of mythic figures. He becomes someone transcendent, an instrument of destiny, a figure conforming to the obligations and demands of a greater plot, a universal story whose author is the Stoic god or divine essence. In Alexandrian terms, he leaves behind the genres of early heroic epic and Greek Alexandrian epic to assume the role of comic hero who in a tragi-comic epic will do battle with figures from tragedy. He has already met and discarded the tragic dramatic heroine Dido, whose final angry moments are part of a dialogue that might have come from the Euripidean stage. Soon he will confront a tragic epic hero, Turnus, whose valiant defense of his land, wild impetuosity, and anger at defeat bear traces of the two exemplars of tragic epic behavior: Achilles and Hector.

We use the word "transcendent" in speaking of Aeneas, or talk of him as the abstraction "comic hero." These are words to describe a character who is distanced, and indeed more often than not the narrator has, curiously enough, left Aeneas out of the action. The great example, surely, occurs when Venus has given Aeneas the shield; he admiringly studies it but, as the narrator warns (8.730) is ignorant of the meaning of the scenes depicted on it. He is *looking* at action, for one thing, rather than engaged in action, and he does not know what it means. All this is significant. Aeneas has a history of being somehow distanced from action. In the *Iliad* he is snatched out of a near-fatal encounter in battle by his mother, Aphrodite (5.315ff.) and then on another occasion by Poseidon (20.321ff.). In the first book of the *Aeneid* too Aeneas is shown gazing at action, this time at wall murals depicting the battles of Troy. The image of Aeneas as onlooker rather than participant in battle is quickly reinforced in his own Book Two narrative when he recounts that during Priam's last grisly moments he himself was watching from cover, and again when he tells how Venus showed him the gods fighting over Troy: with war and battle going on all around him, gods and mortal men engaged in all sorts of combat, he was stayed from action by his mother, stopped, given a chance to observe the scene. Yet again, his journey to the underworld is a voyage of exploration and seeing, not of action. Now in Book Eight, as he receives his new shield, he is once again shown looking on. The poet has used this minor theme to underscore the change that will overtake Aeneas in the final books as he is transformed into a man of action, commits himself to battle, and at the very end kills one of the most attractive and sympathetic characters Virgil could create.

As noted earlier, the poem divides several ways; hence, the reader is forever situated in more than one frame. In the center of the second triad, in the midst of Aeneas's immersion in history—when mythical man, as it were, is made historically concrete—the *Aeneid* radically divides into two halves. Aeneas returns from the underworld at the very close of Book Six; near the beginning of Book Seven is an exordium (37ff.) in which the Muse Erato is invoked and asked for help in narrating coming events, while the narrator announces that he is turning to a grander subject than what has come before. The Trojans have just set foot on the land of Italy; now finally history will begin. The Trojans will exchange their identity as creatures of fable, myth, and legend for that of proto-Romans, creatures of flesh and blood and historical truth. When Odysseus, we remember, is put ashore at Ithaca by the Pheacians, he has slept through the journey from fable, from the never-never Land of Scheria, to the reality of Ithaca, so that he will have no consciousness of the improbable transition from dream or fantasy to reality. Similarly, Aeneas comes up from the underworld by way of the Gate of Ivory, through which, the narrator says, false dreams come. It has all been a myth up to now, the narrator seems to be saying.

That Virgil puts the formal introduction to the second half of his poem thirty-seven lines into it rather than at the very beginning of the seventh book is the kind of violation of form and symmetry guaranteed to make his readers think. It reminds the practiced reader that the poem is as much about literary structure and narrative manner as it is about one man's Herculean labors, the founding of Rome, or world history and Roman destiny. Like the great blues singer Billie Holiday, Virgil contrives to come in after the beat, as it were, which is a deliciously sensual effect. The result is to keep the reader attentive to the way in which the narrator plays off the epic poetry of the past, redefining it while insisting at the same time upon the utter originality of the *Aeneid*.

The hero of this second half of the poem is perhaps Aeneas or perhaps Turnus. Again, one may say that Virgil has taken over from Apollonius a narrative in which two figures demand the reader's equal attention. The narrator of neither the *Iliad* nor the *Odyssey* establishes any serious alternative figure who wars with the main character for the auditor's sympathies. Hector, it is true, is a powerful counterfigure in the *Iliad*, simply because the city of Troy is the important alternative site to the Achaean camp. But one could argue that Hector is seen principally through the reaction of others. He motivates the description of the women in Book Six; he highlights the peculiar quality of Paris in Book Three; he is the true threat to the Achaeans throughout the books in which Achilles withdraws from battle; he is the source of his parents' and wife's woes and concerns as he defends the city and dies. Only in the monologue as he awaits the mad rush of Achilles is Hector revealed as a person.

Turnus, on the other hand, is completely realized in scene after scene in the last books of this poem. He is introduced as a prince of ancient lineage, the intended bridegroom of Lavinia, daughter of King Latinus and Queen Amata. The queen, as the narrator remarks in these early establishing lines, is in haste to make Turnus her son-in-law, motivated by a "remarkable love" (7.57). Thereafter, Juno, still determined to thwart destiny and keep Aeneas from his fated marriage with Lavinia, sends madness upon the earth in the form of a demon named Allecto, who infects Amata and then Turnus. The mild-mannered young man who at first cannot imagine that the arriving Trojans pose any threat to him is driven into a frenzy of masculine competitiveness, territorial anxiety, and sexual possessiveness (7.435ff.). In sum, he is transformed into a Homeric hero. His presumptive mother-in-law rages, as the narrator describes her, like a Euripidean bacchante (7.385ff.). Both are victims of a god. Like Dido before them, raging in love through Carthage, they are offerings for the tragic drama of the losing side which unfolds in these last books. Nothing is sadder than the moment toward the very end when King Latinus begs Turnus to desist (12.19ff.). The scene is a very tortured nod toward the scene of Priam imploring Hector to stay inside Troy. But Latinus speaks in a way figures in a heroic culture do not: he counsels Turnus to quit, since the cause is surely lost, to go home to his lands and find other brides. More remarkably—because heroes, even old Nestor, do not speak in such a fashion—Latinus argues logically and sensibly that since he will certainly ally himself with the Trojans once Turnus is dead, then why should he not do so with Turnus alive and home in safety. The narrator gives Latinus a men-

tality that has come a long way in understanding since Homer's heroic
age. Turnus's answer is heartbreaking:

> The concern for me which you possess, for me, I ask you, drop.
> Let me bargain for glory with my death.
>
> [12.48f.]

The old heroic values still apply; Turnus has learned nothing. He
proudly asserts that in the forthcoming battle he has as much chance
as Aeneas of winning. The goddess mother won't be around, he
sneers, to shield Aeneas by hiding him in a cloud.

In fact, in the *Iliad* scene to which Turnus is obviously referring,
Aphrodite protects Aeneas by throwing her arms about him and putting her folded robe out as a buffer before she snatches him from the
battle; it is in quite a different battle scene, and at a highly significant
moment, that Poseidon protects Aeneas by casting a mist before the
eyes of his opponent. To the experienced reader of the *Iliad*, Turnus's
confusion of the two scenes is fascinating. Virgil certainly knew his *Iliad* well, so the reader must assume the confusion to be deliberate. Obviously, Turnus too knows the *Iliad* story but not well enough. He
ought to know it, of course, since it is presumed to be for all the fictional figures in this story their own history and culture, as the mural
scenes of the Trojan War on the temple walls in Dido's Carthage suggest. Yet he has forgotten or never learned what Poseidon says to justify his entering the battle and saving Aeneas: "Let us take him away
from death . . . since he is destined to survive so that the line of Dar-
danos shall not perish from the earth. . . . Zeus has cursed the generation of Priam, but Aeneas now in turn shall be lord over the
Trojans, he, and his sons, and his line forever" (*Il.* 20.300–308). Turnus's boast at this moment, then, resting on confusion and misun-
derstanding, which the practiced reader would not at all share, gives
rise to that tragic sense of irony so prominent in fifth-century Greek
drama.

As has been remarked, early epic's ubiquitous, conventional heroic
story of military men in triumph and defeat was given a tragic dimension in the *Iliad* by the addition of the story of the fall of Troy.
One could argue that the somber lesson of defeat and death implicit
in every allusion to Troy and the Trojans is also to be applied to
Achilles' struggle to accept the yoke of necessity, imposed first by

Agamemnon and then at last by the very elemental fact of human mortality. What Virgil achieves in the last six books of the *Aeneid* is a colossal dichotomous view: the tragic story of great men in defeat on the field of battle is set alongside the optimistic success story of the man who defeats them. It is a tragedy of history in which those who are obsolescent fall before the onslaught of those who are riding the future's horses. In Shakespeare's *Antony* and *Cleopatra* and Sophocles' *Ajax* the dead or dying or doomed figures who have no place any longer in the world remain center stage, yielding nothing to forces of history that have arrived to take their place: the group who debate Ajax's right to public glory, Octavian who is planning a triumph. Virgil keeps both time's victims and her favorites in the foreground partly by insisting on the equally valid comic and tragic themes invoked in these last six books.

The story of the battle is fairly simple. The Trojans land and go to parley with King Latinus. He receives them graciously and realizes immediately that their king, Aeneas, is the foreign prince who an oracle has prophesied would come for the hand of his daughter Lavinia. Shortly thereafter, Aeneas's son Ascanius, while out hunting, kills a favorite stag of the Latins (the indigenous population); an uproar ensues, and from that the two parties move to war. On the divine level, Juno, who has suddenly discovered that her enemy has managed to make it to Italy, fans the flames of hatred in Amata, the queen, and Turnus, Lavinia's intended. A series of battles follows in which a number of young men and one woman are shown fighting and dying: Nisus, Euryalus, Camilla, Lausus, Pallas, and finally Turnus. Until the mid-twentieth century, criticism generally looked upon the carnage of the last six books as the logical unfolding of the advice Anchises gives to Aeneas in the Underworld:

> Other people shall more subtly make
> bronze into breathing creatures,
> others will draw our living faces from marble,
> others will plead better their cases at court, with the rod
> discover the motions of the heavens
> and learn to tell the rising of the stars.
> But you, o Roman, remember to rule with your power—
> these are your arts—and to impose the law of peace;
> to be merciful to the conquered, and to cast down the proud.
>
> [6.847–53]

The *pax romana* was central to the ideology of empire throughout Western Europe's history. More recently there has been a revision of what had seemed Virgil's enthusiastic endorsement of empire, power, and rule. One might argue that at the time of the Vietnam War a current of disgust at an ill-conceived American imperial ambition altered, especially in America, the traditional reading of this poem. Discounting the praise of Augustus and the imperial enterprise, and focusing more on the deaths of the young men in the latter part of the poem, a wave of American critics insisted that Virgil was saying that the price of empire was too high.

But perhaps Virgil is not talking about this at all. Perhaps Virgil introduces the tragic view of things only to reject it. The triumph of Aeneas over young Turnus, the deaths of all the young and the survival of the aging Trojan prince, are perhaps again part of the overall comic thrust of the poem. To begin with, death is for the young, life for the old. That is the difference between the anguish of Achilles, who frets over his imminent death and the brevity of his life, and the pleasure Odysseus takes at being reinstated once again in his homeland. That is the difference between the old men in certain Aristophanic plays who at the end go off with the girl to a party and the young males who meanwhile gird up for battle. (One thinks as well of the vitality of the aging Oedipus at Colonus, cursing his son and dooming him when he comes for his father's blessing.) That is the difference between the Roman epic—product of an older, wiser civilization, comfortable in having finally arrived at a cultural maturity previously unknown—and the Homeric poems, which are the artifacts of a very new culture, very young, untried. Virgil, one might say, is setting up Rome to play Nestor to Greece's Achilles. The wisdom of age, the balance, the sobriety—these are the qualities of Aeneas compared with the impetuosity, the hysteria, the innocence of the young who go so gloriously to their deaths in the *Aeneid*. This may be said to be the difference between Greece and Rome, as the Romans saw it, so that this poem contains what to the ancient Romans would seem to be all of world history. Furthermore, the Greeks who invented tragic drama, whose epic *Iliad* prefigures the tragic sense of life to be found in those dramas, were far different from the Romans, who did not care for tragedy, whose experience of growth and expansion combined with a far more linear sense of historical time gave them the notion of an ongoing world in which change was possible. This vision of linear history is not tragic, especially when coupled

with the Stoic sense of a beneficent Supreme Being which or who
(depending upon the anthropomorphization) moves all things to that
which is good. A universe seen this way will be fundamentally comic.

Among the many sad deaths recorded in the latter half of the *Aeneid*
are those of the two Trojan lovers, Nisus and Euryalus, and the Latin
allies, father and son, Mezentius and Lausus. Like Turnus, these
figures are presented so sympathetically that the reader requires a
strong will not to capitulate to their point of view. Well, why not
capitulate? Because, true to the dictates of Alexandrian literary theorists, an audience is made of sterner stuff, reads not for the story,
to be swayed by a rush of empathy at the events or the personages
in the narrative. The narrator throughout this poem has insisted upon
distancing the reader from the action. Like the choruses in tragic
drama that protect the audience from too easy, quick, and deep an
emotional identification with the events described and planned in the
dialogue passages, the narrator of the *Aeneid* wants the reader to think
about the action, not simply feel it. Because Virgil has so carefully
and deliberately established the literary antecedents of his poem, has
insisted upon authenticity and category after the fashion of the Alexandrian librarian-poets, he persuades his reader constantly to see
the action in a wider context, not simply to empathize with what
happens but to judge it in terms of its literary history. One of the
special pleasures of reading the *Aeneid* is to force the act of will, to
make the commitment to the central figure of the narrative, Aeneas.

The Nisus and Euryalus episode derives from the story in the tenth
book of the *Iliad* usually called the Doloneia, after Dolon, the principal
victim of Diomedes and Odysseus as they reconnoiter at night in
enemy territory. The Virgilian version has a brace of heroes who set
out not to scout but to sneak through enemy lines with information
for their absent leader, Aeneas. In a way they resemble Dolon. Not
only are they discovered and killed, but their youthful impetuousness
reminds the reader of Dolon's naiveté—or, as actually played by
Homer, stupidity motivated by cupidity, of which there is a touch in
the Nisus and Euryalus episode as well. Yet it is Diomedes and Odysseus to whom the reader is directed in seeking resemblances that will
inspire a reading of this passage; not only are there again two men
on a nighttime expedition, but they encounter sleeping enemies and
kill some of them in very much the same order as in the Homeric
story.

The *Iliad* episode, coming after the ninth book's scene in which
Achilles refuses to return to the fight, is about males in unison whose

union makes for a greater success; it is a strong rebuke through narrated action to the isolation and selfishness of the anguished Achilles, a rebuke equal or superior to the force of the speeches in the ninth book. Dolon is an evil man to look upon, says the narrator. Diomedes and Odysseus treat him contemptuously, cruelly; they decapitate him after promising not to maltreat him. Their subsequent highhearted manner suggests that neither they nor the narrator consider that this behavior has violated any code of heroes. Dolon's physical ugliness is a signal that he is not among his peers; the Homeric poems are consistent in their insistence upon the heroic value of physical beauty.

Dolon has cunning and assertiveness, qualities not unknown to Homer's heroes, but in him the narrator manages to make them suspect. Dolon demands a promise from the Trojans that he will be given Achilles' horses as recompense for his scouting expedition; when he is cornered by Diomedes and Odysseus, he pleads for his life, saying that Hector bribed him with the promise of the horses. His contemptible person somehow makes the negotiation ludicrous and unseemly. In Euripides' play *Rhesus*, Hector is made to want the horses as well, which provokes unseemly negotiation in the play's dialogue between the Trojan prince and Dolon. It is just the sort of incongruity that prefigures the Alexandrian sensibility and suggests ways to understand what Virgil has made of the tenth book.

The Virgilian Nisus has a more complicated view of rewards: "If they give to you what I demand, since fame is quite enough for me . . . ," he says to Euryalus (9.194f.). Material rewards are useful only as love offerings; Euryalus in Greek terms is the beloved, the *eromenos*, to whom Nisus the lover, the *erastes*, gives gifts. As countless anecdotes relate, the *eromenos* is the pursued, the seduced, the wooed, and precious gifts are the conventional means employed by the *erastes*. What Nisus wants for himself is fame; Euryalus can have the material rewards as gifts. Nisus is then some new kind of hero; he does not need the material expression that for the Homeric hero made the glory. But the gifts are still important to this scene. By Greek homoerotic convention the *eromenos* regards the gifts as the material expression of the emotion of the love. Gifts retain their symbolic power as affirmation. Virgil has simply changed the game and the arena.

Nisus loves Euryalus, who is described more than once as beautiful. The sensuality of the boy is marked particularly at the moment of death. The spear breaks his white breast, the blood flows all over his beautiful limbs, says the narrator (9.433f.). Dying, he is compared to a poppy, its head drooping with rainwater. The simile comes from Homer, but Virgil adds the telling detail: the poppy has a weary neck. Flowers, however beautiful, are cold and bloodless. The adjective gives flesh and a sensuous lassitude to the botanical context. The reader is reminded of the sixth-century Greek Tyrtaeus's inspirational elegiacs on the martial spirit in which he envisions with disgust the corpse of an old man fallen on the field of battle as opposed to the beautiful body of a young man.

Nisus loves Euryalus; for the ancients this means desire. Yet despite the younger man's comeliness, one gets the idea that Nisus cares for Euryalus as much as desires him; in other words, he loves him as we moderns understand the term. In the athletic contests of the fifth book, when Nisus slips on blood from a sacrificial animal in the foot race, he manages at the same time to trip up the man coming behind him, leaving the race for Euryalus to win. The act is not heroic in Homeric terms, and modern-day commentators are sometimes repelled: Nisus, it seems, is neither gentleman nor sportsman. But that is the effect Virgil is trying for. He has in Apollonian fashion corrupted the games, which are to be read from the Homeric model of Book Twenty-three of the *Iliad* as conventional masculine heroic competition, by introducing the mischievous, corrupt behavior of the lover. One remembers the portrait of Eros in the third book of the *Argonautica* or the boy lovers of pastoral poetry or the epigrams of the *Anthology*. Furthermore, in the parallel scene from Homer it is Ajax, son of Oïleus, who takes the fall, slipping on dung. He takes his embarrassment in stride and his colleagues laugh at him. After the race in the fifth book of the *Aeneid*, amid the uproar from the defrauded contestant, who is outraged at Euryalus's improbable victory, the narrator remarks that "Euryalus's popularity protects him, and his tears which so become him, and no less pleasing than these is his manliness, coming as it does in so beautiful a body" (5.343ff.). In this athletic contest Nisus and Euryalus are a long distance in manner, body, and sensibility from the rough-and-tumble of the contestants in the Homeric model.

Nisus and Euryalus, the lovers out on a nighttime military expedition, are in the tradition of male bonding which is praised by Phaedrus in Plato's *Symposium*. It was very much the convention in the Spartan army and extolled throughout the rest of Greece. The tradition that the Spartan men who defended the pass at Thermopylae and died there to the last person were all of them loving couples expressed the fifth-century Greek belief in the absolute value of male homosexuality in teaching and maintaining morals, morale, and ethics. The Achaeans of the *Iliad* value males absolutely, but their male bonding appears to have been asexual. What Virgil seems to do is to bring *eros* over to the battlefield. The description of Nisus lying upon the beautiful corpse of Euryalus is from the tradition of erotic lyric poetry. Virgil is confusing genres in an Apollonian fashion. Nisus and Euryalus are a latter-day Diomedes and Odysseus, but their bonding has been complicated and eroticized.

Virgil has further complicated Euryalus's role by giving him a mother. First, Nisus will not take him along because he does not wish to hurt the boy's mother if anything goes wrong. Euryalus spurns this concern, intent on his own share of the anticipated fame. The narrator has him leave her in Ascanius's care, however, provoking sentimental words from both young men which considerably alter the correspondence with the men in *Iliad*, Book Ten. Euryalus is not only a beautiful beloved boy; he is also a dear, caring son. At his death the mother is given Andromache's scene in the twenty-second book of the *Iliad*. This seems to emphasize the loss of youth in battle. Euryalus and his mother, Lausus and his father, Turnus and his prospective mother-in-law—these are the significant relationships of men slain in battle.

The Nisus and Euryalus story is also a tragedy of desire. The *eromenos*, who is traditionally beguiled by the glitter of gifts from the *erastes*, here is attracted to the glitter of the spoils of the fallen in his murderous path. It is Euryalus's desire for glitter that kills him, since he is subsequently spotted by the enemy because of this very glitter. It is Nisus's desire for Euryalus that kills him, as he goes back to defend and avenge his friend in death. Both of them are undone by their lust for blood.

The primary motive in the episode, however, is Nisus's desire for greatness, for fame. He poses the question whether this desire is godsent or whether every man's desire for fame is a god within him. The episode runs its course logically enough from this question to the narrator's exclamation (9.446ff.) after the two young men die— "Fortunate these two, as much as my song has power, no day shall ever take you away from time's memory"—and thereafter to the grisly manifestation of their perverse fame, their heads stuck on pikes for all the Trojans to look across the battlefield and see. The severed heads are a refrain of the descriptions of unusually brutal killing which this attractive twosome is described as having carried out. The gruesome daylight moment in which the heads are visible is ironically introduced by the conventional phase of Dawn leaving the bed of Tithonus, which establishes quite another mood for the day. The reader, going back and forth between the various texts that help in making meaning of this passage, is impressed with young men's self-indulgence, the old-fashioned selfishness, the private love, the viciousness, and the grotesque conclusion—along with the beauty and emotional power of their relationship. Their youth, their love, their beauty, the danger of their mission all imply the tragic end in the beginning. Thus, the narration of this episode is completely satisfying. And yet Nisus and Euryalus seem out of place, as though they ought to be in another poem. They are like so many characters in this poem who fail or confuse the reader by being narrated according to conventions other than those expected.

In the second book, as Aeneas delivers his poem on the fall of Troy before the court at Carthage, he describes (2.469ff.) in vivid detail the moment in which Pyrrhus, the son of Achilles, rushes into the great hall where Priam and members of his family have taken futile refuge. Pyrrhus is in hot pursuit of Priam's son Polites, whom he kills before the old king's eyes. Desperate, the feeble old man girds up to meet his son's killer, who with one swift blow and many a sardonic, sneering remark sends Priam to his death. In the tenth book Aeneas encounters Mezentius on the field, eventually killing both him and his son Lausus. The scene has enough ambiguity to satisfy any reader's appetite for rich narrative. Mezentius has been described in the poem as a vile and cruel man, one who despises the gods and who, as a king or absolute despot, practices the cruelest tortures. The Romans shared the Greek disinclination to assign bad behavior or wrongdoing to the category of what Christians call sin: that is, the knowing transgression of divine law. In Mezentius, however, the narrator has created a sinner; because he despises the gods, Mezentius is evil incarnate, even if his general behavior seems no different from that of any other hero on the battlefield. Throughout the scene in which he and Aeneas fight, the narrator employs language and imagery that mark him as no more and no less than any conventional heroic warrior, stalwart and courageous on the field of battle. When he is wounded by Aeneas, Mezentius instantly becomes vulnerable. His son Lausus leaps forward and with the king's entourage helps him to withdraw from the range of Aeneas's murderous weapons. Aeneas taunts and menaces the young man: "Why do you rush to your death? Why do you try to take on something too big for you? Your filial responsibility [*pietas tua*] betrays you into rashness" (10.811f.). This, needless to say, drives the young man mad; he makes a rush at Aeneas, who stabs him to death. Suddenly at this point the narrator calls Aeneas "Anchisiades," son of Anchises, and remarks that in looking at the dead youth the image of his own filial piety came to mind. Aeneas speaks: "What can Aeneas, the responsible [*pius*], give you to equal the praise you deserve?"

The narrator is to be praised for his courage in putting *pius* into this line. The extraordinary betrayal of the father-son relationship and Aeneas's subsequent killing of the father, who presents himself with unparalleled dignity and courage—echoing, as they do, those scenes in the second book of Pyrrhus killing Priam—require the reader to make up his mind about what indeed *pius Aeneas* means. If the reader accepts the values that the narrator has established for Aeneas, accepts the enlarged and transcendent icon that Aeneas has become, then he or she will be prepared to accept the idea that Lausus in loving his father betrayed the future, betrayed the idea of a community for the luxury of a private emotion. No amount of brilliant heroic hexameter verse can redeem the figures in this tragic drama of failed aspirations and values, which is both the lost cause of the Latins and metaphor for the collapse of the Greek culture the Romans took over. Dante learned this lesson well from his reading of the *Aeneid;* he too demands stern stuff from his reader, as in Canto Five, when the vastly sympathetic story of Francesca da Rimini is played out in the melody of the Italian language. The good Christian reader may sigh and pass on but must first remember to judge Francesca absolutely guilty of the sin and deserving of the punishment. That is the spiritual exercise which reading the *Commedia* inspires.

At the beginning of the *Aeneid*, Aeneas, who is about to drown in a storm, cries out: "Thrice blessed are those who died before the eyes of their fathers beneath the walls of Troy. Son of Tydeus, Diomedes, why did you not kill me . . . so that I might be buried where Hector is, and Sarpedon?" (1.94ff.). The lines echo Odysseus's speech during a similar storm at sea; Odysseus wishes he had been buried at Troy, where he would have had the glory and honor of a grand public funeral. The lines remind one also of Achilles, who, when he is about to be swept to his death by the river god, cries out that he would rather have been killed in battle as his mother promised than die ignominiously in the river. Aeneas wants more than that: he wants the public recognition that heroic action ought to guarantee; he wants therefore his audience; he wants to be lodged in a burying ground that contains the great men of the Homeric tradition; he wants context. He does not want to be in the situation he is in; he does not want to be in this poem. As the narrator undercuts him in the next four books, the reader is more and more convinced of his misfortune in being cast in a story so unsuited to him. When in the final hours of the battle for Troy Venus orders him to let Helen live, she makes his instinctive heroic gesture suspect. Now, as he buckles on his gear for the final showdown with Turnus, Aeneas speaks to his son: "May you learn manliness from me, my son, and the will to accomplish things, worthwhile things to accomplish, but fortune from others" (12.435f.). (The Latin is so elliptical that English translators can hardly help overtranslating: "Disce, puer, virtutem ex me verumque laborem/fortunam ex aliis.") What has this very stiff-lipped and long-suffering successor to Jason, who sighs so often throughout his story, told his son but to pray that somehow he will find himself a better narrator, a better author, a better story, a better genre? Aeneas was born the son of a goddess, a prince of Troy, a warrior on the plains before the city; he has repudiated that heritage, or had it pulled from under him. His triumph is undiminished. But, just as at the end of Apollonius's poem the figure of Hercules once again appears before the crew of the *Argo*, a reminder of a heroic world that once was, so Aeneas remembers past times.

Yet the poem ends in a remarkably abrupt way. "And thus they buried horse-taming Hector" is the final line of the *Iliad*, preceded by the lamentation over Hector's corpse. The lines are few, the movement swift; the matter, however, is so conventional that it is obvious. Virgil's poem does not wind down; the narrator ends so briefly that the reader must imagine much. Turnus, facing his obvious death, asks Aeneas to spare him, acknowledging that he has won the lands, the bride—all is his: "Don't push your hatred further." Turnus also mentions his own aging father, and this most potent of foreboding omens for the males of antiquity in their prime makes Aeneas hesitate—until he sees that Turnus wears the belt of young Pallas, whom he has killed and despoiled. Pallas, the son of the Trojan ally King Evander, who came with his father's blessing to serve with Aeneas has functioned as page, as surrogate son (since myth, history, and story line prevent the true son, Ascanius, from being killed), as a Patroclus figure, as the future, as Aeneas's protegé. Father or surrogate son? Aeneas rejects the salute to the past and chooses to honor the future instead.

The death of Pallas is a momentous personal sorrow, a betrayal by the heavens of Aeneas's successes. The twelfth book then ends with Aeneas's violent rage as he thinks of the death of Pallas; Turnus is the victim upon whom he vents this rage. The reader will think back to the last part of the sixth book as the cavalcade of souls yet to be born is about to end, and Anchises points out Marcellus, who will die young in 23 B.C.E. The death of Marcellus—the young heir to Augustus, son of his sister, betrothed to his daughter—inflicted a personal and political calamity on Augustus and produced a profound shock throughout the newly emerged monolith composed of imperial person, family, nation, and empire. The narrator seems to be returning to this event in the symmetry of the very last lines of this great poem, giving to this successful leader, soldier, suitor, who has consolidated his entire life experience into becoming his people's totem, one last sudden outburst of the private emotion of rage. Virgil has carefully constructed his poem so that the style and genre demand Turnus's death. Turnus must die to ensure the comic ending. The Aeneas who kills him, however, is not totem, icon, symbol, or literary gesture but a male exercising what best expresses the ancient epic warrior-hero: consummate rage.

Further Reading

As one might imagine in the case of poems that have for so long a time been considered so important, the *Iliad*, the *Odyssey*, and the *Aeneid* have generated over the centuries a prodigious amount of commentary. (The *Argonautica*, by contrast, has been virtually ignored.) The scholars of Alexandria set the standard by producing far more commentary on the Homeric epics than on any other text, and there survive in considerably larger amounts the commentaries of Servius, Donatus, and Macrobius on the text of Virgil. To this day more is written about these three epic poems than about anything else that survives from antiquity; indeed, more is written about them than can be read or digested by any one person. It is natural that readers wish to decide what a work "means." That is their way of taking control of an external stimulus, assimilating it or making it their own. Some readers, however, are content with the experience of reading a work. They put it aside with contentment, their assimilation having taken place on an unconscious level. But making meaning, apart from the simple exposition of fact or explication of difficulties, is a very big academic industry. In the literature sector of this industry entry-level jobs, salary increases, academic advancement, tenure, grants, and prizes rest on making meaning in print: hence the vast array of printed material about these poems, most of which seeks to find its niche in the monumental edifice of critical understanding constructed over time, an understanding as elaborate, far-reaching, and all inclusive as the poems themselves. The innocent sampler of these vast reconstructions of the poems will find himself or herself immediately engaged in ideas, perceptions, and evaluations that reflect the legacy of centuries as well as the more recent polemics of the learned. Occasionally they also relate to the poems in question.

What follows is the merest sampling of this vast literature, chosen to illuminate the poems most of all, and limited to pieces in the English language and to those that use minimal or no Greek or Latin to demonstrate their argument. These will give the reader a fair idea of the trends in scholarship that lie behind what is written in this book. Anyone who wishes more may consult the entries for Homer, Apollonius, and Virgil in the pages of *L'année philologique* (Paris: Société d' Edition "Les Belles Lettres"), edited by Juliette Ernst, an annual publication that attempts to list everything published in the field of classics and to provide a précis of the contents of articles and the location of reviews of books. It is probably just as profitable, and certainly much easier, to look into the descriptive two-part survey *Homer Studies, 1978–1983*, by James P. Holoka, published in *Classical World* 83 and 84 (1990, 1991). Although Holoka's work is not up to the minute, it probably does not matter all that much. Like the fashion industry, classical philology is a matter of styles: though it is true that what was said yesterday is no longer of the moment today, it is also the case that almost everything comes around again. There is also a computer-categorized bibliography titled *A Bibliography of Homeric Scholarship: Preliminary Edition, 1930–1970* (Malibu, Calif.: Undena Publications, 1974). This is truly out-of-date but remains interesting because it will show the novice what the areas of interest are for professional Homerists. Virgilians have an easier time of it because annual bibliographies are printed and reviewed in *Vergilius*, a journal devoted, as the title indicates, to the author of the *Aeneid*. See also *The Classical World Bibliography of Vergil*, edited by Walter Donlan (New York: Garland Press, 1978).

As the reader of this book will by now know, the *Iliad* and the *Odyssey* seem to be products of a time when there was no system of writing. Thus, they are truly specimens of oral poetry yet exist as written texts. This inherent tension between the claims of orality and of literacy probably accounts for most of the scholarship of the twen-

tieth century. It has certainly kept the focus on the origin and transmission of the poems more than on any other aspect. The Homeric
Question, as it was called in the nineteenth century, still dominates
the field, even if subliminally.

In 1795 Friedrich August Wolf wrote an essay in which he raised
the problem that poems such as the *Iliad* and the *Odyssey*, which were
most likely composed in a preliterate age, were too long to have been
memorized verbatim and transmitted orally until such time as a system of writing was invented. Wolf's *Prolegomena to Homer*, an interesting and important chapter in European intellectual history, has
been translated into English with an introduction and notes by An-
thony Grafton, Glenn Most, and James E. G. Zetzel (Princeton: Princeton University Press, 1985). For well over a century scholars debated
the questions Wolf raised, coming up with a variety of theories of
composition, most of which depended on the notion that short poems
were stitched together. The principal scholarly activity was finding
the seams. A lucid and comprehensive account of the main nineteenth-century theories may be found in R. C. Jebb, *Homer: An Introduction to the "Iliad" and "Odyssey"* (Boston: Ginn, 1894). J. L. Myres,
Homer and His Critics, edited by Dorothea Grey (London: Routledge
& Kegan Paul, 1958), has very shrewd, penetrating essays about some
late nineteenth- and early twentieth-century scholarship; it is excellent
on the intellectual context, with special emphasis on the role of archaeology.

In the second decade of the twentieth century an American, Milman
Parry, wrote two French theses for his graduate work in Paris in which
he tried to prove with statistical analyses the notion that Homer had
been heir to a long tradition of poetic narrative technique that enabled
him and his colleagues to create, spontaneously through recollection,
two such poems again and again. Parry presented his ideas, enlarged
and refined, to an English-speaking audience in "Studies in the Epic
Technique of Oral Verse-Making," divided into Part 1, "Homer and
the Homeric Style," and Part 2 "The Homeric Language of an Oral
Poetry," in *Harvard Studies in Classical Philology* 41 (1930) and 43 (1932).
These show him to have become convinced that the Homeric poems
were the products of an oral tradition, which, of course, made the
old Homeric problem irrelevant. Parry died very young in 1935, before
he had a chance to develop or correct his ideas in any really significant
way or to develop a school of followers. What he did write has been

gathered with an introductory essay by his son, Adam Parry, in *The Making of Homeric Verse: The Collected Papers of Milman Parry* (Oxford: Oxford University Press, 1971).

In the last years of his life Parry spent considerable time in Yugoslavia because he was convinced that the living tradition of oral poetics among the bards, or *guslars* as they are called there, would provide a convincing analogy for what he was trying to demonstrate in Homeric versemaking. Accompanied by graduate student assistant Albert Bates Lord, who would himself became a very distinguished scholar of oral poetics, he recorded or transcribed oral performances in that area. Lord's "Homer, Parry, and Huso," *American Journal of Archaeology* 52 (1948): 34–44 (reprinted in Parry's *Collected Papers*), is a memoir of that period in Parry's life. After Parry's death Lord continued to study the South Slavic oral poetic production. The results of his investigations are contained in *The Singer of Tales* (Cambridge: Harvard University Press, 1960), in which he first describes the oral poetic technique he encountered in Yugoslavia and then attempts to apply this knowledge to the Homeric epics. The book remains to this day a stimulating approach to the orality of the *Iliad* and the *Odyssey*, although it does not convince those who insist that since nothing recorded by Lord or Parry even approaches the masterpiece quality of the Homeric epics, no genuine analogy can be made between the two poetries.

In the beginning, scholars were loath to take up Parry's ideas. In time, however, most of the American scholarly community adopted the view, and some of the English, too, such as Geoffrey Kirk whose *The Songs of Homer* (Cambridge: Cambridge University Press, 1962), is an excellent survey of what what was known and surmised about the Homeric poems thirty years ago. It is still valuable, although it cannot compare with the far more thorough, authoritative series of essays gathered in *A Companion to Homer*, edited by A. J. A. Wace and F. H. Stubbings (London: Macmillan, 1963). John Miles Foley has tried to establish a poetics appropriate to oral poetic theory. His *Theory of Oral Composition: History and Methodology* (Bloomington: Indiana University Press, 1988) is an excellent account of the development and modification of the theory and its influence on other research into orality. Not to be missed. His *Immanent Art: From Structure to Meaning in Oral Epic* (Bloomington: Indiana University Press, 1991 [reviewed by me in *Bryn Mawr Classical Review* 3, no. 1 (1992): 31–46]) seeks to extract obvious artistry from what others have labeled mechanical functions in oral narrative. He is quite successful at arguing for the encoding in traditional narrative of elements that an audience would endow with significance from their experience of the tradition. He also uses examples from South Slavic poetry that are altogether convincing.

There was always resistance to the notion that oral poetic technique had to be as mechanical as Parry insisted. Parry's Berkeley teacher, George M. Calhoun, wrote an essay in 1935 ("The Art of Formula in Homer—επεα πτεροεντα," *Classical Philology* 30 [1935]: 215–27) challenging Parry's notion that the epithet "winged" in the formulaic phrase "winged words" had no meaning in itself but was a metrical necessity in a phrase which only as a phrase had meaning. But Parry had already introduced a very important aesthetic principle that students of Homer consistently overlook. Speaking of the conventional and stylized language of English Augustan poetry (in "The Traditional Metaphor in Homer," *Collected Papers*, p. 370), Parry remarks that condemnation of this diction "is too simple to be true, for its fails to see that what the words lost in meaning they gained in *charm of correctness*" (my emphasis). However vague "charm of correctness" may be, Parry hit upon one of the most important aesthetic principles and habits of mind of early Greek culture, one that explains much of the ancient Greeks conservatism, their tragic sense of life, their infinite capacity for irony, their obsession with stereotypes.

Still, scholars began to look for more flexibility in the deployment of the formulaic language. Adam Parry discusses the poet's self-conscious use of language in "The Language of Achilles," *Transactions of the American Philological Association* 87 (1956): 1–7 (reprinted in G. S. Kirk, *The Language and Background of Homer* [New York: Barnes and Noble, 1967]). Joseph Russo seeks the personal control of the poet in "Homer against His Tradition," *Arion* 7 (1968): 275–95; *Arion* is a journal consistently devoted among other things to denying the validity of the oral theory. M. M. Willcock, "Mythological Paradeigma in the *Iliad*," *Classical Quarterly* 14 (1964): 141–54, offers some attractive suggestions about how traditional myth stories have been reshaped by a presumably self-conscious narrator. *Yale Classical Studies* 20 (1966) was entirely given over to revisionist essays, the most important being Adam Parry's "Have We Homer's *Iliad*" (pp. 177–216). The essays focus on recovering the self-conscious artistry, the intentional manipulation of the traditional material, which one would more likely posit for a literate writer of narrative. This approach earned the immediate rebuke of Albert Bates Lord ("Homer as an Oral Poet," *Harvard Studies in Classical Philology* 72 [1967]: 1–46).

Adam Parry introduced the 1971 collection of his father's papers with a thoughtful critical survey of the various approaches to oral theory, concluding with a call for more study of poetic control of the language. Norman Austin shortly thereafter, in *Archery at the Dark of the Moon* (Berkeley: University of California Press, 1975), launched an attack on the elder Parry's use of statistics, noting that the distribution of certain traditional epithets in the *Odyssey* seem to reflect conscious patterning rather than random happening. Other studies have since observed that certain formulaic language seems to appear in speeches as though consciously giving flavor or color in this fashion. Yet another more recent study (David Shive, *Naming Achilles* [Oxford: Oxford University Press, 1987]) has again attacked the Parry statistical method. The controversy continues. The emergence of the computer should give the new generation of Homerists a kind of control never before possible over these very lengthy texts. Statistics, however, is a very subtle, complex, intellectual discipline in which classicists are rarely if ever trained, and their use of statistics invariably looks naive to professionals. But happily or ludicrously, such is the abysmal separation of intellectual and cultural interests in late twentieth-century America that few classicists will ever know statistics, and statisticians are unlikely to draw to their attention the absurdities perpetrated.

H. M. and N. K. Chadwick created an invaluable treasure-house of fact about early narrative poetry from around the world in *The Growth of Literature* (Cambridge: Cambridge University Press, 1932–40); see especially the two-hundred-page "General Survey" at the close of the third volume. This material was more or less digested and refocused by one of the few classicists with a real understanding of literature, the arts, and aesthetics, C. M. Bowra, in his *Heroic Poetry* (New York: St. Martin's Press, 1961), who is also responsible for the chapters on meter, style, and composition in Wace and Stubbing's *Companion* (cited above). The oral theory, however, does not yet dominate these surveys as it does Ruth Finnegan's *Oral Poetry: Its Nature, Significance, and Social Context* (Cambridge: Cambridge University Press, 1977), which is largely a field investigation of this kind of poetry. Finnegan's discovery that in some places the oral poet could also use writing and that the two practices were not incompatible seemed to fly in the face of the Parry-Lord insistence on the oral poet's illiteracy or preliteracy as a kind of qualification of orality. Suddenly

Homerists who wanted to be oralists but who also wanted a poet self-conscious enough to necessitate the hypothesis of a text could eat their cake and have it too.

The Germans took to the Parry-Lord theory slowly and reluctantly. The prevalent critical position in Germany is known as neoanalysis, since it was the German classical establishment of the nineteenth century which established analysis as the game plan for the Homeric Question: that is to say, the investigation of the sources for the various parts of the *Iliad* and the *Odyssey*, on Wolf's presumption that nothing so large could have come down whole and integral. Neoanalysis looks for other texts that are alluded to in the Homeric poems. The *Aithiopis*, a poem from the so-called Epic Cycle, which details the death of Achilles, among other things, is a notable candidate for their attentions. Although poems of the Epic Cycle, extant only in fragments, were said by the ancients to have been composed (whatever that means in this context) *after* the *Iliad* and the *Odyssey*, they nonetheless provide a ready quarry for elements of the mosaic of allusion that neoanalysts find in the Homeric texts. It is not always clear, of course, whether the neoanalysts are referring to an established text or to a kind of fixed oral tradition, repeated more or less exactly over time, since most of them acknowledge that the Homeric poems were generated in some kind of context in which orality was the predominant feature. Readers should consult Walter Kullman, "Oral Poetry Theory and Neoanalysis in Homeric Research," *Greek, Roman, and Byzantine Studies* 25 (1984): 307–23, for a presentation in English of this important direction in German Homer scholarship. The neoanalyst argument, needless to say, has spread beyond the borders of Germany; see, for instance, Mark Edward Clark and William D. E. Coulson, "Memnon and Sarpedon," *Museum Helveticum* 35 (1978): 65–73, for a discussion of the way in which the death of Memnon in the *Aithiopis* shapes the scene of the death of Sarpedon in the sixteenth book of the *Iliad*. M. A. Katz, who is influenced by and dependent upon the neoanalytic school, has a generous selection of quotations, citations, and bibliography from that school to buttress her arguments in *Penelope's Renown: Meaning and Indeterminacy in the "Odyssey"* (Princeton: Princeton University Press, 1991 [reviewed by me in *Bryn Mawr Classical Review* 2, no. 6 (1991): 369–73]). This book argues for a more important, more authoritative Penelope in the *Odyssey*, built from a combination of traditional story lines combined from other narratives.

America's own Gregory Nagy has developed a theory that will

account both for what some would call individuality and for the conventional notion of tradition. He argues from the position that this poetry is a phenomenon common in Indo-European language and metrics and therefore allows the researcher to seek analogies throughout the narrative traditions of this group; he argues, furthermore, that there is a commonality to oral poetic practice which allows the researcher to use analogies from around the world. In *The Best of the Achaeans* (Baltimore: Johns Hopkins University Press, 1979) and *Pindar's Homer* (Baltimore: Johns Hopkins University Press, 1990), Nagy argues that the Homeric poems are the end result of a tradition of praise-blame poetry or, more specifically, poetry chanted to mark or commemorate the death or grave cult of local heroes. It is his theory that over time the tradition lost its locality and topicality as it was disseminated over space, and this was a trend to be described as pan-Hellenism (in which movement the Epic Cycle poems represent specimens of epic narrative not yet divorced from the local cults, local heroes, and regional topicality). Thus the poems are completely of the tradition, renewed, re-created, recollected on each occasion of performance; they are therefore fixed and fluid at the same time, altogether original and conventional at the same time, in the fashion of the performance of Dixieland jazz, but growing ever more fixed and less fluid as creator-performers were replaced by reciter-performers, who maintained the poems until the time in which they were written down. Thus over time the poets of the tradition could invent the most incredible subtleties and narrative connections, which became part of the routines, the *shticks*, as it were. The tradition grew strong enough to constitute for critical purposes what we could call a text, which allows for the notion that the *Odyssey* consciously (in some sense of that word) recalls, alludes to, the *Iliad*. The thesis of Nagy's earlier book turns on the resonance of the *Iliad* in the *Odyssey* narrative. Thus Nagy, too, is also able to eat his cake and have it. Nagy is an important figure in current Homer studies and not to be overlooked. He has, however, a dense and difficult prose style; one might be advised to dip into his chapter in *The Cambridge History of Literary Criticism*, edited by G. A. Kennedy (Cambridge: Cambridge University Press, 1989), 1:1–77, titled "Early Greek Views of Poets and Poetry," which presents his ideas in somewhat, but only somewhat, simpler fashion. Belief in the self-conscious relationship between the *Iliad* and the *Odyssey* underlies Pietro Pucci's *Odysseus Polutropos: Intertextual Readings in the "Odyssey" and the "Iliad"* (Ithaca:

Cornell University Press, 1987). This is a consistently interesting and insightful book that reveals a number of coincidences between the poems. Because it demands the existence of texts for its argument, it does not convince me. I cannot accept the notion of texts in the period of gestation, something that seems to me essential for any argument for sensible intertextual meaning.

There are those as well who choose to believe that Homer made a text of his poem and that his technique was not much different from that of any other poet of the Western European literary tradition. Two books by Paolo Vivante, *The Homeric Imagination: A Study of Homer's Poetic Perception of Reality* (Bloomington: Indiana University Press, 1970) and *The Epithets in Homer: A Study in Poetic Values* (New Haven: Yale University Press, 1982), are unabashedly committed to a close reading of the text, advancing the argument that every element of the narrative is there for purposes that have nothing to do with making formulaic phrase–filled, orally generated hexameter lines. To my mind, Vivante reads each epithet as making sense in its context, which seems to deny exactly what is so important in Parry's observation of "the charm of correctness." See, however, James Redfield, "The Proem of the *Iliad:* Homer's Art," *Classical Philology* 74 (1979): 105–8, for a very good close reading that one would think demands a text. See also the excellent study by Mark Edwards, *Homer: Poet of the "Iliad"* (Baltimore: Johns Hopkins University Press, 1987), with excellent close readings of various passages of the poem, together with intelligent and penetrating analyses of various relevant scholarly opinions.

Increasingly, critics are reading tight authorial control into the text. See, for example, M. M. Willcock "Ad Hoc Invention in the *Iliad*," *Harvard Studies in Classical Philology* 81 (1977): 41–53. One can read more of Willcock's ideas in his *Companion to the "Iliad"* (Chicago: University of Chicago Press, 1976), a commentary on Richmond Lattimore's translation. Still other scholars, however, point to the numerous passages that seem to refute tight authorial control; these they offer as absolute evidence of the oral performance of the poem. See, for instance, F. W. Combellack, "Some Formulary Illogicalities in Homer," *Transactions of the American Philological Association* 96 (1965): 41–56; Bernard Fenik, *Studies in the "Odyssey,"* Hermes Einzelschriften Heft 30 (Wiesbaden: Steiner, 1974), pp. 50–53, 124–26; D. G. Miller, *Improvisation, Typology, Culture, and "the New Orthodoxy": How "Oral" Is Homer?* (Washington, D.C.: University Press of America, 1982). This last is, in addition, a consistently lucid, witty, utterly convincing argument for the complete orality of the two poems; Miller introduces instance after instance from the text to substantiate his claims. If the reader has time to read but one book on the subject of Homer as an oral poet, this is the one I recommend.

Increasingly, Homer critics wish to refute the celebrated saying of Erich Auerbach: "The Homeric poems conceal nothing, they contain no teaching and no secret second meaning. Homer can be analyzed . . . but he cannot be interpreted" ("Odysseus' Scar," in *Mimesis*, translated by Willard Trask [Princeton: Princeton University Press, 1953]). In the same essay, Auerbach compares the narrative style of Homer and that of the authors of the Genesis narrative, arguing that Homer offers a myriad of details that establish the scene and the happening, whereas the Genesis narrative is so exceedingly sparse that the reader is constantly required to invest in the narrative his or her own interpretation. The readers of this book will see the point he is making if they simply compare the story of Abraham taking Isaac to the mountain (particularly if they follow the commentary and criticism of E. A. Speiser in the Anchor Bible) with Homer's anecdote of how Odysseus acquired his scar; one can see how Kierkegaard can make so much meaning from the former passage.

This is not to say that there is no "meaning" in the Homeric poems, of course, that the audience or reader cannot make meaning, but that the narrative style *seems* to inhibit it. As I have said elsewhere, Homer "gives the *illusion* of telling us everything. He overpowers us with detail, alternative stories; the characters bombard us with their observations on everything that takes place. We are helpless before their onslaught. This is the poetry of oral presentation: the poet knows that we do not have the text and cannot reflect. He keeps at us, hectoring, seducing, amusing, but always demanding our submission to his narrative. In that sense he tells us everything. . . . Homer never *invites* us to make meaning. That is important. It must remain unconscious. We are also not in league with the author ready to make sense of the narrative. He pretends to be its slave as well" (Charles Rowan Beye, *Epic and Romance in the "Argonautica" of Apollonius* [Carbondale: Southern Illinois University Press, 1982], pp. 11–12). Since Homer tells his audience everything necessary to take in the scene, it seems utterly foreign to his technique that he would suggest in a subtle way that Penelope recognizes the beggar as her husband in disguise. But such an interpretation is popular. The following three essays are important arguments for that view, which I however, now cannot tolerate: P. W. Harsh "Penelope and Odysseus in *Odyssey* XIX," *American Journal of Philology* 71 (1950): 1–21 (with which I completely agreed when I first wrote about Homer); Anne Amory, "The Reunion of Odysseus and Penelope," in C. H. Taylor, ed. *Essays on the Odyssey: Selected Modern Criticism* (Bloomington: University of Indiana Press, 1963), pp. 100–121; J. J. Winkler, "Penelope's Cunning and Homer's," in *The Constraints of Desire* (New York: Routledge, 1990), pp. 129–61. Yet readers are advised to look into Michael Lynn-George, *Epos: Word, Narrative, and the "Iliad"* (Houndsmills, Eng., 1988), who takes on Auerbach to refute him with the very scar passage itself.

So far I have been surveying trends in Homer criticism. In what follows I mention sources that will direct the reader to further discussion of various aspects of the Homeric poems and their contexts. A particularly stimulating caution in the matter of criticism is Ian Morris, "The Use and Abuse of Homer," *Classical Antiquity* 5 (1986): 209–21, who has valuable observations to make about the solid evidence that survives and how it is useful or not in discussing the poems.

A reading of the poems that transcends the discussions of origins and transmission, one of the few books by a trained classicist in which aesthetics is the guiding principle, is the Sather Lectures of S. E. Bassett, *The Poetry of Homer* (Berkeley: University of California Press, 1938). Bassett is not altogether indifferent to the problems raised by the Homeric Question. He quickly lays them to rest, however, in his first chapter. Then, having established his belief in treating the poems as poetry, he proceeds to an excellent discussion of what he calls epic illusion—that is, the kind of mood and image of reality that oral epic poetry creates—followed by a sensitive account of the way he imagines that Homer manipulated his audience. Thereafter, Bassett discusses details of the poetic language, endowing individual words and phrases with far more meaning than Parry would allow. In the same tradition is Jasper Griffin, *Homer on Life and Death* (Oxford: Oxford University Press, 1980), who is especially good at finding parallels from the Hebrew books of the Bible and other Near Eastern texts in his analysis of the religious ideas and notions of godhead that inform the Homeric poems.

An article on the psychology of an oral culture, as interesting and informative as the day it was written, is J. A. Russo and Bennett Simon, "Homeric Psychology and the Oral Epic Tradition," *Journal of the History of Ideas* 29 (1968): 483–98. It discusses the way the inner self is portrayed through exterior description, how meditation is described in dialogue with another (for instance, when Achilles and Athena talk of his suppressing the urge to murder Agamemnon). The authors relate this to the psychology of oral performance, to the way in which the poem is external to the poet who asks the Muse to give it to him. They consider to what degree the poet's manner relates to the way of thinking and speaking of his contemporary audience.

Thomas Van Nortwick explores the bonded males, or alter ego male companion, in the *Iliad*, the Gilgamesh poem, and the *Aeneid* in *Somewhere I Have Never Traveled* (New York: Oxford University Press, 1991 [reviewed by me in *Bryn Mawr Classical Review* 2, no. 7 (1991): 444–47]), a series of essays that also looks at the subject of masculinity from a twentieth-century perspective, using especially the ideas of Carl Jung about the Shadow figure. Van Nortwick's interpretation makes of the loss of Patroclus and Enkidu an affirmation, a healing process, part of growing, rather than an element of tragedy. See also Beye, "The Epic of Gilgamesh, the Bible, and Homer: Some Narrative Parallels," in *Mnemai: Classical Studies in Memory of Karl K. Hulley* (Chico, Calif.: Scholars Press, 1984), pp. 7–20, in which I argue that these narratives construct the life of a male from infancy to adulthood to old age and death.

Typicality is addressed in J. I. Armstrong, "The Arming Motif in the *Iliad*," *American Journal of Philology* 79 (1958): 337–54; Bernard Fenik, *Typical Battle Scenes in the "Iliad,"* Hermes Einzelschriften Heft 21 (Wiesbaden: Steiner, 1968); and M. W. Edwards, "Type-Scenes and Homeric Hospitality," *Transactions of the American Philological Association* 105 (1975): 51–72. Beye, "Male and Female in the Homeric Poems," *Ramus* 3 (1974): 87–101, lies behind many of the remarks I make about women in this book.

Passages that have commonly been categorized as digressions are reevaluated by Norman Austin ("The Function of Digression in the *Iliad*" *Greek, Roman, and Byzantine Studies* 7 [1966]: 295–312), who sees them not at all as legitimate digressions but as elements integral to the narrative, which offer instructive forms of behavior in contrast with or in complement to the action of the main story, as devices to mark moments that are decisive for the direction of the story, as means to stop time briefly.

Ring composition was first addressed by J. L. Myres in "The Last Book of the *Iliad*," *Journal of Hellenic Studies* 52 (1932): 264–96, who wished to ascribe this narrative patterning to the same aesthetic impulse that marks the symmetry of geometric vase painting. See also E. T. Owen, *The Story of the "Iliad,"* 2d ed. (Bristol: Bristol Classical Press, 1989); and C. H. Whitman's chapter "The Geometric Structure of the *Iliad*," in his *Homer and the Heroic Tradition* (Cambridge: Harvard University Press, 1958). A long chart in this latter book, showing all the correspondences throughout the *Iliad* as established by Whitman, demonstrates both the weaknesses and the strengths of such schematization. See also M. L. Lang, "Reverberations and Mythology in the *Iliad*," in *Approaches to Homer*, edited by C. A. Rubino and C. W. Shelmerdine (Austin: University of Texas Press, 1983), pp. 140–63, which deals with correspondences in the story.

Structuring of the narrative is also to be found in the rehearsal of scenes. See Thomas Van Nortwick's excellent article on the relationship between the Nausicaa-Odysseus scene and the Penelope–beggar/Odysseus scene: "Penelope and Nausicaa," *Transactions of the American Philological Association* 109 (1974): 269–76. The traditional folktale, by arousing expectations in the auditor or reader, imposes its own kind of structuring in a narrative. See D. L. Page's chapter "Odysseus and Polyphemus," a very informative account of the versions of the Polyphemus story worldwide, in his *Homeric "Odyssey"* (Oxford: Oxford University Press, 1955). W. J. Woodhouse, *The Composition of Homer's "Odyssey"* (Oxford: Oxford University Press, 1930), is a witty, insightful account of various techniques of storytelling which the author identifies in the *Odyssey* as coming from folktale or fairytale. Page argues for the personal control of the poet over his material, whereas Woodhouse sees these folktale structures as having a power of their own to shape the narrative. Page's remarks on the Polyphemus story ought to be read in conjunction with Justin Glenn, "The Polyphemus Myth: Its Origin and Interpretation," *Greece and Rome* 25 (1978): 141–55, a psychoanalytic interpretation of the myth.

The characterization of the principals in these stories has been treated often enough, sometimes in a more valuable fashion than others. S. Farron, "The Character of Hector," *Acta Classica* 21 (1978): 39–58, attempts to establish a provocative divide between what the narrator has to say of Hector and how the narrator shows other characters experiencing him. James Redfield, *Nature and Culture in the "Iliad": The Tragedy of Hector* (Chicago: University of Chicago Press, 1975), describes the doom of the socialized man, a kind of personalization of the tragedy that Northrop Frye in his *Anatomy of Criticism*

(Princeton: Princeton University Press, 1957) identified in the collapse of the city of Troy. T. W. MacCary, *Childlike Achilles: Ontogeny and Phylogeny in the "Iliad"* (New York: Columbia University Press, 1982), is a provocative exercise in Freudian theory which establishes that Achilles has a pre-Oedipal psychology. As one might expect, Odysseus's character has excited an audience of critics. See especially W. B. Stanford, *Ulysses Theme* (Oxford: Oxford University Press, 1954), which has four excellent chapters on the Homeric Odysseus. These are notable demonstrations of the complexity of the character who provided material for the host of works discussed and criticized by Stanford in this superb survey; the book is one of those rare pieces by a professional classicist which reveals sophisticated critical faculties operating at every turn. Stanford proceeds to discuss the Odysseus/Ulysses figure throughout Western literature. Another gifted critic is George Dimock, whose "Name of Odysseus," *Hudson Review* 9 (1956): 52–70 (reprinted in George Steiner and Robert Fagles, *Homer* [Englewood Cliffs, N.J.: Prentice-Hall, 1962]), addresses the peculiar strain or stain of personality that is inspired by the anecdote of Autolycus's naming the baby. See as well the sixth chapter of W. G. Thalmann, *Conventions of Form and Thought in Early Greek Poetry* (Baltimore: Johns Hopkins University Press, 1984). Sheila Murnaghan's particularly interesting book, *Disguise and Recognition in the Odyssey* (Princeton: Princeton University Press 1987), looks at the contradiction inherent in a man's disguising himself and lying about himself in a culture in which public recognition is one's principal means of validating oneself.

The religious background can be studied in M. P. Nilsson, *The Minoan-Mycenean Religion and Its Survival in Greek Religion*, 2d ed. (Lund: Glerup, 1968). See more recently Jasper Griffin's *Homer on Life and Death* (cited above), in which religion is emphasized with interesting parallels from the Hebrew Bible and other Near Eastern texts. In this connection one should consult C. H. Gordon, *Homer and the Bible: The Origin and Character of East Mediterranean Literature*, 2d ed. (Ventnor, N.J.: Ventnor Publishers, 1967), in which Gordon discusses parallel passages, motifs, and attitudes. Jasper Griffin, "The Divine Audience and the Religion of the *Iliad*," *Classical Quarterly* 28 (1978): 1–22, suggests that the gods are more spectators than anything else, an idea important in helping auditors to define themselves as well. One might even argue that the audiences for Homeric epic, habituated to identifying with the gods and thus possessed of tragic irony, were acculturated into a similar position of watchfulness when viewing the tragic drama. D. C. Feeney, *Gods in the Epic: Poets and Critics of the Classical Tradition* (Oxford: Clarendon Press, 1991), argues in a magisterial review of the divine presence in all the extant Greek and Latin epic poems that their depiction is true to a convention for epic gods rather than obedient to the religious ideas of the time.

One cannot know the historical context of the Homeric poems. The Bronze Age is best described by Emily Vermeule, *Greece in the Bronze Age* (Chicago: University of Chicago Press, 1964), who states in her introduction that she flatly refuses to use any evidence garnered from the texts. M. I. Finley has taken details from the *Odyssey* to create a sociological view of its world in *The World of Odysseus*, 2d ed. (New York: Penguin, 1979) See also A. M. Snodgrass, *The Dark Age of Greece: An Archaeological Survey of the Eleventh to the Eighth Centuries* B.C. (Edinburgh: Edinburgh University Press, 1971), and *Archaic Greece: The Age of Experiment* (London: Dent, 1980), the best explanations of what is currently known from archaeological investigation. Battle narratives are better understood after reading Hans Van Wees, "Leaders of Men? Military Organization in the *Iliad*," *Classical Quarterly* 36 (1986): 285–303, and "Kings in Combat: Battles and Heroes in the *Iliad*," *Classical Quarterly* 38 (1988): 1–24.

The pieces of epic poetry that preceded, coexisted with, or followed the *Iliad* and the *Odyssey* as we now have them survive only in the merest fragments. There is very little we can know about them. Jasper Griffin, "The Epic Cycle and the Uniqueness of Homer," *Journal of Hellenic Studies* 97 (1977): 39–53, makes important distinctions between the Homeric masterpieces and those poems thought to be more or less contemporaneous with them. G. L. Huxley, *Greek Epic Poetry from Eumelos to Panyassis* (Cambridge: Harvard University Press, 1969), is a survey of what little remains from writers after the Epic Cycle poets down to the man who was considered to be Herodotus's uncle and the last great epic poet. Huxley has little to say about literary critical problems, confining himself largely to dating the epics and assessing their political nuances. In trying to recover the skeletal outline of the stories, however, Huxley is at his best.

The third century witnessed a renaissance of letters in the ancient Greek world, centered at Alexandria, hence called the Alexandrian Age. This fascinating period is well treated, and very fully, in P. M. Fraser, *Ptolemaic Alexandria* (Oxford: Oxford University Press, 1972). It was a time when poets could expect that their audiences would be familiar with the masterpieces of the Greek literary tradition. To gain some understanding of it all, readers of this book are directed to my *Ancient Greek Literature and Society*, 2d ed. (Ithaca: Cornell University Press, 1987). In my *Epic and Romance in the "Argonautica" of Apollonius* (cited above) there is a fairly comprehensive bibliographical essay for the *Argonautica* (pp. 169–78). The reader is encouraged to read J. F. Carspecken, "Apollonius Rhodius and the Homeric Epic," *Yale Classical Studies* 13 (1952): 33–144, which is remarkable for its literary acuity; and Gilbert Lawall, "Apollonius' *Argonautica:* Jason as Anti-Hero," *Yale Classical Studies* 19 (1966): 121–69. It is interesting to observe how scholars write to the prevailing ethos. Lawall's anti-hero is for the fifties going on sixties as surely as Carspecken, with his hero lost in a crowd, wrote for the forties going on fifties. And I, in "Jason as Love-Hero in Apollonios' *Argonautika*," *Greek, Roman, and Byzantine Studies* 10 (1969): 31–55, was writing to the great sexual revolution that occupied the late 1960s going on into the 1970s.

The literature of scholarship surrounding the *Aeneid* is as vast as that which plucks at the vitals of the *Iliad* and *Odyssey*. I am in the process of adding to it with a book about the influence of Apollonius on Virgil, tentatively titled *Virgil's Apollonian "Aeneid."* The reader would be wise to look into H. W. Prescott, *The Development of Virgil's Art* (Chicago: University of Chicago Press, 1936), an adaptation for an American audience of the writings of the great German Virgilian scholar Richard Heinze, whose ideas still seem sound enough to merit knowing. Prescott is also good on Virgil's sources. For the background to Virgil, see Wendell Clausen's excellent essay "The New Direction in Latin Poetry," in *The Cambridge History of Classical Literature*, edited by E. J. Kenney (Cambridge: Cambridge University Press, 1982), 2:178–206; and James Zetzel's chapter on Catullus in *Ancient Writers: Greece and Rome*, edited by J. T. Luce (New York: Scribner, 1982).

Viktor Pöschl, *The Art of Virgil: Image and Symbol in the "Aeneid"* (Ann Arbor: University of Michigan Press, 1962), discusses the nexus of imagery in the poem and Virgil's creation of symbols. See in this connection Michael Putnam, *The Poetry of the "Aeneid"* (Ithaca: Cornell University Press, 1988), for illuminating discussion of the repetitions and echoes throughout the text. All cited passages are translated to permit the reader to see clearly into the workings of the poem's language. This book is particularly valuable because Putnam treats some of the least discussed, less accessible books. He is an early exponent of the pessimistic tone of the *Aeneid*. See M. Owen Lee, *Fathers and*

Sons in Virgil's "Aeneid" (Albany: State University of New York Press, 1979), which looks at Jungian archetypes in the poem. W. R. Johnson, *Darkness Visible: A Study of Virgil's "Aeneid"* (Berkeley: University of California Press, 1976), is very good at reading what some negative critics call Virgil's vagueness and imprecision as the poet's deliberately impressionistic narrative style. Johnson has excellent things to say as well about the great trend in Virgilian criticism that established a more somber reading of the poem.

Brooks Otis, *Virgil: A Study in Civilized Poetry* (Oxford: Clarendon Press, 1963), proceeds from the assumption that Virgil thought himself in competition with Homer and that the *Aeneid* was an attempt to go the archaic poems one better in genre, theme, and technique. It is not clear that there is quite the close identification that Otis imagines. I, for one, would introduce Apollonius as a rather large filter through which the tradition had to pass. An interesting Christianizing subtext to Otis's criticism of the *Aeneid* reminds his readers that for centuries the Church appropriated this pagan poem as one of its own. See Otis on Virgilian narrative technique in his very good survey "Virgilian Narrative Technique in the Light of His Precursors and His Successors," *Studies in Philology* 73 (1976): 1–20. Readers who would like to examine more closely the possible connections between Homer and Virgil would do well to look into K. W. Gransden, *Virgil's Iliad: An Essay on Epic Narrative* (Cambridge: Cambridge University Press, 1984).

Kenneth Quinn, *The Aeneid: A Critical Description* (Ann Arbor: University of Michigan Press, 1968), is consistently interesting and instructive on each book of the poem. Gordon Williams, *Tradition and Originality in Roman Poetry* (Oxford: Clarendon Press, 1968), helps outline the vast knowledge of culture, history, and literature which Virgil and his audience possessed. Williams, does not believe that Virgil brought over the *context* of the original, or that his readers did when they recognized an allusion in the Virgilian text. He tends to consider allusions as so many notches in Virgil's belt of borrowing. P. R. Hardie, *Virgil's "Aeneid": Cosmos and Imperium* (Oxford: Clarendon Press, 1986), discusses the relation between the universe created by Virgil and the imperial reality in which he lived. S. F. Wiltshire, *Public and Private in Vergil's "Aeneid"* (Amherst: University of Massachusetts Press, 1989), helps contextualize the poem, focusing on ideas and attitudes in the public life, balancing them against private behavior; from this process the author develops an interpretation of the *Aeneid* that is more optimistic, more affirming of society and the Augustan dispensation than is currently popular. Consult A. S. Long, *Hellenistic Philosophy: Stoics, Epicureans, Sceptics*, 2d ed. (Berkeley: University of California, 1986), for the tenets of Stoicism, a philosophy that became almost a personal religion for great numbers of Romans.

There has sprung up a new field of study investigating how later ages took to these facts, called for want of anything better in English by the German term *Rezeptionsgeschichte* (i.e., reception history). Frank Kermode's *The Classic* (Cambridge: Harvard University Press, 1983) is an excellent contribution to this field. The first chapter particularly is a suggestive essay about the history of the *Aeneid* as a cultural icon throughout the centuries since its publication. Nowadays the Homeric poems are very much preferred, but this was certainly not the case before the nineteenth century. The subject is long and complicated; see for starters S. Shepard, "Scaliger on Homer and Virgil: A Study in Literary Prejudice," *Emerita* 29 (1961): 313–40. J. K. Newman, *The Classical Epic Tradition* (Madison: University of Wisconsin Press, 1986), brings the reader from Aristotelian theorizing on epic through antiquity, the Middle Ages, and modern Europe to Tolstoy's *War and Peace* and film director Sergei Eisenstein's many epics on celluloid. For something with greater wit and less depth but sometimes better literary critical judgment, see J. B. Hainsworth, *The Idea of Epic* (Berkeley: University of California Press, 1991), which covers the emergence and decline of the epic genre. Hainsworth is interested in the genre's failure as much as in its success, as well as its transmutations (see, for example, his interesting remarks on Akira Kurosawa). As my own contribution to *Rezeptionsgeschichte*, see my "Gilgamesh, Lolita, and Huckleberry Finn," *Classical and Modern Literature* 9 (1988): 39–50, and "Sunt Lacrimae Rerum," *Parnassus: Poetry in Review* 10, no. 2 (1982): 75–95, a discussion of Hector Berlioz's use of the *Aeneid* in his *Les Troyens*. Homer's reception in later ages is analyzed by Howard Clarke in *Homer's Readers: An Historical Introduction to the "Iliad" and the "Odyssey"* (Newark: University of Delaware Press, 1981), which is one of the ways to get at a reading of the poems themselves. One might also consult H. A. Mason, *To Homer through Pope* (New York: Barnes & Noble, 1972), doing the same thing on a smaller scale, with the proper attention to how a translation is both a commentary and a reading. See also G. deF. Lord, *Homeric Renaissance: The Odyssey of George Chapman* (New Haven: Yale University Press, 1956) and Kirsti Simonsuuri

Homer's Original Genius: Eighteenth Century Notions of the Early Greek Epic (Cambridge: Cambridge University Press, 1979). Volumes 7–10 of the Twickenham Edition of Pope's works contain his translation of the *Iliad* and the *Odyssey*, edited by Maynard Mack (New Haven: Yale University Press, 1967), which is exceptionally valuable as instruction into how the eighteenth century understood the Greek and read the poems. The reader may also benefit from Taylor Corse, *Dryden's "Aeneid": The English Virgil* (Newark: University of Delaware Press, 1991). It is difficult to understand nowadays that once upon a time translators could assume that their English readers knew the Greek or the Latin and were interested to see how a verbal construct in either of those languages was made over into English and thus into a new work of art, an English reading, as well as a kind of commentary on the original text.

Most readers today will need translation to get *any* of the meaning. Alexander Pope translated the Homeric poems, sometimes with the assistance of his minions; Dryden translated the *Aeneid* (and also the first book of the *Iliad*). These, of course, are excellent pieces of poetry, insofar as translations rise to that standard. Their excellence lies in the use of a poetic diction, which will remind the reader that the ancient originals were made in language not at all like the common usage on the street. Their gravest fault is that they rhyme, thus creating couplets, whereas the originals, like mighty rivers, flow majestically yet with a quick current. Contemporary translations suffer from the fact that no English poetic diction survives in the twentieth century; Richmond Lattimore's introduction to his translation of the *Iliad* (Chicago: University of Chicago Press, 1961) bemoans that loss. Twentieth-century poetic language rarely goes beyond the journalese of a newspaper, but then, twentieth-century readers know little else but the pages of the *New York Times*. Richmond Lattimore and Robert Fitzgerald each translated both Homeric epics. (Fitzgerald's translations are published by Doubleday, Garden City, 1989, 1990.) Those who prefer the former (his *Odyssey* is published by Harper & Row, New York 1975) do so usually because they sense that he is absolutely faithful to the original Greek; this means being faithful, for instance, to each repeated epithet, a practice that can, as the reader will imagine, bore some to madness. No one is going to be ravished by Parry's "charm of correctness." Robert Fagles has translated the *Iliad* (New York: Viking, 1990), and he is a very good poet-translator, as anyone who has encountered his *Oresteia* knows; still, he too must labor with the fact that the English language today has no distinction when it comes to poetry of this sort. The result can sometimes be a little chatty.

Fitzgerald has also translated the *Aeneid* (New York: Vintage, 1990), as has Allen Mandelbaum (New York: Bantam, 1981); unlike the very good translation of C. Day Lewis (Garden City: Doubleday, 1953), these versions are many lines longer than the original. One can hardly expect English—pimpled over with prepositions, definite articles, and compound verbs—to be shrunk to the elegant minimalism of Virgil's expressively deft tightening of the inflected Latin language, but Mandelbaum's translation is fluent, which is a great virtue. No translation of the *Aeneid* can fully succeed, however, because the story is so much less important than the extraordinary musicality of the language, which, of course, does not survive translation. Certainly the chance to mouth and sound the Latin of Virgil's *Georgics* and *Aeneid* and Horace's *Odes* is sufficient justification for the study of that language

The truly exciting translation of Homer is that of Christopher Logue, who has translated portions of the *Iliad* very freely indeed and announces that he is out to do the rest, with some additions of his own (Hector and Priam at home with Andromache, Hecuba, and the baby—that sort of thing). See his *War Music: An Account of Books 16 to 19 of Homer's Iliad* (New York: Farrar Straus Giroux, 1987), and his more recent *Kings: An Account of Books 1–4* (New York: Farrar Straus Giroux, 1991). Perhaps because he has written so many screenplays, he instinctively elicits the cinematic possibilities in those lines. The translation is brilliant, beautiful, recalling the *Iliad* to the point that the reader aches, and yet Logue is utterly free and often far, far from the text.

For the journal *Parnassus: Poetry in Review* I have written three essays on some of these translations: "Tackling Homer's *Iliad*," *Parnassus* 4 (1975–76): 137–49; "Fitzgerald's *Aeneid*," *Parnassus* 11, no. 2 (1983–84): 213–35; and "Logue's Homeric Battles," *Parnassus* 14, no. 2 (1987–88): 93–107.

E. V. Rieu has made a prose translation of the *Argonautica* (*The Voyage of the Argo* [Baltimore: Penguin, 1971]) which is witty and elegant and gets the tone just right. His prose *Odyssey* (revised by C. H. Rieu in consultation with Peter V. Jones [London: Penguin, 1991]) is not bad at all and sometimes reads like a screenplay or suggests comedies of the 1930s. When Athena reveals herself to Odysseus on Ithaca, the reader may imagine Carole Lombard putting in an appearance, smiling that smile and saying: "Odysseus, you sly puss."

The Latin language requires some effort to learn, and the *Aeneid* is hard for the beginning student because of its elegant economy, subtlety, and allusiveness. Readers of the *Iliad* and the *Odyssey*, however, might be surprised to discover that it is not all that difficult to learn Homeric Greek and thus engage in the altogether delectable pastime of reading the two poems in the original. Stop to consider that once upon a time every English schoolboy, and in this country every pupil in Jesuit schools, learned Greek; obviously, it does not require any great supply of brains. Those who fear that they have passed too far along life's journey should take heart from the example of I. F. Stone, who in his seventies learned Platonic Greek well enough to write a best-selling book about the *Apology*. Let the prospective students get Clyde Pharr's *Homeric Greek* (Norman: University of Oklahoma Press, 1970). This will lead them through the first book of the *Iliad*, propped up by generous excurses on all the grammar and vocabulary. Pharr has an old-fashioned sense of humor that he no doubt thought would appeal to schoolboys; it seems a trifle silly at times, but that will be part of the fun. Then let the readers arm themselves with R. J. Cunliffe, *A Lexicon of the Homeric Dialect* (Norman: University of Oklahoma Press, 1963), and the text to the *Iliad* and the *Odyssey* as printed in the Loeb Classical Library, published by Harvard University Press; the latter provides the Greek on the left and a workable translation by A. T. Murray on the right. As time goes by, the formulaic nature of Homeric verse will give students real competence at getting the sense, and the English translation will save them from having to look up all the rare words that dot the narrative. As this author can testify, a lifetime of reading these two poems can never exhaust their infinite capacity to give joy, to teach, and to reaffirm the value of human existence. If there were nothing else to read, the *Iliad* and the *Odyssey* would be a sufficiency.

Index